HOUSEWIFE

HOUSEWIFE

Home re making
in a Transgender Marriage

For Judy
with light & love!
Kristin Collier

KRISTIN K. COLLIER

Library of Congress Cataloging-in-Publication Data 2016914891

ISBN: 978-0-9977901-0-8

Published by: Abbondanza Publishing, LLC

www.kristinkcollier.com

The memories collected here are recorded with the greatest accuracy that my lens allows. Others are bound to have differing views of events, and I only claim to share my story as it pertains to this narrative. There are no composite characters, but most names and many identifying characteristics have been changed to protect the privacy of others.

Editing by Carole Audet
Cover and content design by Renee and Mark D'Antoni
Cover and interior woodcuts by Katy G. Collier
Cover photo by Sherri Phillips

For Seda, who turned the light on before I was ready
and grew my capacity for love in all ways.

Contents

PART THREE

PART FOUR

PART FIVE

PART SIX

Prologue

RECENTLY, I RAN into a friend from high school while walking through my hometown in California.

"Kristin!" she said. "I haven't seen you in ages. The last time I saw you in Eureka, you were pregnant and married to—I can't remember his name, but he was good looking! I bet your baby's all grown up now. Do you have more kids? Same husband?"

"Well, that's a bit of a story," I said, not for the first time. She listened, rapt, while I brought her up to speed.

We love to celebrate what's gone well with our friends, but stories of struggle and triumph are what inspire us, especially when they begin with the seemingly unremarkable. So began my tale . . . with a housewife, me, comfortable with her gender role, her husband, and domestic life in every way until something went unexpectedly awry. In 2005, my inner and outer worlds collided and converged when my husband was diagnosed with gender dysphoria (GD) and transitioned to live the rest of his life as a woman.

Gender dysphoria, or transgenderism, was previously known as gender identity disorder (GID) in the Diagnostic and Statistical Manual of Mental Disorders (DSM) published by the American Psychiatric Association. GD is a medical condition that affects people "several orders of magnitude higher than earlier estimates indicated," says Thomas Bevan in *The Psychobiology of Transsexuality and Transgenderism: A New View Based on Scientific*

Evidence. There is no statistical consensus to date, but Bevan uses "survey and estimation approaches . . . [to] set a best conservative estimate of . . . male to female transgenderism . . . [at] at least 1% . . . [and] 0.5% for female to male transgender frequency."[1] However, in the experience of every transperson and transtherapist we know, there are about as many transmen as transwomen. Physiological differences have been found in the brains of some transgender people,[2] so whether one should call GD a condition or a naturally occurring variance is debatable. Effective medical treatment has been established as hormone therapy, electrolysis, and gender confirmation surgery.[3]

Almost ten years into our marriage, my husband's diagnosis and commitment to treatment resulted in a radical transformation of our lives as a couple and as a family, but the change did not happen overnight. My spouse had experienced some type of inner disharmony for as long as he could remember. This nameless dissonance had materialized since his youth in a form of self-loathing that left me bewildered from the time I came to know him well. Looking back, there were other signs of transgenderism, but they were without context, so those few events took no place in our comprehension or memory. We now see that this was a period of denial for us both. Even after counselors told us that the problem was likely GD, we had no social framework that would help us to understand or share our challenges with others, so my husband and I kept our secret locked up tight. We did not formally agree to this; we just couldn't see any other way. Our family structure began to morph, and there were few models we could look to in its redesign.

Over time, we found people who could help us. In early transition, I went to the library one morning after summoning the courage to check out books of others' experiences with GD. I found only *My Husband Betty*,[4] by Helen Boyd. It was helpful to read about another woman wrestling with what appeared to be the same dilemma, but Boyd did not have children and we did. Later, my husband and I stumbled onto a significant resource in Jennifer Finney Boylan's memoir, *She's Not There.*[5] Though Boylan was a parent and made mention of her boys, who were nearly the same ages as ours, her book too had little information on the nuts and bolts of how a family transitioned together. It was, understandably, not her focus. *Where could I find the perspective of a housewife and mother who had been caught off-guard?* I wondered. I felt sorry for myself. I couldn't tell some days whose work was harder, my spouse's or mine.

I have attempted to write the book that I was longing for at that time. It is my story, as a wife and mother, and the chronicle of my husband's male-to-female transition is not always the centerpiece. Gender confusion exploded and reshaped our family, and this transformation took place within the context of my vital daily work as a housewife. The mundane irony of our reality juxtaposed to the archetype did not escape me.

Our family looked picture-perfect on the outside (and the outside is so important!), while on the inside my world had shattered. As I picked up the pieces, I became more open to unconventional ways of meeting my own and our family's needs. The ensuing story, which contains the journey of three other romantic relationships, is about my own peace making with gender stereotypes and cultural norms as I sought to hold us all with compassion. While my husband struggled to make sense of his inner and outer experiences of gender, I redefined gender for myself. In so doing, I felt the need to harmonize my inner and outer worlds of loving unconditionally and serving generously while not allowing my joy and lifework to be hindered by an imbalance of domestic servitude based on gender stereotypes.

Our family's story is somewhat unique in that we miraculously learned how to remain deeply connected to one another as we muddled through this multi-layered transition together. It was no easy feat. We had the help and support of Nonviolent Communication[6] and our mentors and friends who lovingly practiced it. Looking back, I see that our commitment to living compassionate, simple, and wholesome lives guided and informed the way we grew together.

I unabashedly share my story from a variety of angles, and I include the practical details of life with kids, because Seda's gender transition took place in that topography. Transition cannot happen in isolation. "Trans" *means* that you are shifting from one thing, space, or idea into another, which requires something outside of yourself, a territory. For those who are transgender, that territory includes their self-identified gender, but it also includes how people in their world see them; this largely subconscious merging of inner and outer experience shapes the way they feel and express their gender.

In my experience, those of us who aren't genderqueer[7] are largely unaware of this map. We are settled and easy with our identity as male or female because our cultural backdrop mirrors our experience as an expected norm. When the identities of people around us begin to shift, we suddenly see our edges and are often surprised to witness how our own gender is also co-created by inner and outer experience. My husband never had the sense that he could choose whether to explore his gender and, frankly, I did not feel in choice about exploring mine.

Someone recently pointed out to me that gender transition is a potentially erroneous concept, because the person going through that transition is anchoring more firmly to who they are while the rest of the world must transition to accept this truth. As such, the transition described in this story is my own, and I am in good company with countless others who are adjusting daily to comprehend the inner truths of loved ones. The territory in which I transitioned included our home, garden, and community.

I believe that transparency around gender transition is critically important if our world is to understand that gender dysphoria falls within the realm of normal and daily affects the lives of families and communities around us. In order for society-at-large to accept and support transpeople and their families, transfamilies must at times become visible and detail their experiences; communities can then witness our likenesses rather than setting us apart as "other," as so often happens when a group is feared and misunderstood.

"Violence begins where knowledge ends," said Abraham Lincoln. When people better understand gender transition and what it requires of a family and community, they will also understand how to help. For this reason, I encourage the curious, offering readers an opportunity to become educated and more effective allies. It is my hope that this story contributes to those who are seeking information, companionship, and the inspiration to grow their capacity for love.

Part One

Second Birth

AT MIDNIGHT, THE contractions strengthened and followed one another in tight succession. I gripped the upholstered arms of my chair then heaved myself up to standing. Taking a breath, I relaxed my hands, arms, neck, and face. Breathing quietly, I let the tension drain from my feet, legs, hips, and back as I began to sway. Would this baby come on the day he was due? I shook my head in disbelief and stared at the hardwood floor. I didn't think that happened. "Get the camera," I said to my husband.

Fred went to the closet and returned, camera in hand. We hadn't taken any photographs in the third trimester, and our window was closing fast. I splayed my fingers wide over my pale, round belly, silently encouraging its tightening muscles to squeeze our baby downward. In a black sports bra and leggings, I posed, smiling, as Fred angled the camera and clicked the shutter. From the back, I didn't even look pregnant.

Sam would be our second baby, and the first was enough of a handful that I hadn't had a chance to give this new addition the attention I felt he was due. My reading and meditative preparation had been spotty. I'd created no birth art to explore my innermost hopes and fears, and the bedroom contained almost nothing new with the baby in mind. In my anticipation to birth Sam, the only thing I'd changed was my hair, which clung tightly to my head in corn rows lovingly braided by a friend. I thought that would be a clever way to get my hair out of my face and not have to brush it for a month.

At 2:00 a.m., I called my friends and family and asked if they would come and care for Trinidad, so I could give birth to our baby at the hospital. My sister-in-law Janet, an OB/GYN nurse, listened carefully to my voice to estimate how far along I was. I paused for a contraction and then offered detailed instructions about how to pick up Trinidad from a neighbor's when it was time to bring him to the hospital to meet his baby brother. Gauging my cheerful enthusiasm, Janet determined that I was in early labor and told me she'd see me later.

At the hospital, the admitting nurse asked me not to be disappointed if I wasn't very far along. I was clearly enjoying myself too much to be in the throes of labor. Fred and I whispered to each other and broke out in laughter every few minutes. Seeing Fred alone was a rare treat. Since we'd given birth to Trinidad two years ago, we had managed to spend roughly five hours away from our son, and that time was taken in small chunks. Trinidad wanted to be only with Mama or Daddy, and after several attempts to encourage him otherwise, we had relinquished ourselves to spending "couple" time together as a family. The nurse checked my cervix and announced with some gravity that I was six centimeters dilated, and the baby's head was fully engaged. I was indeed in heavy labor.

"You're having a water birth?" she asked.

"Yes," I said. We had looked forward to the opportunity to birth this baby under water since we'd seen the serene videos of mamas and babies in the Black Sea. At least I had those images to hold onto! Fred beamed at me, dark hair and beard framing his handsome face. I smiled back.

"Well, they'd better get that tub set up quickly!" the nurse said.

Fred and I found our room and set down our things. I had walked up the stairs, all three flights, as I'd learned to do in my first pregnancy. The rocking motion of the hips while ascending stairs brought the baby down. I knew that easy birthing required discipline, relaxation, and effort, and I engaged in the work joyfully. As I stood in our room, arms around my husband's neck, I realized that no more stairs were needed. Our baby burrowed its head deep into the cradle of my pelvis, and my belly tightened in a caress around him. I pressed my cheek into Fred's shoulder, and he rested a hand gently at the nape of my neck.

This man had been my harbor for almost nine years. I looked up and saw Fred's blue eyes twinkle with anticipation then lost myself in those calm waters as the next contraction rocked me. Fred grasped both of my shoulders with broad, strong hands while we swayed together in silence.

At eighteen, I had sworn never to marry. I'd planned to go to New York and study theater. Before heading east, I'd stopped in Wyoming to help my father. Within a month, I met Fred, an eccentric rancher's son. When he wasn't engineering on a fishing boat in Alaska, he spent time with his family in Wyoming. We met in a writer's group at the public library. Shortly after, he asked me out to dinner—the first formal date I'd ever been on. I found myself engaged to be married three months later. Fred and I held our own private ceremony in the living room of his cottage by candlelight that summer; one year later, we celebrated the commitment with a traditional wedding.

I had many friends and acquaintances who complained about their mates, but I didn't have any major dissatisfaction with Fred. He always shifted his perspective to better understand me when I was upset and quickly rectified every conflict to the best of his ability.

Once, when yet another china coffee cup fell and broke because he'd stacked the dishes too high, he suddenly saw my pain as his own. "Oh my gosh—is it the same as if you'd taken my woodworking tools and used them on concrete?" he asked, then shook his head and sighed, appalled by his previous blindness. He apologized deeply as he held me crying. Fred was perfect.

We never fought. We never even argued, with one exception: we disagreed about where the mid-west started. I said it included eastern Wyoming and he vehemently disagreed, refusing to be a mid-westerner, even for my benefit. After jumping up and down in an alley one cold winter night trying to prove my point, we both stopped and looked at each other, suppressing a smile. One snort of laughter broke the dam, and we both surrendered, shaking with mirth, at the absurdity of our dispute. We decided to let it go. At the same time. One mind.

Fred was relieved to witness my ease in birthing Sam. During contractions, I turned inward and, despite my lack of planning around images for meditation, the most amazing inner landscape opened before me. A rainbow made of water appeared—a vertical river flowing in all colors. There on the river, shooting downstream in his own tiny kayak, lay my baby Sam. As the contraction eased, I opened my eyes and smiled, happily envisioning our baby barreling down to join us.

I rested in a warm Jacuzzi bathtub as the nurses filled a portable hot tub with water. Lying on my back slowed Sam's descent considerably. The heat, relaxation, position, and my heart all asked him to wait just a bit so we could make everything perfect. Sam, wise and reasonable from the start, collaborated with us in creating a beautiful and harmonious birth.

Fred and I spoke softly to one another between contractions, examining our lives together as lovers and parents. We marveled at how much we'd grown since Trinidad had entered into our lives, and we celebrated the depth of love we felt for one another. I stroked Fred's forearm with one finger as he smiled down at me.

There was nowhere to go, nothing to do but to enjoy one another as we had during so many long drives in the countryside in that spacious time before children came into our lives. My elbow slid slowly down the side of the acrylic tub as we talked, and I accidentally hit the button for the Jacuzzi jets. I shrieked when the air came on full force with a grinding sound, as loud as the Jake brake on a semi-truck. Fred and I burst into peals of laughter when we realized what I'd done.

The nurses looked confused. Intensive labor is not expected to be fun. Nevertheless, this marathon effort of body and spirit turned out to be the sweetest date I remembered having with my husband. The hot tub filled in an hour or so, and the nurses shuttled me out of the Jacuzzi and into my room where the birthing tub waited. My midwife sat beside it on a cushioned bench while she filled out paperwork.

"Oh . . . I think I'm going to have to push!" I told her as I made my way slowly to the tub, noticing the only edge of anxiety that I'd experienced all night.

"All right. Let your body do its work," she said, smiling. Then she looked back down through her reading glasses perched on the end of her nose while she continued her notes, one knee tucked neatly beneath her.

I nodded and relaxed. As I climbed into the tub, a nurse brought a release form and asked if several other nurses could watch the birth too, as they hadn't seen a baby born into water by such a jubilant mother before. I grinned while I signed their papers. They were apologetic about the timing, but I was not troubled in the least.

I called my husband to join me. He stripped down to his swim trunks and climbed in behind, enfolding me in his arms. I bobbed and swayed as I found a comfortable place so that my pelvis, sweet bony cradle, could allow our baby fair passage. Holding the side of the tub, I squatted with my back to Fred who stood at the tub's center.

"Ohhhh . . . " I called out, deep and low, as I gave one long push.

"I feel him there!" I sang out to my midwife. The baby was crowning already, a sensation bright and searing. It was familiar, having birthed before, but still shockingly new.

"Go ahead then," said my midwife, leaning forward only a little.

I pushed again as the urge came. Sam's whole head slid out from between my thighs. I reached down and felt his face with my fingertips. I will never forget how rubbery his tiny nose, eyes, and lips felt underwater, and how I came to know his features before my eyes ever took them in. Fred began breathing harder, surprised that it was all happening so quickly. The pauses between contractions seemed to last forever. I wanted to hold my little Sam! Again, the urge gripped me, and I sent my baby downward and out of my body like a fish into water.

"Catch him!" called the midwife to my husband. Sam bobbed up like a cork, arms waving, propelling himself upward before his first breath. In an instant, Fred came to life, his large hands groping to wrap around the pale, fragile body of our second born son. Our baby arched his back and broke the surface of the water, turning his head to open one eye. I raised my leg and stepped over the cord that bound us as I received him, tiny fingers opening and closing to the air.

Settling back down into the water to keep us all warm, I nestled against my husband. This baby was so tiny and perfect. Sam opened the other eye a slit and regarded me calmly, likely wondering, as I was, whether we'd met some place before. He took a deep breath and settled himself against me with a small grunt of recognition. Fred pulled me close, and we both looked down in wonder at what we had created. There had been no pain.

House Fire

REMARKABLY, FROM THE first day we brought him home, baby Sam slept through the night, other than to wake for nursing. He joined our family seamlessly, delighted to watch and listen to the big brother he'd come to know through the wall of my belly. I recovered from the birth quickly and found myself bicycling to playdates with both of my children in the bike trailer after only a few days. Everything about this second birth seemed so much easier than the first—until Sam turned six weeks old in April of 2003.

I'm not sure what woke me. I stared up at the ceiling in the dark and listened to sharp cracks and pops from somewhere nearby. I shook Fred.

"What?" he asked thickly.

"There's a sound," I said.

"Mmm. It's just the cat." He rolled over.

"No!" I said, sitting up. The dog, terrified of loud popping noises, stood panting over me, saliva dripping from her tongue. I stared blankly into the dark. "There's something happening."

Fred roused himself from bed. Trinidad slept on beside me. My husband straightened himself slowly, walked to a nearby window, and pulled open the blind. Yellow and orange light flickered back at us through the frosted glass. Fire.

"Oh my God!" Fred said, disbelieving. I grabbed Sam and

sprinted to the living room. For a moment I paused, floating on adrenaline.

"Mama!" called Trinidad sleepily from the bedroom. I had forgotten him! My brain was hard-wired to know that I had one baby, but Sam's lifespan of six weeks had not yet burned its impression into my long-term memory. I ran back to gather my toddler.

Fred called the fire department as I stepped out onto the porch, children in my arms, dog pressed against my bare legs. I paused long enough to consider that I was wearing no more than a T-shirt. Shaking my head, I decided that it was enough and dashed down the front steps to cross the street and hand off my children to the neighbors. The wide-eyed young woman who answered the door took Sam in one arm and rested her other hand on Trinidad's head as her husband ran with me back to the duplex.

Dumbfounded, I did not know what to retrieve as the flames leapt from the unit attached to ours. My neighbor encouraged me to take photo albums and the laptop computer. I grabbed an armful of clothes from the closet as well. Fred carried three albums under one arm and our laptop in the other. The phone line had gone dead at the end of his call to 911. Our house suddenly flooded with smoke. We all crouched low and made our way to the front door as the long red engines pulled into our driveway.

I sat on my neighbor's couch holding our children as firefighters shot their hoses through the windows and doors of the unit next to ours. I watched them through the large plate glass window as if they were figures moving on a screen. Fred stood beside them, watching as the smoke descended into our quiet nest. Black and thick, it penetrated unseen cracks and left its dark, filmy thumbprint across our every possession. An electrical problem had started the fire next door, and all the occupants were out for the night. One had celebrated her birthday and returned the next day to discover that the fire had consumed everything she owned.

At three o'clock in the morning, the fire chief walked us back through our home. "There was no fire separation between the two sides of the duplex," he explained. "I don't know how you made it. The smoke came into your side because the fire broke into the roof rafters. Another few minutes and the ceiling would have dropped. You are all incredibly lucky to be alive."

I looked around in wonder. My home still looked so tidy. Aside from muddy boot prints on the carpet, everything appeared the same, only in a darker shade of gray. The fact that our home had nearly been destroyed unnerved me. The cooling rack in the kitchen stood stacked with peanut butter cookies that Trinidad and I had baked together the night before. I fought an impulse to pass them out to the firefighters. Our home had been badly damaged. We would have to move and start over. This had not been the plan.

A Vase of Flowers

THE NEXT NIGHT, we moved into a loaner house. Fred had been working for a housing developer as a designer and drafting technician. His company heard of our loss and offered us a three-story house that they had purchased with the intention of subdividing its four-acre property. The developer had little interest in the house itself and kindly rented it to us for the same price we'd paid for our one-bedroom duplex. At the edge of city and country, our newly borrowed home stood high on a rural highway with an expansive grassy hill at the back. Below us, houses stacked neatly in tighter and tighter formation as the city beneath lit up the gently sloping valley. Our view was spectacular.

We arrived well after sunset, toting our daypacks and white paper bags from Burger King. The electricity had not yet been turned on. It was early April, and the temperatures hovered around freezing. No heat had warmed the house for months. We found a downstairs bedroom by flashlight, threw down borrowed sleeping bags, and burrowed into them to keep warm. We ate under the covers and talked little.

I kept my hands on both boys through the night, their bodies warming as they drifted into sleep. I lay awake staring into the dark and feeling uncertain. There had been a fire, yes, and it was past. Sleeping in a house I had only been able to inspect by flashlight was disconcerting, but why did I feel both eerily sad and hyper-vigilant? Fred fell asleep on the other side of the boys. There were no mysterious clicks or bangs, no footsteps, and no rustling. I could not put my finger on what it was that made me so ill at ease, but I could not settle. Slipping in and out of sleep, I kept watch on my family through the night.

In the morning, I still felt strange. This was not a happy house. I don't know what had happened there, but my hair stood on end when I walked down the hall. I had never experienced such a feeling before. Cryptic writings covered the bathroom walls where mirrors and paintings once hung. A man professed love for his wife Betty, but other notes were dark in tone and indecipherable in meaning. An upstairs studio bore locks on both sides of the door. I went up there only twice. Both times, my stomach tightened and my eyes filled with tears. Fred had the same feeling. Others noticed, too. We closed the doors to the upstairs and downstairs and lived only on the middle level. Fred and I had been living in six hundred square-foot houses for most of our lives together. We tried to create a sense of home here and take comfort. It was not easy. The house did not fit us at all.

Later that afternoon, I went to the grocery store and bought a small, locally made juice in the prettiest bottle I could find. Fred looked at me curiously. Such an indulgence seemed well beyond our means, but he did not ask why. I drank it up, rinsed the bottle, and filled it with water. I cut tulips from the yard and arranged them carefully in this makeshift vase.

I set the small bouquet on our mantel. The broad, waxy petals of brilliant yellow and red captured the wholesome lightness and goodness of the outdoors. Everything was out of order, but I did what I could. This place was going to have to be our home.

Going Back

A WEEK LATER, I prepared to visit my mother in California. I didn't know what else to do with a new baby, a toddler, a house fire, and a terrifying new home. I packed up and drove south while Fred continued with his job at the design firm.

Halfway to Eureka, I made my first stop in Grants Pass at a McDonald's, the only affordable place I knew to be warm and welcoming to a young family at eight o'clock in the morning. The tile floor shone under fluorescent lights as I turned to maneuver through the heavy glass door with both of the children in my arms.

Sam stretched and grunted. He had slept for the first three-hour leg of our journey. I marveled at his easy temperament. I set Trinidad down, and he pulled me hard to the register. After studying the menu above, I looked down at the polished stainless steel counter and noticed a dark yellow streak of mustard. "I'm not going to put my sleeve in that," I thought.

I placed my order with a pleasant young woman and then told her, "You might want to clean this mustard up before you set something in it."

She raised her eyebrows in surprise and whipped out a white terry cloth rag to wipe it up with. I turned away from the counter and looked down to discover that I *had* in fact gotten my sleeve in the mustard. I must have leaned on the counter too, because a yellow smudge had tracked itself clear across the front of my best sweater.

With a sigh, I took Trinidad's hand and headed off to the rest room with the kids to clean up. As I set my seven-week-old baby on the counter, I noticed that he had a yellow stain on his leg. I gulped.

It had been two years since I'd left the front lines of leaky infant cloth diapers and had since serenely forgotten the short-comings of ill-fitted nylon diaper covers. Mortified and blushing fiercely, I cleaned up my children, grabbed our order, chased Trinidad twice around the restaurant, and blazed south to reach my childhood home by early afternoon.

I spent about a week in Eureka; I don't recall how we occupied ourselves there. What I remember most was the phone conversation I had with Fred the day before I returned to Oregon.

"I want to talk to you when you get home," he said.

"Sure. About what?" I immediately broke out in a cold sweat, and my shirt grew damp in places, sticking to me under my arms. I waved them a little, shrugged, and subconsciously urged myself not to create a problem where there was none. This talk didn't have to be about something worrisome at all. It was probably just a setback connected with the house fire. Insurance, maybe.

"It's about . . . well, it's complicated," he said.

My heart raced. I set Sam down in his bouncy chair and walked over to the window chewing on the edge of my thumb. "Okay. Just give me a word, huh? Something so I have an idea?"

"Well, it's about . . . clothes," he said.

Memories flooded in unbidden: my best red dress ripped with his apologies, a negligee smelling of male sweat that he gifted to me on our first Christmas, his horror at being caught after a second dress turned up torn. These events from our history together lived underground. I didn't know where they existed for him and, frankly, I didn't want to know. They had remained buried for me until now. I put his words together with what there were no words for before: he wanted to wear women's clothes.

"Women's clothes," he said. I nodded and felt light-headed. Into my silence, he cracked open uncertainly. "I'm not sure why, but I don't think it's a phase, or I wouldn't want to talk to you about it. I don't understand it, but somehow it's a part of me, and it's really big. I can't pretend it's not there anymore. I'm not sure what this means, Kristin, but I'm working on it. I'll tell you all about it when you get home. We can go for a walk," he said.

"Uh-huh," I said. "I love you. We'll figure it out."

"We will," he said.

"I'll see you tonight."

"I love you," he said. "Goodbye." I set the phone gently into its cradle and stood staring at the wall, vaguely hearing the sound of Trinidad prattling to his grandmother behind me.

Women's clothes. So, what of that? Was it really such a big deal? For men in general, no. I read Dear Abby. She said not to question his size thirteen red stiletto heels as long as they stayed locked in the suitcase at the back of the closet. But was it a problem for *my husband* to wear women's clothes? Yes. Not because it was wrong—it just didn't *suit* him. There was no part of the man I married—not the part that liked to be with me, not the part that liked to be alone, not the part that grew up on a ranch, not the part that fished in Alaska—that I could see in women's clothes. To wear women's clothes, he would have to be a different person. It would mean that I didn't know this man I had married ten years ago, that he was as mysterious to me as a stranger on the street. But, inexplicably, somehow this was the case.

Worse yet, I married him thinking that I knew him, so I must have been—must in fact be—delusional. This thought stopped me cold. I knew that I was stressed out and stretched with being a new mom, but I couldn't be delusional, too, could I? No. And I didn't have the energy to clean up after someone else who *was* delusional. It made no sense. No other marker in our lives suggested that my husband was anything other than what I'd believed him to be. Something doesn't come of nothing. Does it?

Maybe I was just making too big of a deal out of this. Maybe my husband was all of what I thought he was, and he also had this encapsulated part of his personality that wanted to sometimes look like a girl. Couldn't I bend to grant him that? Couldn't I support this person I loved in exploring his inclination to wear women's clothes? It probably wouldn't lead to anything and might even fade away over time. We had such a satisfying marital and family relationship. If there was nothing missing there, what else could he possibly need? Couldn't I afford him space, and perhaps privacy, to explore who he was as an individual? I think Dear Abby would have said, "Yes!"

I tried imagining myself being a person who could be open to her husband occasionally dressing in skirts, heels, and blouses. I shuddered when I thought of *him*, heavy and bearded, dressed as *her*. I felt nauseated when I imagined it. *How could a skirt be so horrible on someone?* I wondered, confused.

I thought of myself as liberal and artistic. I had been brought up with these values and also saw myself as a bit of a maverick, bent on self-reliance. I had even fancied myself a bit of a gender bender as a teen—a tomboy of sorts. But if he sometimes wanted to be a she . . . well, where could you take that? What did it do to a marriage, a family?

"Kris, what's wrong?" my mother asked. I hadn't noticed her standing beside me.

"Oh, nothing really. It's not much of anything. It's . . . " I stopped myself and looked down at my feet. How could I tell her what I didn't have words for myself?

"I just . . . Fred's going through some soul-searching, trying to figure out who he is. You know he was raised so conservatively in Wyoming. His dad over-criticized him . . . and was very strict about what kind of clothes he wore. He always had to wear, um, boy clothes. Like classic boys'—or men's—clothes. Overalls and cowboy hats. He's working through that now. He was just telling me about it. Not anything big, just kind of . . . trying to figure stuff out." I looked away. I could feel her eyes searching, but I couldn't meet them, not without crying.

I couldn't tell yet if there was anything to cry about. I took a breath. And then exhaled. I smiled and turned to sit down with my children. I said words and made toy cars and people go up and down on the Fisher Price elevator. The sound of the bell and my children's laughter clanged in my head, but I didn't really hear. Their grandpa played with us, too, and I smiled at him, grateful that I could be left alone with my thoughts.

I couldn't tell my mother that I had known better than to leave Fred alone for a week, that he started drinking when things got quiet and hated himself for reasons that I couldn't understand. Fred's shadow had emerged in phone calls to me in the past and found its way into letters anxiously counting the days until my return. I couldn't tell my mother about the seasonal depression that left him at home for hours some mornings, spinning his wheels in the greenish glow of internet news reports, trying to personally collect and contain the scope of despair and destruction in the world. When I could not rouse him to attend to his family during these times, I took over as best I could. I couldn't tell my mom that I did not know the extent of his dark side, or how it would affect our children or me. I did not yet know how to let my eyes get accustomed to the dark.

I simply couldn't see a thing.

Snapshots 2003

There is a Zen-like ornamental garden ten feet from the busy rural highway where we now live in this borrowed house. I do not relax at all when I watch my toddler play here.

Two days after the fire, a friend thinks to give me underwear, for which I am grateful. I wear the same skirt for the first ten days after we lose our home, even to my kitchen shows as a consultant for Pampered Chef. It is a moss green linen skirt that falls to my ankles. I feel like a pioneer.

Our clothes are returned from the cleaners, where they had been sent by our insurance company. It has been a month since the fire. They are bundled three or four to a package, tightly wrapped in transparent plastic. Trinidad stacks them like blocks then climbs the mountain to look out our living room picture window. He can see the city and beyond.

I pay $60 to restore a basic collection of spices for rudimentary cooking. I never knew what treasures I'd owned.

In the grocery store, I hold Sam to my breast with one arm while Trinidad rides in the cart, grabbing what he can off the shelves. I stare with wide eyes at the packaged food before me.

All color. Something is missing. I am very still and then sud-
denly, as if emerging from deep water, I fill my lungs with air
and the world around me comes alive again. I forget that I have
this problem, not remembering to breathe. I am surprised by it
again and again.

I prune the grape arbor that stretches the length of our front
walk. It bleeds and bleeds clear sap for weeks. I am appalled that
I made those cuts. I cannot stand its crying.

In the outdoor equipment store, Trinidad runs squealing and
hides among the tents. He is all the way across the store from
me, and I stand motionless, disoriented, and embarrassed. I call
to him but my voice sounds like it's underwater. I have a list in
my hand, people walk all around me, and I think, "To them, I
look like a housewife going about her day. But so do all of these
other ladies. Who else in this room has just been through a fire?
Who else has a husband who wants to wear dresses?"

One morning in May, two-year-old Trinidad enters the kitchen
naked and puts on his yellow and black striped rubber bee boots.
He opens the front door and stands in a patch of lemon-colored
sunlight. "I'm going out," he says.

There is no fire escape plan from our bedroom window on the
second floor in our borrowed house. I imagine jumping out,
snapping both legs, and lying there to break my children's fall
as my husband tosses them out to me one at a time. This vision
is far from the Hollywood exit I would like it to be.

I get a massive breast infection while nursing my infant son.
Fred is unable to come home from work as my temperature
peaks at 103.5. I lie in bed, delirious, nursing Sam. I somehow
manage to give detailed instructions to Trinidad for one obstacle

course after another, waiting for Fred to get home from work.
"Run to the living room, jump twice on the sofa, touch the
refrigerator in the kitchen, then come back."

My husband tells me that while I was at my mother's, he wore a
skirt all the time. It swished around his ankles as he danced up
and down the hall, and my husband had an epiphany: he was
meant to be a woman.

Everything is clear. To him.

Part Two

Starting Over

IN AUGUST 2003, we found a house to rent. It had hardwood floors, a separate office, and space for a garden. I finally felt ready to tackle growing our own food again. We were ecstatic with the find.

Fred asked me if he could do the space clearing, a meditative ritual we had used to clear and bless our past three homes. He offered to clap or ring bells around the empty space to move stuck energy and arrange cut flowers on tiny altars that were in line of sight with each other from room to room. He would then sprinkle river water while setting intentions for our new space. I felt sad about giving this job to him because I loved to do space clearings; he had performed the last one when I'd been pregnant. But there was much to be done in the transition, especially juggling an infant and toddler, so I consented and he did the honors.

Fred walked me through the house after the clearing, and I admired the wide picture window in the living room. Every one of our houses had featured such a window. Perhaps this manifested from a desire to see and be seen, integrating the inner life of the family with the community outside. I looked past the table Fred had covered with small bouquets and happily regarded the open back door that led from kitchen to patio. I had always wanted a direct connection with the outdoors from the sacred hearth of our home where all our meals were prepared and eaten. With gratitude and amazement, I walked through the generously sized bedroom and office, each adorned with a small altar containing tiny bouquets from the yard. This was the largest and best-situated house Fred and I had shared together. I wondered how the rent was so low in this popular college and family neighborhood. I shook my head and marveled at our luck.

"Thank you so much for letting me do the space clearing," Fred said. I smiled, bouncing the baby on one hip as we walked together to the kitchen.

"I just really wanted to do it this time. I wanted to have a strong connection to our home because this is the place that matters most to me. This is the center of our world, you know? It's where we eat, live, and grow. It's where you are," he said and touched my cheek. "I love you so much."

"I love you too," I said. "Thanks for doing it."

I began to let go of my disappointment at not being the family spokesperson for our intentions in this new space. At least I had collected the river water, leaning far out over the Willamette River to skim its surface, holding our baby in a sling tight against my belly. The water sparkled in its captive glass, and it felt strangely like some extension of me. I dipped my fingers in and traced a wet finger across Sam's cheek. He grinned up at me.

I had lived the first two years of my life by the Trinity River in Northern California, and the smell of water rushing through earth and trees imprinted itself on my being. As a teen, I took my English setter and a jar of lemonade, drove my car an hour up into the mountains, and then lay on the hot, round stones at the river's edge. As friends went to parties, sporting events, and the shopping mall in our small coastal town, I sought time alone inland, by the river where I felt happy, whole, and at peace.

I was proud of myself back then for discovering a way out of the chaos that infected my home. At fourteen, my mother had divorced my stepfather and I'd been glad of it—there would be no more broken dishes to clean up. When she cut her ties with him, my mom set herself loose on the world and discovered that the crucible of speed and cocaine helped her reach deep through decades of pain to shape the broken bits of her life into art. The sharp edges of my mother's world made it difficult for me to find my home with her again. I took to sleeping at friends' houses, my grandparents', or in the front seat of my car with a thick comforter and a Snoopy alarm clock on the dashboard. That was when I rediscovered the river and a way out. The river has had a calming effect on me ever since.

"The house looked so beautiful with all the flowers and candles," Fred said. "I wish you could have seen it. I felt so full of gratitude and love holding our intentions as I walked through our home to bless it."

I imagined each of the intentions on our list: to cultivate community, to learn and grow, to live in harmony with each other and the earth, to express creativity with joy . . .

"And I added one more," he told me shyly.

"What's that?" I asked.

"I added the intention that there would be a space here for me as a woman. To dress and feel myself as one." He paused nervously as my face fell. "I had to, Kristin. I have to be true to myself, and that means that I've got to make a space for this part of me, whatever it is, whatever that means. I don't understand it. I just know I have to do it."

He watched my tears fall in silence. I couldn't look at him. I trusted him, always had. But this was some kind of a trick; something didn't add up. Either everything he'd said and been before he had these feelings was false, or the feelings themselves were a sham. It seemed that my husband was doing something horribly cruel to our family, and I couldn't understand why. Fred was not a cruel man. I no longer knew how to be with him, and I turned away. He rested a hand on my shoulder.

"I'm sorry it's so scary," he said. "I wish it wasn't. But I just can't push it away anymore. It would kill me."

That night, I broke down and called a friend. I held the receiver tightly in my hand while the phone rang. My heart pounded hard in my chest. Was this the right thing to do? The right time? My palm turned sweaty, and I wiped it on my jeans.

"Hello?" said Michelle.

"Hi, it's me," I said. "Listen, I have a problem." Michelle had been my best friend and confidante for several years, the one I'd called at 3:00 a.m. on the night of the house fire. Still, this was the biggest terror I'd ever faced. I hoped she was up to the task.

"What is it, Kristin?"

I swallowed hard and closed my eyes. "Some part of Fred wants to be a woman."

Silence. I wished I hadn't tried to do this on the phone. But I was desperate! I couldn't hold it in any longer. I couldn't keep it to myself. She had to understand.

"Kristin, that's not natural," she said, matter-of-factly. "That's not God's way."

This time, I held my end of the line in silence. If this wasn't God's way, then it could be righted. But what if it wasn't wrong? How could I know for sure? It broke my heart, it threatened our family, but what if Fred's truth was still full of light and love anyway, even if I couldn't understand or benefit from it? Is marriage really in God's plan if it ends like this? Is everything always meant to be?

"Kristin," she said. "We have to pray."

No Man's Land

IN THE AUTUMN, we flew back to Wyoming to visit Fred's family, and none of them knew our secret. Fred's brother had been killed in a logging accident two years before, and his sister DeeDee now lived in a care facility after weathering a car accident that left her a quadriplegic with the mental faculties of a very sweet six-year-old. I wasn't excited for Fred's parents to learn that the third of their four children was not who they thought he was.

This was our first vacation as a family in years, and I felt uncomfortable leaving the home we had just barely settled into after months of living like nomads. I felt like a doll on display, two cherubic children clinging to my skirt. I smiled and nodded, hugged and exclaimed, while inside I felt hollow and confused. Was this my family? If Fred changed on the outside, would I even be a part of this world anymore? Would he?

His mother held each one of us in turn with tears in her eyes. She had been waiting for this moment to have us both in the flesh, to see our children, to discover how Fred and I had actualized ourselves as a family. She looked so proud. "If only you knew," I thought. "If only you knew."

Fred followed me like a puppy through the bed and breakfast inn, happily exploring the realm of womanhood vicariously through my every move. He perched on the edge of the bathroom counter to watch me apply mascara. I looked at him sideways. This was not in our contract.

"Is that how you keep it from gumming up?" he marveled.

My stomach turned. I did not look away from the mirror. Was I somehow encouraging his fantasy of being a woman by performing my feminine rituals in his presence? I shoved the black wand back into its silver tube and dropped it with a clank into my toiletries bag.

Fred backed up quickly to let me through the bathroom door then bounced along behind me as I dug through my duffel bag for something to wear.

"Ooh. I love that color!" he said when I pulled out a burgundy cowl-neck sweater. "And it's so soft. Has that got angora in it?"

"No," I said curtly. "It's an alpaca-wool blend."

Out of the corner of my eye, I saw my eldest son standing beside an end table, drawing. I crossed the room in three strides, snatched the pencil out of Trinidad's hand, and replaced it with his wooden car. "Pencils are for paper," I said, quickly erasing the mark he had made. Fred brushed a finger across my carnelian bracelet as I moved to set the pencil down.

"Would you just stop?" I snapped. He stood up straight and suddenly understood that I didn't share his excitement. I did not want to be a part of this change with him. I wasn't even sure if I wanted to be with him anymore. And here we were with a new baby and a toddler visiting his family in the little town where he grew up. I wanted to bolt.

"I'm sorry," he said. "I'm just . . . I have so much to learn."

I sat down heavily on a loveseat printed with autumn colors, feeling nauseated. Little Sam, propped beside me on pillows, began to cry. I reached for him. "Well. Would you like to know how to nurse the baby?" I asked, feeling suddenly mean and liking it.

"That's not fair," he said. "I will probably never get to do that." He pouted.

"Oh. *Probably not,* huh? Ya think? You're a man. You have a man's body, and it can't do this. Nor do you *consider* whether your baby is hungry, right? Because that's a woman thing. And I can tell you that woman things are *not* all fun. It's not all dress up and blissful motherhood, lovey-dovey eye-gazing. It's spit up and poopy diapers and making dinner while you fill orders for your business because your husband is at work doing ONE job. It's packing your bags as fast as your toddler unpacks them and making enough food for the trip while your husband is answering emails and researching what? Breast implants?" He blanched.

"I'm sorry, but that kind of focus on yourself is not allowed once a woman becomes a parent. You failed the test." I looked down at my watch, remembering that Fred's mother was due to pick us up in fifteen minutes. It was not a good time to have this conversation. But, when was it ever?

"Kristin," he said, looking down.

I hated myself. I was not being kind.

"You know, I remember when you used to look at the curve of my wrist with longing. Not for the wrist to be yours. You wanted *me.* I was your woman. You admired me when I put on a unitard or a skirt. You liked the shape of me. Right? Wasn't that the case? You didn't size up my clothes so you could wear them later. Or is that just what I'm telling myself? Is it?" My face contorted as I began to cry.

"Don't, honey," he said. "Don't do this."

I bowed my head sobbing over the nursing child, and Sam slid his mouth off my breast with a smacking sound. His eyes squeezed shut, then he opened his mouth wide and began to cry with me, his face turning purple.

"Oh Jesus," said Fred. "Stop it, Kristin. I love you. I have always loved you. I can't help this. I don't want it to hurt you. I just can't pretend this isn't a part of me. Well, okay, maybe I can try. I don't know for how long, though. Honey, please."

He put his arm around me and the crying baby and began to rock with us. Trinidad came down the hall, wooden car in hand, stepping heavily, his weight swinging from side to side. He stood by my knee and reached up with both chubby arms.

"Up, Mama," he said. He pushed Sam's leg off mine to make room for himself.

I moaned softly, tears continuing to fall as I stroked Trinidad's soft, blonde hair. He ran his car up and down my arm.

"We don't know what any of this means," Fred reminded me. "It may be just a part of myself that I'm really seeing for the first time. And I'm letting it in. I'm not saying that I actually want to change my body to *be* a woman physically. I don't want to let you go. Not ever. I would never do anything to make that happen."

"I know," I said, relaxing into him, my tears still falling.

"You saved me, you know? I don't know what I would have done without you. I was lonely and depressed and had no direction. You came along and all that changed. I've never felt so connected to anyone in my whole life as I do to you. You're everything to me."

"You are to me, too," I said. "I don't know how we did this for each other, but we did. We saved each other. And now we have a family. I didn't get this far to watch it all fall apart, Fred. We've done a good job as parents, but they're still so little. I want them to have a family, a home, both parents, something normal. Something I didn't have." He squeezed me hard.

"I want that, too," he said. I nodded.

"I'm so afraid," I said.

"I know," he said. "This is totally terrifying! You think I'm not scared? I don't understand it, and you don't understand it, but we shouldn't make ourselves crazy by thinking up what *could* happen. We just don't know. We really have no idea."

"What *is* a woman?" I asked that night as the children lay sleeping on either side of me. Fred had always been somewhat passive and unsure in bed, and with his newly expressed gender confusion, we were both avoiding sex entirely.

"I don't know," said Fred quietly. "I just know I am one."

I lay in bed in the dark working this out for myself. A woman served. But a man served also, in his way. A woman stretched fully, beyond even herself, to be sure that all needs were held. She was more malleable and capable of squeezing through impossibly small gaps, only to show herself larger than life on the other side. An octopus.

Baby Sam began to grunt and root for my breast in the dark, his delicate hands patting at my side while his nose pushed toward me, seeking connection. I rolled over to face him, lifted my nightshirt, and offered him a breast. He latched on soundlessly. Trinidad reached into the gap where I had been, searching for me with his outstretched arm. He touched my back then rolled toward me in his sleep until his body nestled against mine.

"It's not possible for you to be a woman," I told Fred the next the morning when I found him in the bathroom shaving. "If you were, you could live with this and not make any outward changes. You would just be who you are on the inside to hold our family together. For us."

Fred looked down at his razor, defeated. Shaving cream dripped into the sink. How could any part of me rejoice in hurting him? I felt the poison of my own words. Who was I to tell him how to live? Or to put the children and me before his own integrity? How could I make these demands and be a woman myself?

If only his exploration had not called into question my identity too. My identity as a partner, a woman, and even as a human being—all were shaken. I would have to redefine myself in so many ways. It wasn't fair.

Fred rapped his razor on the side of the sink twice and rinsed it off, scowling. I turned and swung out of the room, feeling miserable. Trinidad ran along behind me.

"You can't be a woman," I hissed into the dark on our last night in Wyoming. The children slept beside us, exhausted by their first encounters with snow. The inn was silent, and, far from city lights, darkness filled every gap in the room around us.

"You weren't raised as a woman. You didn't experience the thousands of tiny invisible conditionings that make you feminine in our culture. And, more than that, you never experienced the many ways that society told you no. No, you're not safe here because you're a woman. No, you probably won't have the focus to go into that profession, being female. No, you won't be able to support a family by yourself."

"Kristin, what has ever stopped you? From anything?"

"It's not that women believe all of those no's as we grow up, Fred. We just create our identities in relationship to them. I'm a damn fine shot with a gun, *for a girl*. I can arm wrestle a good number of men to a standstill, even though my father has chided me for doing so because it hurt their egos. I love being a sexy wench in heels, a red silk camisole, and tap pants even though that's stereotypical. I don't think these choices are right or wrong on my part. They're just ways that I've expressed myself, with all due resistance, in the culture that raised me as a woman."

"Hmmm," he said. I stared up into the darkness.

"I'm not an expert on this. I don't pretend to see all of the things that are gendered in my world or to have cultivated an enlightened feminist perspective that allows me full autonomy. I'm not sure I could exist separately from the culture that defines me in my role as a woman. I like being the woman I am. And as that woman, I'm here to tell you: you're not one."

Fred considered that for a while. Under cover of dark, I silently cheered my own victory. I could not see a single hole in this argument. He would have to bend to reason.

"Does that make sense?" I asked after a few minutes.

"Yes, it does," he said, tired. I knew I had won the argument, but at what cost?

"I don't know what to tell you. I just can't go on as I have been," he said. "I am not a man." The darkness seemed to swallow us. I could hear the clock on the wall ticking, and I suddenly couldn't bear the sound. Lying between my two sleeping children, I felt trapped.

All of those classes in college—the gender studies, the literary theory—only suggested the map of this treacherous territory I found myself lost in.

No man's land.

Giving Thanks

IT WAS OUR first Thanksgiving in the new house. I had purchased the requisite bird, and it sat thawing on the kitchen counter. I had gotten out of bed reluctantly not wanting to disturb Sam, but still he woke. I pushed through my closet to find a skirt and blouse that would help me feel festive. I had a hard time pulling them on over and around the baby who wanted to nurse non-stop. I broke Sam's latch on my breast in order to button my blouse with both hands, and I saw a green trail of snot sliding down one of his cheeks. I grabbed a clean cloth diaper and wiped his face. We were both sick. Angry sick. And we wanted to go back to bed.

I shuffled to the kitchen in my slippers, one arm around Sam in the sling who had settled back into nursing with his eyes tightly closed, wet cheek pressed against my breast. I could understand his determination to keep the light out. My head pounded and my throat was sore. Trinidad called to me from the bedroom. Why couldn't he just get up and come out to talk to me? I pulled hard on the sides of the plastic stuffing bag to open it. The seam gave way suddenly so that the bag split and stuffing cubes flew in all directions. I was in no mood to be thankful.

Fred's light was on in the office outside. I knew he was writing and had been since five o'clock in the morning. This was his schedule and had been for the past few years. Wake at five, brew coffee, and sit at the computer. Since we had moved here and he set that awful intention to make a place for himself as a woman, he had been very excited about writing. I guessed that this ritual was done wearing women's clothes.

I was not about to go find out. I didn't have the energy to walk outside across the breezeway and knock on his door. Trinidad now wailed from the other room, and Sam couldn't manage to get his mouth onto my breast while I bent double picking up stuffing cubes from the floor. Tears welled in Sam's eyes again and, nodding his head, he opened his mouth in a silent howl. Trinidad coughed roughly and fastened himself to the expectation that I would rescue him. I could hear it in the pitch of his cry. The bread cubes were a damned mess. I picked them up one by one and threw them all in a bowl. I set the bowl on the counter then adjusted Sam's searching mouth so that it found my nipple. I straightened my shoulders, adjusted the sling, and walked slowly back to the bedroom.

I sat with Trin awhile on the bed, comforting him, while Sam fell back to sleep at my breast. I tried to carefully slip the sling away from me so as to leave Sam lying propped on some pillows on our king size mattress on the floor, but he woke as soon as his body left mine. The blessed quiet was broken by his bawling, and I hoisted the cotton sling over my head and shoulder like a yoke. I sat rocking Sam on the bed while I stroked Trinidad's hair and spoke softly to them.

I heard the back door swing open and Fred refilling his coffee in the kitchen. I'm sure he heard us in the bedroom and saw my progress toward Thanksgiving dinner.

"Good morning," he called as he came through the hallway to find us where we sat.

"Good morning," I said.

"Is there anything I can help with?" he asked.

"Hmmm," I said. "How about you make Thanksgiving dinner, and I'll just do the kids today?"

He grimaced but said nothing. The man could build a fence, balance the checkbook, and do the dishes, but he had no interest in cooking. I once stopped by his house unannounced when we were dating and found him heating a can of soup—still in the can—in a pan of water on the stovetop.

"You tell me what to do, and I'll try," he said.

"Okay, can you chop potatoes?"

"Sure," he said. He was not smiling. "How many do you want?"

"I don't know." It was so hard to visualize what I wanted and explain it to someone else. It was almost as if I could no longer use my brain to process and communicate, but instead my hands knew how many, how small, how long to stir or knead. My breast knew when the baby was hungry. My feet started walking child-ward, seeming to know when the crying had gone on too long and needed to be tended to. Why didn't Fred's body know these things, too? And why wasn't I a better teacher?

"Try five? And let me see what that looks like."

"How big do you want them chopped?"

"Mama! I want to go outside!" said Trinidad, his voice breaking in the middle. He started coughing so his little body bent and heaved while my hand rested on his back. He began to cry.

"I wanna go outside!"

"I know," I said, pushing myself up onto one arm on the bed. Sam jerked his head off my breast suddenly and snorted, lips pressed tightly together. He made a chewing expression with his eyes closed, tongue tucked against the roof of his mouth, sucking at an imaginary nipple while he slept. I turned to face Fred. He looked pale and alarmed.

"I don't know what to do," he said.

"Cut the potatoes," I said.

"Let's go!" cried Trinidad.

"Okay, hold on," I said.

Fred looked at me sadly. "Kristin, you're sick. You should go back to bed."

"That's a great idea," I said, reaching over with the cloth to wipe Trinidad's nose.

"No, seriously. You don't look good."

"Thanks," I said. "Who's gonna cook?"

"I don't know," he said. "We don't have to have Thanksgiving dinner."

"Okay," I said. "But we do have to eat. We're all going to get hungry. And I haven't even started the stuffing."

"Okay. I'll do that. How do I do that?"

"Just do the potatoes, please?"

"Mama! You're not listening." Trinidad climbed out of the bed with his pajamas on, tugged at my skirt, and then coughed again.

"Okay, look—you need some medicine. We can go outside, but first you get medicine."

"Yeah," said Trinidad. I wrapped my arm more tightly around Sam and got up off the bed, walking past Fred to the kitchen. I opened a cabinet with one hand and dug for the homeopathic cough remedy. Turning my body sideways so Sam didn't hit the counter, I unscrewed the cap and poured the thick, honey-scented syrup to the correct dosage mark then handed it down to my three-year-old.

"God, I'd love a cup of tea," I said to no one in particular.

"Why don't you get one and go back to bed?" said Fred. "I'll take Trin out for a walk."

"No, Mama! I go with you, Mama!" Trin shouted, pulling at my skirt. Sam's little head jerked, and he sucked in a bellyful of air before opening his mouth to cry. I rocked Sam with one hand and gripped the top of my skirt with the other to keep Trin from taking it down with him.

"I don't know what to do," said Fred.

"Well, I don't either," I said. The stuffing cubes sat in a bowl on the counter, and I couldn't remember how my mother made hers. She was so unreliable if you called her for a recipe, too. She never had anything written down. It was all in her head, but when she told me it never came out right. How did stuff come out right when she did it? Was it all in her hands? Was that her problem, too?

"I don't know," said Fred. "I guess I'll just go back out and write. At least I can get something done there. You call me if you need me," he said.

"Potatoes," I said.

"Right," he grimaced and grabbed the cutting board.

"Outside!" said Trinidad. "Go outside!"

I stood swaying my hips back and forth, quieting Sam who had begun to nurse again. My nipples were sore. "God, please grant me the patience, the energy, and the ability to be grateful on this Thanksgiving," I thought. "And please . . . I need that *now.*"

Fathers

I KNEW THAT, overall, I had picked a good husband. Fred would have done anything for me if I could name it. Sometimes begrudgingly, sure, but we all have moments of suspended motivation. He adored me, and once he truly realized my need, he was there for me. He worked hard at the things he was good at—building, repairing, basic caregiving—and also did what I asked of him.

More challenging for our relationship was the integration of Fred's personal life. He had very few friends and spent most of his time on the computer, whether socially or while writing his fantasy novel. Because he got up early each morning, he was exhausted and unable to do much after eight o'clock at night. He was in bed by eight-thirty or nine most nights while I continued to do housework, feed, and care for our children until ten or eleven.

I wondered if he subconsciously wanted to be unavailable to us. He thought he was gaining extra time for himself in the day by getting up early, but then he was with us for only about two hours after he got home from work. That did not leave much time to spend with family or to help around the house. I craved connection with him. The kids did not complain because they had never really bonded with him, and I felt confused and disappointed about that. If Fred spent more time with them, would that help? The question was rhetorical, because he was not willing to shift his schedule. Fred's writing time was precious to him, and I supported that.

To grant me respite, Fred had occasionally tried to occupy the boys on his own but it had rarely worked out the way we intended despite the fact that Fred had been a stay-at-home dad for over a year. After Trinidad was born, I took maternity leave for a couple of months, then Fred stepped in as the primary caregiver while I went back to work as a lead tutor for several home programs serving preschoolers diagnosed with autism under the auspices of our local university. Every few hours, Fred would bring Trinidad to me for nursing. This went on for almost two years. During that time, Fred took Trin on many walks in the woods near our home, successfully acclimating him to the outdoors and fostering in him a love of nature that he still has today. Nonetheless, whenever I got home, Trinidad would have no more of his father; he would direct his attention only to me for meeting all of his needs.

Years later, Fred told me about how he struggled when Trinidad would cry for me during the day. Sometimes the crying would go on and on, and he could find no way to console our son. Fred had dropped to his knees on the floor, angry and frustrated, pounding the carpet with his fist. Whether this heightened Trinidad's emotional response, then or in the future, I will never know. But I do know that it left his father feeling helpless and unsuccessful in yet another aspect of his life.

I saw this happening and had no idea how to stop it. Just as Trin had determined he would not take a bottle (we tried on more than several occasions), he had also decided that I was his primary comfort. Trin spent time with his dad building with blocks or getting rides in the laundry basket and laughing with glee as long as he knew I was in the next room. Then, if Trin needed anything, he would come find me.

I myself had suffered separation anxiety when I was young. My mother would get calls from the preschool because I'd cried so hard that I'd made myself throw up. They called to ask her almost daily to come and get me. I remember feeling terribly alone there. I was also confused and scared, unsure of when and whether my mom would return. I felt completely safe and happy when I was with her. She and I did everything together when she wasn't working, and I loved her boundlessly—as you might love an angel—with adoration, trepidation, and always worry for the time when you might find yourself navigating alone. So, understandably, I felt for my son.

As for what kind of father I wanted for my children, I did not have much in the way of models to help me decipher. In my childhood, this is what I knew: it is the mother's job to provide food when the father does not. It is also her job to meet every other need beyond food, at least when she is not struggling to get enough cash to put food on the table, and it is the mother's job to protect the children from their father. I knew I did not want to be put in the role of protecting my children from their father, and I thought I had found such certainty with Fred. He was kind and gentle in every way.

In fact, Fred's temperament was very easy-going in comparison to the high-strung intensity of my personality. I would hash out every last detail of a plan, as well as a plan B and C, to ensure success. This took a fair amount of energy and some anxiety, too. Fred would smile, wink, give me a hug, and trust it would all work out fine. I relaxed into that trust time and again, and it served me. He made sure we came through every crisis in one piece. We never went hungry, and we had a roof over our heads the day after the house fire thanks to his efforts. He was an excellent helpmate in most ways.

However, there was a gap where my desire to have more and better exceeded his own. The degree to which I kept the children engaged and the house clean, as well as my efforts at preparing wholesome meals, was somewhat beyond what he would have personally ventured to achieve, though he enjoyed what I created nonetheless.

Do the majority of men have a socially constructed expectation that women will take care of them and the household, or are they naturally disinclined to do those things for themselves and simply would not do them if left to their own devices? It is a rare thing in my limited experience to see a man and woman agree about how a household should be managed and partner equitably to keep it that way, but perhaps this is also true of men living with men and women living with women. What I don't appreciate is the conventional/stereotypical expectation that a woman will keep the house for an entire family, even if working full time outside the home, while a man is entitled to rest and refuel at his abode as long as he is holding some outside job.

In my youth, my mother worked as a dog groomer to pay our bills while my stepfather spent years unemployed, lying on the couch watching television. I was given a list of chores to do daily, and my stepfather inspected each of my tasks, demanding that I vacuum the entire kitchen over if I missed a thread or some dog hair in one spot. I don't recall my stepfather physically hurting me, but he occasionally beat my mother because, according to her, his ego was wounded from being out of work. "You don't know what that does to a man," she said.

My biological father had been a workaholic, driving long-haul trucks across the nation and stopping to visit his wife and baby girl midway at our home in Kansas. He beat my mother for a different reason, and that began while I was still in utero. It seems that some men who spend all day in a truck fixate on the possibility that their wife is having fun with another *available* man. My father would drink to try to get that idea out of his head, and the drinking became a habit he couldn't shake, even when my mother was around.

He was a loving husband and father, and he was an angry drunk. I was almost three years old when my mother and I returned to California for the holidays, and I did not see my biological father again until I was fourteen. She refused to let him visit without being present herself, because she feared he'd take me. My father refused to pay child support for a child he wasn't allowed to see on his own terms.

Fred certainly performed better than either of my father figures. He did everything I asked and was not abusive in any way while he cared for Trinidad during his period of unemployment. He even did his best to keep up with the laundry, shopping, and some of the cooking.

Fred's efforts were a drastic improvement over his own father's. For much of Fred's youth, his father had scrutinized his children's work much the way my stepfather had. He rarely left the house to do it, preferring instead to manage their ranch chores from his comfortable chair in the kitchen. Fred fed the cows, broke the ice on the water troughs, brought the sheep in, and then answered a barrage of questions about the minutiae of these tasks.

Fred's father likely suffered from obsessive-compulsive disorder and spent the last third of his life indoors picking up individual crumbs from the floor and rummaging through the garbage in case someone had accidentally thrown out something important. Like a spoon. Fred knew he did not want to be that kind of father, but neither of us had great role models to look to for guidance.

And now my children's father wanted to be a woman. I did not have a plan for this challenge, but I would soon have to devise one. Being the mother I'd most wanted to be had helped heal the wounds I'd suffered as a child in a broken and dysfunctional home. I wanted to continue on that path of healing and had no intention of letting go of the exceptional love I felt for my husband. Even if he saw himself as my wife.

Therapy

FRED HAD STARTED seeing a therapist after I returned from my mother's, following the house fire. He had taken charge of his healing, and my job was to wait on the sidelines until he got it sorted out. Fred's first counselor saw his gender exploration as a necessary part of his undeniable artistic persona. She gave him movies to watch about other artists and musicians that had struggled with their gender and/or sexuality. Fred began to see his creativity as the cause of his dilemma, and he dug more deeply into his writing. His novel's main character was, in fact, a woman.

"I am an artist," Fred declared, as if that explained everything.

"You are?" I asked. "You are? And that makes you a woman, too? Because being an artist doesn't make me a man at all."

He looked at me. I could tell that he'd forgotten that I might describe myself as an artist. While he had struggled to write a book over the past decade, I had channeled my creativity into dinner, flower gardens, and décor. I sang and danced in meadows and at the park. I drew and painted cards for friends and relatives. I wrote poetry between breast feedings. My life was so full of meeting basic needs that the only way I could maintain my art was to express it in small ways from dawn to dusk. I shook inside when I saw that he had missed that.

"I am an artist, too," I said slowly. My lips pressed together into a thin line.

"You're right," he said. He took me in his arms. "I'm sorry, I somehow didn't see that. You are much more an artist than I am. You never stop creating all day long."

My irritation was not quick to dissolve. I put my arms around him but my jaw was set with fury at how easy it was to become invisible. Now you see me, now you don't. This is the problem with being a housewife. If you're lucky. Otherwise, you're just invisible most of the time.

Fred got a new therapist.

Nonviolent Communication

OUR LOCAL La Leche League hosted their regional conference in Eugene that October. I accepted their invitation to attend as a vendor with products from my business with Pampered Chef. I brought my children and a trunk-load of kitchen tools to set up in the conference center's lobby. I looked at the schedule of events and discovered there was a topic every hour that I wanted to listen in on. Surprised at being so engaged by the content of the conference, I scanned the brochure once more and realized that each workshop I felt drawn to, one out of several offered each hour, was presented by the keynote speaker, Inbal Kashtan.

Kashtan's work caught my attention because it centered on acceptance and peaceful resolution of conflict. Her topics ranged from navigating intimate partnerships to deepening love and integrity within families. While my toddlers played in the hall nearby, I stood at the door listening to her teachings of Nonviolent Communication (NVC).

Also called Compassionate Communication, NVC teaches that every behavior, thought, and action is an attempt to meet a need. In order to more deeply connect with ourselves and each other, we can seek to understand and hold dear the needs behind everyone's actions, including our own, even if we disagree with the strategies that have been employed to meet those needs. This premise resonated with my previous experience in teaching children diagnosed with autism. It made sense and I wanted more.

I immediately picked up a copy of Kashtan's book *Parenting From Your Heart*, and I read it cover to cover. I thoughtfully completed the exercises within, noticing that a successful practice of NVC was more difficult to achieve than a theoretical understanding of it. I agreed with the concepts, but when I tried to differentiate a universal need from a strategy to meet that need, I sometimes felt confused. I also had trouble imagining what unmet needs might prompt certain feelings or behaviors. I spent hours studying and writing about my experience as I tried to superimpose this new modality onto my life and parenting.

Initially, I was drawn to NVC to support safety and peace between me and my children. I recognized that my patience had shrunk with the addition of a second child. One morning, I caught myself plunking Trinidad down unceremoniously on the floor and lacing up the shoes on his little feet too tightly while he squirmed and protested. I needed some constructive way to let off steam and connect with the love I knew I had for this child.

I had grown up with domestic violence and did not want to repeat the pattern. I was not even tempted to until I had children. Now, as they began to walk, talk, and promote their own agendas, I found myself desperate for a sense of quiet inner focus. I knew I wanted to stay in my heart, even with the less comfortable emotions, and I wanted to model that for my children. I just didn't quite know how to do it.

Six months later, I contacted a local NVC instructor who agreed to teach classes if I organized them. I gathered several parents, and we met at local parks weekly. Fred, appreciating the value of this work, decided to manage childcare for participants on a playground nearby. Our instructor did not have children of her own but had been teaching NVC in our community for a few years. She asked me to help translate NVC into the world of parenting.

I agreed and quickly embraced the intellectual and heart work of exploring feelings and needs while stewarding children and families. As I delved more deeply into my NVC practice, I found it easy to support others in doing the same. I continued my education by taking teleclasses and workshops in our vicinity. What had initially sprung from a desire to deepen my patience and connection with the boys became a beacon in my relationship with Fred. I learned to sit with my feelings, to express them at all volumes, and to hold the needs behind them with tender care, whether the needs were met or not. I learned to detach myself from shame and blame. This became my growing edge, and I worked it daily.

Snapshots 2004

*Our new house is in the perfect neighborhood, but it is remark-
ably isolated. It faces a neighbor's side yard across the street,
and all of our adjacent neighbors' houses face away from ours.
I had not foreseen this isolation. The boys and I are in our front
yard often, but few people notice or care. We are strangely alone.*

*I take walks by the river with my husband and two small
children, sorely missing our old dog who died of cancer when
we moved into the new house. Trin and Sam throw rocks at the
water's edge while Fred rages against the many faults of our
political system and his father's parenting. He feels helpless and
despondent. No amount of empathy appears to soothe him. I
am exhausted and consider shooting him to put him out of his
misery. (This is only half a joke.)*

*I want another baby. I'm afraid to have one with Fred because
our family could be on the brink of extinction. I'm tempted to
conceive before it disintegrates, so I can have one more child
with this person I adore beyond reason. My inner stockbroker
determines that it is not a wise investment to have a baby now. I
decide to plan for a new dog instead.*

*Sam is all-powerful. He is a tiny, half-frail-looking creature,
but anything he wants he somehow gets his hands on. All of*

his development has come ahead of schedule—rolling over, crawling, and walking. I decide to toilet-train him at less than a year, and he agrees. This convinces his brother that he is to be reckoned with as a peer, and Trinidad has never failed since to take him quite seriously.

Fred and I spend hours trying to work out what is going on inside of him. The children are around, on top of, and between us, but we cannot wait to have these conversations alone. I cry into his shoulder as quietly as possible. Trinidad is enraged and hysterical much of the time. He will not sleep, eat, or play without me nearby. I don't see that he may be feeding off my energy, my pressure cooker tempest of hysterical anger and confusion. I just think that my life is rather exceptionally difficult.

Fred takes the boys for a walk in the park. As soon as my family is out the door and around the corner, I scream and tear at my hair. I fall to my knees on the cold hardwood floor. With tight fists, I stretch out my already-baggy T-shirt as I sob and writhe. I think of shaving my head, binding my breasts, denying the hold gender has on me. I want to hurt myself. I am terrified and alone. I wonder how many people in a five-mile radius are in the midst of this same crisis and do not tell a soul.

Heather

FRED CONTINUED TO work diligently on his novel from five to seven o'clock every morning in our detached, six by seven foot home office. Once part of a storage shed, the tiny room boasted a low ceiling, dirty white paint, and an aluminum-framed window covered by a white vinyl blind. Fred typed diligently there at his desktop computer, making real progress on his novel at last. He told me he felt relieved to live the life of a woman through his heroine, Ellen. I was glad that he had fully turned his attention to creating something rather than floundering with despair over everything in our world that was broken.

I got out of bed a couple of hours later than Fred did every day, and in the winter months, it was still dark at that time. I gingerly peeked between the slats of our bedroom blinds across the yard into his office to see what he was wearing. From a distance, I could make out a woman's blouse, maybe a scarf. If he stood up, I could see the top of a skirt. I recoiled as my eyes probed deeper, trying to make out every detail from across the yard. I wanted to see it all, to know, to discern our fate, but I was terrified as it unveiled itself in the early morning light. My heart raced and my stomach turned so I thought I would vomit. My ears became hot and a distant whirring sounded deep inside of me. Every morning, this feeling lasted for hours as I tried to remember what was next on my list to get done. Finally, I could take no more and asked Fred to shut the blinds while he worked. He obliged.

My husband developed a persona to match his feminine aspect. Her name was Heather, and she was very soft, feminine, and determined to be seen. He timidly told me about her, in the third person. He said he was exploring her, learning from her. He clearly valued her internal companionship. I thought he might be nuts.

One night, I asked Fred if I could talk to Heather. He said yes. Lying in bed in the dark, I asked her who she was, why she wanted to come out in our world. She described herself and said plaintively that she had been locked away for so long, it was unbearable. She had to get out or she (and he) would go crazy. My eyes grew wide in the dark. Heather spoke in a lilting falsetto. I did not dare to look at the side of my husband's face. I didn't know this person I lay next to. Maybe *I* was nuts.

Observing that possibility, I decided to go whole hog and asked Heather if she wanted to have sex with me. She shyly agreed. My heart raced as I closed my eyes and felt a woman through my husband in the dark. I stroked her cheek, her neck, and the curved back of her ear. I kissed her eyelids and traced her high cheekbone with my tongue. She responded with tiny gasps and moans, lifting her chin higher to me. I grew excited.

I thought maybe I could make this work. I dominated Heather. I sucked and rode and ravaged her. It was fun. I wasn't sure whom the dick belonged to, but I was glad for its presence. "A penis between us," we later joked. I wasn't sure that I wanted Heather around all the time, but her presence sparked a "top" in me that I hadn't fully realized until then. (A lesbian friend explained to me the dynamic of tops and bottoms in relationships. The top is a dominant energy and the bottom is more submissive. As I understand it, these tendencies can shift in different aspects of the relationship—sex, domesticity, professional life, etc.)

Years later, I realized that Fred had never taken a dominant role in our sex life. He'd always hoped that I would lead. The Heather phase of our relationship helped me to be fully there for him in the way he'd most longed for sexually. I stretched now for him as he had, for more than a decade, stretched for me.

When we woke up the next morning, Heather didn't want to say hello. I never slept with her again. Over the course of the next two years, she spoke out less and became more and more integrated as Fred fully acknowledged the feminine aspects of himself. Several years later, we'd both nearly forgotten that she ever was.

Smelling the Coffee

I WORE MANY hats trying to keep our household in order through tough economic times. I spent my evenings presenting kitchen shows and my days parenting. Fred had lost his job with the design/build firm that had housed us after the fire and now helped me with Pampered Chef bookwork when he wasn't looking for employment as an architectural intern. He even bravely performed a couple of kitchen shows. I got up early to do the laundry and prepare food for the day. I hung wet clothes indoors to dry through the winter. Our little house steamed and sweated.

As I sorted whites from colors one morning, I lifted an undergarment I didn't recognize from the pile. The pink lace edging triggered a gag reflex when I noticed the pantie's size. It was clearly not mine. I'd often suppressed a fear of discovering some other woman in our relationship, but I never would have guessed that I would meet her this way. I held the garment at arms length and flipped it with a finger into the washing machine.

I looked down and saw a bra that matched the pantie. What on earth did he put in that? Socks? I didn't wear a bra myself. My mother had once pointed out that if you can put a bra on backward and get the same support, you're likely better off without it. I couldn't imagine wearing one without a need to. Fred was just not my kind of woman.

The back door swung open. I froze, clutching the pink lace. A leg covered in navy stockings stepped through the threshold on a moderately heeled shoe. What legs! I scanned upward to a tight, round bottom clad in a business-length short skirt topped with a blue-striped sweater. Dang. She looked cute from behind. I hid in plain sight with my hands on her bra. She didn't see me but stepped brightly across the kitchen to refill her coffee cup. Then she turned and the goatee beard caused something inside me to fall.

"Oh! I'm sorry," said my husband, crossing his arms over his chest. The spell had been broken. My eyes fell and then worked their way slowly upward again. Fred did have nice legs.

"I didn't realize you were up," he said. "I usually change my clothes before I come inside, even for coffee. I didn't mean to upset you."

He reached a hand tentatively out as if to embrace me, and then dropped it and drew back.

"I'll be more careful next time," he said.

I moved my leaden feet one after another to cross the room. I reached out and wrapped my arms around him. What in the world was happening to us? I cried into his hard, pokey bust. I told him it was okay. I handed him his bra.

"I'd rather you did your own laundry," I said.

An Ocean between Us

MY FRIEND BEA called from Germany.

"How are things going, Earthling?" She caught me in a tender spot. I was so used to holding it together, focusing on the trials and tribulations of parenting while living with the transgender elephant in the room. I was usually good at hiding what was really on my mind twenty-four hours a day, but that day, she found me worn a little thin.

"Um . . . my husband wants to dress like a woman," I said. Admittedly, it was a moment of weakness, and thankfully Bea lived across the ocean. How could word get out? The silence crackled.

"Oh . . . tell me about that," said Bea. She was politic, my friend Bea. She listened wholly, and her curiosity seemed bottomless and true. I told her everything.

"Wow. I watched a movie about that recently," she said. "You have to see it. And, you won't believe this, but I have a friend who went through the same thing with her husband, whose name is now Lila."

As Bea told me about her friend and her friend's former husband, a light went on. I had been to a conference with Lila a couple of years ago, and I had been transfixed with everything about her throughout the workshop we attended together. Her (if that was her chosen pronoun—I hadn't been sure at the time) hair hung down past her shoulders, and she wore a skirt, though her five o'clock shadow matched her deep, masculine voice. She worked for a computer chip manufacturer, and I was perplexed by the degree of serious respect given to her by everyone in the room despite what I perceived to be her incongruous appearance. They didn't seem confused or put off by her gender presentation at all. I don't even remember the topic of the workshop because I was utterly distracted by Lila's appearance.

I remember asking Fred what he thought of the transwoman's presentation.

"I don't know," he said. "I mean, I'm interested, sure, but I don't want to ask." I remembered now how small and withdrawn he had looked when he'd said that.

"So where is Lila now?" I asked Bea.

"Oh, she's in Portland, selling Mary Kay," Bea said. "You should have Fred look her up. She could set him up with a great facial." I wondered how on earth Lila made a living with that. I hoped her beard was gone. I knew what a chore it was to get a good base coat across the stubble, because I'd seen Fred try when he thought I wasn't looking.

Well, I mused, this happens more than I thought. There *are* other transpeople out there in various stages of metamorphosis. They are folks like us, trying to make a living while raising a family and sitting on a secret that could bust it all apart.

"Yeah," said Bea, "you know what the problem with that is don't you?"

"The problem with what?" I asked.

"Well, he wants to wear women's clothes now. Then he'll want to spend more and more time dressed that way. Then, it's transition. And, I'll tell you what, girlfriend. There isn't any room for you in that."

"You mean . . . ?"

"Yep. If he's got it like you say he's got it, your marriage is just about over. That's what happens."

"Oh." I said. I had been leaning against the kitchen stove, phone gripped tightly in one hand. Slowly, I slid down to sit on the cold, avocado and rust-colored linoleum. Silently, I wept.

"I'm sorry, sweetie," she said. "That's just how it happens."

Harvest

FRED AND I tore down the dilapidated structure that provided a covered patio between the house and office. The light that flooded our newfound space astonished us. The dead patch of earth in front of the office quickly grew lush with weeds, and I decided to plant an herb garden there. I got out a shovel and dug the old, moldy-smelling earthen clay from between concrete walkways. Trinidad inspected the hole for dinosaur bones while Sam collected pretty rocks and put them in yoghurt containers.

I ordered fresh compost from a landscaping company, and it was delivered in a mound that my children climbed as if Mount Everest itself had popped up in the back alley. We filled in the hole between house and office with hills and mounds that hugged a winding stone footpath. Silver thyme cascaded down one slope beside rosemary, marjoram, and parsley. Other sages and thymes peppered the walkway with blooms of blue and violet offset by the brilliant orange and yellow of marigolds and nasturtiums. Our neighbors Ben and Katherine stopped to talk and admire our efforts. I gave them a tour of our vegetable garden behind the office, too.

Potatoes, beans, tomatoes, corn, and squash grew abundantly, but most impressive were the enormous bushes of sweet basil. I stuffed a black plastic garbage bag with load after load of it one day—around fifteen pounds in all. I took this bounty to the back porch where Trinidad and I laid it gently in buckets of cool water to rinse. Then we spread it across terrycloth towels to dry in the shade. The sweet scent of basil rose up, intoxicating. I picked off the leaves and ran them through a food processor, grinding them to a paste. Trinidad, old world style, crushed them by hand with garlic in a mortar and pestle.

"That's how the women of Genoa did it," I told him. "They invented pesto to feed their sailor husbands who worked at sea. It was the only green, flavorful leaf they could keep fresh for weeks with garlic in olive oil. Now, it's a luxury sauce for the rich and for us, the cleverly frugal who grow so much basil in our garden."

Trinidad and I revered the process. Basil is holy in India, recognized as a healing herb. Sam watched and tasted, swaying beside us on his spindly toddler legs. Trinidad and I spent all afternoon reducing our harvest to a small number of jars that I hoped would feed and heal us, no matter the storms to come.

She's Not There

FRED AND I stood at the back door and watched Trinidad collect bugs. Sam toddled along after him, looking into jars without lifting the lids, trying to follow his brother's instructions. I stared over the top of a six-foot fence between our yard and the alley while Fred told me that he didn't think he was a transsexual. Maybe he was only transgender, he said. He didn't need to have a full sex change. He just had to figure out how to live with this woman inside him.

"You'd better look at all the options," I said. "You'd better find out what it's like for people who do make a full transition, because that choice is at one end of the transgender spectrum. You've got to understand the whole spectrum to know where you fall."

I hated the words coming out of my mouth. My heart sank when I said them, and I had an eerie floating sensation while I gazed down the back alley. Why did I take this role in pushing him forward to certainty? Because I wanted clarity myself. I wanted peace and harmony for him so I might also be able to relax, to sink back down into my mother body and just worry about the boys and myself for a while. I was tired but well aware that we were nowhere near finished with this piece of work.

"I don't want to transition, though," he said. "Where would that leave you and the kids?"

"You need to know what's true for you. You have to look at all the possibilities just like I do."

I didn't know that courage would taste like so much bile at the back of my throat. I did not know that urging my husband to seek his truth would become my own truth even though it felt like a kamikaze mission. I saw the vehicle of our marriage spinning madly out of control, but I could only clutch at the steering wheel and turn with the spin in hopes of correcting our path. Sometimes, I could only hold on for the ride.

My eyes did not leave the top of the fence. A squirrel picked her way along it then stretched out full length on the top bar in the shade. Her belly draped down over the side of the running board; she was pregnant. We called the squirrel Ivy, and this would be her first litter as far as we could tell. The boys and I watched her progress daily. Today, she looked hot and uncomfortable.

"Are there people you could talk to about this?" I asked. "People in our community who have made the change?"

"Yes," he said. "There's a male-to-female transsexual that I could meet with. I've got her number. She used to be a butcher and, after two suicide attempts, she realized she had to transition to survive."

"Okay," I said. "Good."

That afternoon, we went to the library. We came home with books on dinosaurs, bugs, castles, and transsexuals. Fred and I picked our first reads. I chose a clinical book describing the process of identifying and supporting the transsexual, and he chose an autobiography of a male-to-female transsexual titled *She's Not There,* by Jennifer Finney Boylan. Fred took his read out to the office and disappeared for a while. I lay in the hammock watching the kids play and read through tears.

It could be us, I thought. These case studies sounded familiar. This could be what Fred was going through. The sun was out, and our boys jammed rocks into their pockets while loading up the red wagon with weeds I'd left in a pile by the garden. My tears fell hot and steady. I cloistered my fear and the beginning of my knowing. There was no context for it—not in the grocery

store, not in playgroup, not even in our hip college neighborhood. I'd never known anyone with such a problem. This sort of
thing only happened on Oprah, and we didn't have cable.

"Did you learn anything?" I asked Fred when we swapped
books a few days later.

"Yeah—this is a well-written account of Jenny Boylan's
life and transition, but I don't think it's me. Pretty interesting,
though," he said.

I felt cold inside as I looked at the cover—a woman's lower
body clad in tight jeans; sexy and appealing. The clothes made
the body clearly feminine. Could it possibly be that easy? I
cracked open the book warily.

Three hours later, Fred came to find me on our bed. I was
reading about the life of James-then-Jenny Boylan. I read that
Jenny had a wife and two young sons, and that the family had
come to terms with Jenny's true identity. The family constel-
lation was so much like ours that I shuddered. Also akin was
James's love for his wife—so much like Fred's love for me. It
was a tough transition, but they stuck it out and were still
together—though it didn't say exactly what together meant at
the time. I sobbed uncontrollably, chapter after chapter.

"Where is Jenny's wife's story?" I sputtered to Fred. "How
did she feel going through this? What was she thinking? How
did she survive the not-knowing, day after day, and finally the
knowing? Why can't I hear from her?"

"It's okay, Kristin," Fred said softly, his arm around me.
"It's okay. It's not us. I don't see that being us."

"I think it might be, Fred," I said. "I think it might be."

The next week, Fred met with the former butcher. She
assured my husband that her transition was life-saving and a
decision that made it possible for her to continue supporting
her wife and family. She would never leave her wife, no matter what. They were old school that way. Fred asked the butcher
if I could talk with her wife. She said, "Yes, of course. I can't

imagine that she would be opposed to that. She has really accepted the whole thing now."

I wanted to know that they really made it work. I wanted to know how—the nuts and bolts: sex, attraction, day-to-day routines of makeup and coffee. I needed to see it happen to real people. I needed a context.

I rang the butcher's wife three times. She did not return my calls.

A Birthday Wish

FRED JOINED A writers group that met once a week. In addition to working on his novel, Fred began to explore his inner feminine side in personal essays. It took courage to share his process with the group and, happily, Fred found that his companions accepted and embraced his shifting identity. With an enormous sense of relief at being able to out himself to a small portion of the world, Fred attended some of their meetings dressed as his female persona.

In October of 2004, Fred turned forty-four. I decided to throw a party for him and invite his friends from the writers group. They were his only local friends, other than those he had met through me. Fred had never really cultivated a circle of friends on his own. During football season, he went out to watch a few games with my friend's husband. Otherwise, we did things together or he pursued his interests alone.

On the night of the party, I baked Fred's favorite chocolate cake. The boys and I walked around the neighborhood and collected tiny, brightly colored leaves to place at the edges and in the center of the cake over the glossy, sour cream-chocolate frosting. I decorated the living room and extended our table to seat ten.

The guests arrived on time and gifts collected at the end of the long table. I watched the writers banter back and forth with my husband. It was a pleasure for me to see him appreciated and valued in his work. Fred smiled, laughed, and appeared very comfortable with them. I was the one on the outside this time, and I didn't mind the role reversal. I glowed to see him so joyful and at ease with his friends and welcomed the opportunity to bring this community into our home, our family.

I set the cake before my husband, lights dimmed and candles blazing. Fred silently made his wish and blew out the candles. Everyone clapped and the cake was served. Trinidad and Sam sat beside me and devoured their servings in just a few bites. The group included me in their conversation out of consideration, but mostly they were excited to gather outside of their regular Tuesday night meeting. With great animation, they attended to one another, happily discussing their lives outside of writing.

I collected empty plates as Fred reached to open his first gift. I returned from the kitchen to see our guests leaning in close as Fred pulled a pink vinyl purse from the sparkling tissue. The bag bore an art deco image of a woman emblazoned across the front and a long pink zipper ran down one side. My breath caught in my throat. I looked at the boys. They watched with curiosity.

I had no idea what to do. This was clearly a gift for Fred's feminine side. I had never seen that part of him acknowledged beyond the privacy of our home; indeed, I had rarely spent time with it myself. The children, now four and almost two years old, had no concept of gender in any conscious sense and only knew their father as he showed up in jeans and a chamois shirt. It hadn't occurred to me that bringing the writers group into our home would open Fred's gender exploration to our children.

My heart raced and I began to sweat as Fred, blushing, unzipped the pink pouch. He reached in and carefully pulled a pair of black fishnet stockings from the purse. The woman who had offered the gift began to rise out of her seat with excitement. "I wasn't sure if they would fit," she said. "They only came in one size." Jewelry, too, spilled out of the bag and onto the table.

Fred picked up the pieces one at a time, gently stroked the stockings, and then shifted his gaze to me. I stood still in the threshold between living room and kitchen, knuckles pressed against my lips. How would I survive this moment? I did not want to walk away from Fred's friends. I wanted to honor the acceptance and kinship he had found there. This group had saved him personally and cultivated his talents as a writer.

At the same time, my insides turned to ice. This was our home. Fred and I chose how much of his feminine exploration would be revealed here. Every day, we walked a fine line of being honest with each other and ourselves about our feelings as Fred spent time in Heather's shoes. Never had it occurred to me that Fred's "other woman" would find her way into the living room over cake and birthday wishes.

Our boys took in the situation with interest but no apparent confusion. I wanted to scoop them up and run out the door to God-knows-where. Only one local friend, Michelle, knew of our plight, and she was hardly accepting. Where would we go? What would we do?

As I churned internally and my head began to pound, laughter and the clinking of wine glasses played on before me. Friends leaned across the table to share witticisms and pat each other knowingly on the hand about long-time inside jokes. Torn, Fred looked to them with wonder then back at me beseechingly, fully perceiving the jagged trap I found myself in. He half rose to come to me, but I shook my head and left the room.

My husband would celebrate no more birthdays. Our community reflected it back to me clearly: she had moved on without me.

Medicine Dream 1

I AM IN a classroom while a group of students discuss political figures who have died in office over the course of history. I sit with my mind blank, unable to think of any as my peers rattle off facts and figures. I feel embarrassed at my inadequacy and think to myself, amused, "What do I know about death? I have a dog who died."

I look to the wall where a spice rack hangs, and I think of a story I know in which Death was once considered an ambassador from another world. He picked people up and carried them across the threshold as a mother picks up her children from school. One day, in the story, Death did not come for people anymore, and then everyone grew afraid of Death because they were afraid to cross over alone. Death then became a word for the transformation that people made in isolation. There was something missing—a guardian, a guide.

I start thinking about insanity, about how people sometimes see things to keep themselves from being alone. I sit back in my chair in the classroom, musing to myself that this seeing is likely an act of God to keep people from feeling isolated and separate.

Suddenly, I am pulled bodily and spiritually out of my chair to the classroom door. A bright light issues from beneath and around it. I throw open the door and am nearly blinded by the light. I am clear that I am looking at God, and to go through this door is to die.

It is enough to look, and with gratitude, I turn and run back into the classroom. I fall to my knees. "I am your child in God!" I cry.

The experience of the light is now in my heart and between my hands. It grows so intensely bright and beautiful that I try to expand on my words to meet it. "I am your child in Buddha!" I say.

The light goes out. I am pulled by the heart, dragged to the door, and it flies open again. The brilliance is all-encompassing and wordlessly communicates that my last statement was somehow wrong, at least for me.

I turn, run back into the room and kneel. "I am your child in Christ!" I say with my head bowed.

The light dims, and then gently a voice more female than male speaks these words: "How do you feel when you say that?"

I pause a moment and say, "It's not right."

The voice leads me back to the door, or perhaps the door of my heart opens, and I witness the light within. "I am your child in God, just God!" I blurt. And that's enough, I think.

Again, I experience the rapturous light in my heart and hands, and it pulses in me, accompanied by my ecstasy and gratitude.

The voice, a little tired but patient, tells me, "Good. Now let's go home and get some rest."

I collapse onto a couch and wake up.

Moving into Manhood, Killing Time

TOGETHER WITH HIS new therapist, Fred finally accessed a dark, dismal childhood trauma to process. An almost-memory, the fuzzy recollection could well have been the seed to a gender confusion that lasted some forty years. Fred scraped at the memory, the trauma, in his mind like it was a fresh leather hide to be tanned and stretched taut to dry in the bright sunlight. In therapy, he opened his eyes to events that he had suppressed and opened his heart to feel what he could not feel as a small child overwhelmed by pain. He soaked and stirred that hide of trauma in bitter alum to soften the fibers that they might bend to his will. He rubbed his pain against all of the hard spots in his world, inner and outer.

I grew tired of the rubbing. I grew tired of hearing his anger at the people involved, his bitterness at not being protected. But yes, I grieved with him. I grieved and grieved.

I grew tired of the waiting. Healing takes time. But the process brought me hope. What if this trauma was the cause of his confusion? Could it indeed be healed and left behind? Might we be a white-picket-fence family once more?

Fred worked this memory, the pale leather hide of his trauma, inch by inch with hands now calloused against the softening hide of his pain. He grew tired from processing so much.

I could not find his heart because the work of healing was too demanding. The leather of his memory slowly yielded to him, one finger-width at a time. It tendered and eased, silky to the touch. We marveled at his craft, his success in moving through the pain. He looked up from it, wild with excitement. His clothes would be made of this now—his outward appearance would reflect that the war had been won. Soft and durable was the hide—pain and love embraced together. And there would be no need for women's clothes now that he understood this about himself, now that he had moved on.

I dared not become too excited. What if it did not last, this wholeness my husband experienced after the realization and healing of trauma? What if the euphoria of recognition subsided and Heather reared her head again, this time to be reckoned with?

Fred took his box of women's clothes to Goodwill. He didn't need them anymore, he said. I celebrated, yes, but the experience of my husband's perceived gender dysphoria had changed us. Denial could not be recaptured. We had seen a map of that territory; we had a compass in hand. If we found ourselves there again, we knew the various routes and destinations that could be chosen. Both of us were now clad in the soft hide of Fred's childhood pain transformed, a trophy cloak, and it was all we could wear to protect us in the journey ahead. Blissful ignorance and shock were no longer available to us for killing time.

Here we were, a normal family once again.

Snapshots 2005

I become a bit crazy about getting a dog. I keep a journal of my experience as if the puppy were a baby in gestation. I read several books on border terriers and order a puppy from a reputable breeder. I save a thousand dollars over the course of a year and throw a puppy shower when she arrives so that all of our friends can meet her. I serve hot dogs for lunch. I completely delete this puppy shower from my memory and only recall it when I discover the guest list six years later. Then, I find it very weird.

I meet Marie and Olivia, six doors down, who have a cairn terrier pup named Tamsin. I visit them a few times a week in the evening, amazed that my kids finally accept their father so I can slip away on my own for an hour or two. Marie and Olivia offer me wine and mixed drinks, stimulating discussion about books and people, and an adorable dog to play with. I forever think of them as my angels-in-hard-times.

A seven-year-old boy from down the street comes to our house every afternoon. He tells me about his day at school and eats a snack. I don't know who his parents are or why they never seem to be home. The boy tells me that our neighbor Ben Blakeman, two doors down on the alley, has proposed that they sail to Hawaii together. I think it's wonderful that another adult is nurturing this urchin with me. I wonder if I can join them.

I notice that the grocery store aisles look like racetracks—long and straight. In the fruit section, I lose my children completely. They are not grabbing at fruit; they are laughing and playing. I move on past the freezer section, elbows on the cart handle, and they finally look up, see I am missing, and go in search. I recover the boys effortlessly, but later an older woman announces loudly to her husband that she has finally found the mother of "those children who were lost in the produce department." I explain quietly that I like to give them the opportunity to pay attention to their surroundings and where their safety net is. "Are you sure that's the message you want to give them?" she snaps at me. I shake my head in wonder that she will judge me as a parent based on this one experience. I smile thinking she doesn't know that people pay me to teach parenting classes.

Fred launches his own business as a house designer and builder. He acquires tools and a commercial van from a friend going out of business. We name the van "Hope," and within a month, Fred has garnered enough clients to work full time.

Together, our family paints each room of our home in bright pastel and earth tones. It takes months to accomplish. The backside of the front door is a golden "Denver Omelet" with the handprints of each member of our family in a different panel and color. We sign them all.

My dear friend Anna gets married in Germany and invites us to attend the ceremony. She and her husband sponsor our travel so that we may be a part of their celebration. Our children are flower boys and, during the reception, Sam discovers sparkling water. After drinking a liter of it, he also discovers he can find his own way to the restroom on the next floor down via the glass elevator. Anna asks about Fred's battle of the sexes. I tell her it is remarkably over, and we are free.

Limbo

BY JUNE 2005, I had completed a vegetable garden, a flower garden for the boys, an undulating herb garden, and several border gardens in our yard. The landlord marched up the concrete walk on a sunny afternoon, and, under our magnificent magnolia, she handed me a thirty-day notice to leave. She had sold our home.

Ben Blakeman, the music teacher down the back alley who owned the sailboat, got wind of our dilemma and walked us around a six block radius of the neighborhood to check in with other landlords he knew. For the first time, I felt valued and welcomed in our community. We looked at a variety of houses and finally talked with Sarah Mae, a neighbor who invited us to rent and then buy her house on Juniper Street, just across from where she lived.

We moved into Sarah Mae's house and much of our furniture sat outside and cracked that hot July, because the house was too small to accommodate it. Dry rot ate at one wall beneath the siding, so our loan application was turned down. Again, we were faced with a deadline to move within weeks. Between house hunting excursions, I watched our children vigilantly at our transitional home so they didn't fall into the aboveground goldfish pond and drown. No fence contained our new puppy, and she took it upon herself to meet the neighbors while I focused on keeping the boys safe.

Each morning, we picked blackberries from the wild bram-bles that skirted the alley behind our house and we made cob-blers, pies, and crisps. Such sweet abundance helped us set our sites on the expectation of goodness to come.

Part Three

Moving On

TWO DAYS BEFORE our month was up on Juniper Street, we discovered a two-bedroom house on 62nd Avenue. The lot measured almost a quarter acre, including a seasonal pond and a tall willow tree for climbing. It was a good buy in a kid-friendly neighborhood, and we barely managed to procure a variable, interest-only loan so we could snap it up before the house hit the market. Considering we had two cats, a dog, a family of four, and only self-employment to carry us, we considered ourselves lucky.

I did the space clearing this time. Before I even began, I entered the living room and stood awhile, running my hands through the air inches from the perimeter walls. I was struck by the sadness I felt in that room. Our family life had regained an even keel since Fred boxed up Heather's clothes and sent them off to Goodwill. But here, the energy felt heavy with grief and conflict. I remembered then that the last two or three times the house had sold, its sale had been pressed by divorce.

I sank to the hardwood floor and cried for the house and its inhabitants, for heartbreak and dreams shattered. I gave empathy to the house. I had never done that before. At the end of the grieving, I made a promise that we would be different. Ours would be a home of peace, laughter, and love. This would be a home to raise our boys in.

I blessed our house with intentions of truth, love, light, and connection. I blessed it with the intention of building community and growing ourselves with as little footprint on the earth as possible. I held it sacred as a place that would support us all in finding grace, come what may.

Live and Learn

IN JULY OF 2006, I took a leap in my study of Nonviolent Communication. I was accepted as a participant for BayNVC's Parent Peer Leadership Program. The program was in its first year, designed and presented by my mentor, Inbal Kashtan. The nine-month course would include an eight-day Family Camp followed by weekly teleclasses, empathy support calls, and writing opportunities.

I packed up our kids and headed to Napa Valley for the camp. Fred stayed home to work and support my ongoing education. I deeply appreciated the way he championed my every cause. I was also grateful that he had embarked on this course of study beside me, growing his compassion to show up more heartfully for our children and each other.

Family Camp proved to be a challenging and rich experience for the boys and me. During morning workshops, I uncovered and explored my own triggers in preparation to effectively teach NVC to others. The boys participated in the children's program with the support of my sweet niece, but Sam snuck in to sit with me quietly for more than a few sessions.

Trinidad, now five, performed his first magic trick beside the swimming pool. "See what I have?" he asked a friend and me holding up a rock. Then he said some magic words while rubbing the rock between his palms. He kept his eyes on ours until he had slipped the rock carefully into his pocket. Then he opened his hands, eyes wide, demonstrating the wonder he expected from us both.

"It's gone!" he said. We cheered, clapped him on the back, and encouraged him to perform his trick at the talent show, which he did with aplomb. As I sought a path of honesty and transparency, my eldest son took his first steps down the path of illusion. As a family, we seemed to be mostly inside out.

After five days at camp, my stomach started to tighten. I thought of the last time I'd been away from Fred, after the house fire. When I had returned home then, Fred had a new female persona to share. I knew he had grown and healed since, but still I worried. Whenever I'd left my husband for any length of time, the duration had been a living hell for him as he encountered his demons alone. I got empathy for my concerns from fellow campers.

On the day before our return, Fred called to check in. He said he had important things to talk with me about and wondered if we could meet as soon as I pulled into town, before either of us returned home for the day. My worst fears, I guessed, were about to be realized. I arranged to meet him at a park, and a friend came to take our boys.

Fred and I sat where the sun shone brightly on a grassy knoll at the park three blocks from our home. Children on tricycles and in strollers wheeled down the concrete path below us. Mothers called to their kids at the playground, and the creek eased along its marshy banks as it had done a thousand days before.

In terror, I met with the man I'd married. Who was he now? Was he lost to me? Did I even want him? Fred's face looked worried, pale, and drawn. Our hug was filled with apprehension. Where mutual love and attraction once flowed, now fear and uncertainty coursed; we hardly knew each other, hardly knew ourselves.

"I can't do it anymore," Fred said. "I've tried being a man. I've been everything on my list that would make me one. I've been a soldier, a firefighter, a rancher, a fisherman, a husband, and a father. And still, I'm not me. I need to be true to who I am," he said.

"Even if it means losing us?" I asked.

"I hope it won't," he said. "I dearly hope it won't. And I don't know how it's all going to work out in the end. But I'm afraid I'm going to kill myself if I go on living like this."

"You're suicidal?" I asked.

"Every day," he said. "The only thing that stops me is that I can't figure out a way to do it so that the kids won't know I killed myself. I don't want to leave them with that."

"Oh, Fred."

"I'm so sorry," he said. "I didn't want it to be like this. I don't want to hurt you. I love you with all my heart. You're the best thing that's ever happened to me. And so are our kids. But I can't live this lie. I can't do it anymore. I cannot live with myself in such deceit. Not in front of you, not in front of God. I am sorry, Kristin. I am so, so sorry."

If our previous experience with gender dysphoria was a gift, it was in this way: I managed to remember how to put my feet back on the path to home so I could fulfill my role as a mother while inside, my heart broke open.

A Call for Help

THE NEXT MORNING, I drove to the edge of town and parked at the Ridgeline trailhead. I sat in our station wagon and stared down at my cell phone. Our beautiful home, children, pets, and community—all of it was at stake. The precious fabric of our lives would unravel as soon as our secret was out and we committed to moving forward on this path. I felt terrified and alone.

Despite my worst fears, I couldn't keep the secret. Only days before, I had agreed to be a regular empathy buddy with Maria from Family Camp, and I needed empathy now. With shaking fingers, I dialed her phone number.

"Maria," I said, "my husband believes that he is a woman and wants to transition so he can live as one."

There was a soft groan on the other end of the line. I burst into tears. I got out of my car and paced up and down the gravel parking lot, phone pressed hard against my ear. A cool morning fog clung to the trees around me and slowly gave way to sun that stretched its orange glow over the hillside while I cried.

"What do I do?" I begged. "What do I do?"

Maria had no experience in these matters. Very few people had.

"What's going to happen? Do we divorce each other and go on as single people? Maria, I don't want to be single! I hated that. I don't want any other husband. I want *my* husband. I want Fred. This isn't fair!"

"No," Maria said sadly. "No, it's not fair at all."

"I don't get it. This is not the man I married! Was everything we've had for the past fourteen years a lie? Where have I been that I didn't see we'd end up like this? I thought I had this fairy-tale life. I thought I was lucky. But I was duped! I was so stupid, Maria. How could I be so stupid?" I sobbed, covering my mouth with one hand, crouching in the tall grass, and rocking back and forth.

"Kristin," she soothed. "You were not stupid. You could not have seen this coming. It's not your fault."

"I hate this! But I love my husband. Where is he? Is he dead? Can he come back? I don't think he can. I think he's gone, Maria. I think he's gone." I sat down on the damp earth, my back bowed, unable to see through the grass that surrounded me. "He's gone."

"Kristin . . . this is incomprehensible. Did this just come out of nowhere?"

I told her the story of the past few years, holding nothing back. Maria was quiet. "What happens with our kids? Don't you think he would have thought of that? What impact this has on them? It's so selfish, Maria. I can't believe it! I don't care if it's right or wrong, it's just selfish!"

"I don't understand it, Kristin," she said. "I'm not sure how he can do this to you and the boys. I don't get it."

"I don't either," I said, defeated. "I don't get it at all. And I don't know what to do when I get off the phone. I don't want to go home. It's horrible being home. It's all ruined. I grew into a woman with this man. Now even that seems like a lie. I've become who I am as a person, a mother, a wife *with him*. And now I'm—I'm really no one at all," I sniffed.

"Well, I'm a mother," I said. "Because when I get home, somebody's gonna be hungry, I can count on that." I giggled a little and then groaned. "God, this is so hard."

"If you need to get out at any time," said Maria, "you and the children can come here." There were no easy outs. Only listening, space, and time for clarity to surface amongst us all.

It would take time.

On the Trail

I TOOK THE PUPPY, and I walked. I walked the Ridgeline trail every day after I dropped Trinidad off at the Waldorf kindergarten. I walked deep down into the woods then followed the winding trail up the ridge, peeling off sweaters, scarves, and sometimes even a coat as I went. I left my clothes hanging from the branches of trees so I could collect them upon my return. It was rare that I saw anyone else on the trail so early in the morning. The dog and I had it all to ourselves.

Rosie ran ahead. She tore up one side of the ridge and down the other, hot on the scent of squirrels, deer, and all things that leave their marks on the forest floor. I watched her with pride and delight, vicariously living her thrill of freedom and exploration. As I waded through grief and the shattered pieces of my marriage and family, Rosie's exuberant play bookmarked the possibility of joy in my world.

If my husband really was a woman for all the world to see, what did that make me? Was I to become a lesbian? A divorcée? But it hardly seemed like divorce; our relationship had not failed. How could we navigate this course, both individually and as a couple? I had never felt so separate from Fred.

Rosie and I walked for thirty minutes into the forest before turning back. I tried to return to the house before Sam woke up. He wanted his mama in the mornings, and Fred needed to work on his design business. But still—sixty minutes of time just to commune with my thoughts and the trees! It was the great indulgence of the day.

Sometimes, I would step quietly across the forest floor without breaking a twig, soundlessly balanced. Sometimes, I would tear down the path at breakneck speed, my heart pounding, trying to outrun my fears and the reality of the changes upon us. Sometimes, I would walk with a wide, swinging gait, my hair hanging long before my face as I stooped, sobbed, and moaned a song of grieving. I knelt and pressed my hands against the damp, soft earth. I asked for endurance, strength, and love. I leaned into the silent and accepting community of trees.

Every morning, I walked through the open meadow and deep forest to a place where the trees opened wide to an expansive view of our city. I came to that spot and cleared my mind, let go of my grief and thoughts, if only for a moment. In that space, I opened my heart and my spirit to a prayer. Sometimes, I brought a question and posed it to the stillness, fully trusting that an answer would come forward. Other times, the question would emerge in a self-made answer.

One cold morning in December, such an insight was offered after I stood a few minutes on my prayer spot. I felt open and had no desire in my heart. I was empty of all expectation of knowing, drained of grief, exhausted by loving. And there, not ten feet in front of me, a hummingbird appeared in the fog. She hovered, regarding me with one eye, perhaps resonating with my search for nourishment. She did not doubt, but swiftly crossed the clearing in one magnificent arc. She landed on a branch for just a moment, so I could wonder at her in the early morning light.

What would feed this tiny bird? I didn't know, but I was sure its appetite would lead it unerringly to food and life. It had thus far—the bird existed! Here on the cold valley floor, a hummingbird sustained itself hourly, certain that it would be provided for.

My heart opened into the infinite wonder of possibility. I would be fed. No matter the fog, the winter spell, the mystery before us, something would be offered, and I would be there to receive it. The tiny sprite before me was nourishment in itself, leaping into the air and whizzing high above my head into gray. There is no colorless place where flight is not possible.

Hormones

I SPENT HOURS online Googling "transsexual" with "married," grappling with all of the possible trajectories. I found a few entries—predominantly love stories where the couples had stayed together. Most of them also admitted to being sexless unions after transition, or they simply omitted any detail about their sex lives, which I found utterly disappointing. I combed through each account carefully, trying to understand how they did it, what their lives were like.

Finally, I stumbled onto the TransFamily Spouse Yahoo Group.[1] I had never asked for membership to a Yahoo Group before, but this was a group I knew I wanted to belong to. I signed up and waited impatiently for the moderator to accept me. After a few days, I was given the green light. I sat at my computer in our unheated garage, wringing my hands in the winter cold as their site slowly downloaded onto my screen for the first time. At last, I was in.

The stories of my companions blurred behind my tears. Here were the partners of both female-to-male and male-to-female transsexuals. Some had children. They spoke of their anger, frustration, fear, joy, and love as their partners embarked willy-nilly or with fear and trepidation onto paths of self-discovery. They spoke of anguish at losing intimacy on so many levels and celebration at discovering that they maintained optimism nonetheless. They talked about the ways that they and their partners supported each other through transition, usually with a fair stock of ingenuity and humor. These people demonstrated the honesty, transparency, and courage that I had been so desperately seeking. I introduced myself.

Within weeks, Fred's transition took off at full tilt. As a member of TransFamily Spouses, I garnered a better understanding of the male to female transition process: a psychologist specializing in trans issues would be needed, then hormone therapy, electrolysis, and finally a goal would be set for gender confirmation surgery to cover changes in the lower half of her body. Some transwomen augmented these therapies with plastic surgery to shift bone mass and accentuate the feminine aspects of their faces. Such surgeries were not in our budget. But, at some point, we would have to come out to our families—both Fred's and my own—and inform our community as well.

I found that there was a wide range of "out-ness" amongst trans folks and their partners. Some people who were trans went out in their preferred gender only at specific times and places, and the rest of their lives appeared relatively unaffected by their transgender identity. Others lived in integrity with their identified gender and passed flawlessly. A few lived double lives and showed up one way for work or with extended family and quite another when they were at home or with friends. Some did not adhere to one pronoun or another but straddled the line between, identifying with both genders simultaneously or, conversely, identifying with neither, and using pronouns like they, their, and them. All of these options had their ups and downs, and most spouses were willing to share their experience with candor and care.

Here, at last, was a place I could connect with other partners, some of them mothers, who lived with the same rare challenges I did. Here were people who could describe to me the dosages and effects of various hormones and testosterone blockers. I asked about changes in skin tone and fat migration when Fred's face sagged with the chemical cocktail that seemed to put everything inside him on the move after hormone therapy began. I asked about gaffs "to tuck away those inconvenient hanger-downers," even though we never actually got one. No questions were out of line, and I became a resource for others braving the terror of early transition. Again, I took note of the ways that reading and writing served to bring us together, to help us process and comprehend this dilemma. I hoped to write a book someday and encouraged others in the group to do so as well. I thought perhaps we could even write something collaboratively.

Unfortunately, I was told that some senior members of the group had been discussing whether to write something and deemed themselves much more qualified than a beginner like me to be sharing stories about transition. Feeling vulnerable and slightly ashamed, I bowed to their judgment and stopped journaling for awhile, a choice I would live to regret. The carefully examined experience of beginners is a rare find indeed, and I encourage all learners to track their progress so that their fresh perspectives may benefit others. There is no one more qualified to report than a person experiencing something firsthand.

Fred and I made an appointment with Reid Vanderburgh, a therapist specializing in transgender issues just north of us in Portland. We both spent time in Reid's office exploring our present and future. Reid immediately wrote Fred a referral letter to take to a doctor so he could begin prescription hormone therapy. He said that Fred had addressed his past trauma, and now gender dysphoria was the only work left on the table. Reid felt confident that a full transition, male-to-female, would be best for Fred's mental and emotional health.

I sat with Reid alone and talked to him about my worst fears. What if I was no longer attracted to *her*? He said that could happen. What if she was a very homely woman? I knew that this was a terribly unenlightened question, and I'm embarrassed that I felt moved to ask it. Truthfully, though, I was accustomed to having a very handsome *husband*, and I had no idea how that would translate, nor how I would cope with the results.

Changing gender is a big enough jump without losing attractiveness, too. Reid smiled as I laid my questions on the table.

"Beautiful men tend to make beautiful women," he said. I told him all of the varieties of relationships I'd seen people shift through over the course of transition so far, and he only nodded in agreement. "It's hard to know what's coming in your marriage," he said. "You two will decide as you move along. The changes will take several years to complete, really. You may not even settle on something until then."

After the sessions with Reid, our family walked along the river under gray skies. I felt oddly alone, even as I tried to fully witness and champion the newly expressed woman beside me. She still had a beard, and that did make it difficult. Part of my loneliness was due to singularly holding a picture of something that few others shared. In fact, most of the world looked at my husband and saw a man. Most people looked at us and saw a happy, nuclear family.

The boys walked single-file along a driftwood log and reached out to us for a liftoff. We picked them up, one at a time, and swung them around before setting them down on the sandy beach. If only Fred and I could carry each other so easily. If only we could help bear the burden of each other's pain.

The prescriptions for estradiol (estrogen replacement) and spironolactone (a testosterone-blocker) were filled before we arrived home in Eugene. Our course was set with destination uncertain.

Show and Tell

FRED AND I spent a few minutes of every day wondering aloud to each other whether we'd make it work. From the time that Fred announced that he had to go forward in transition, I don't remember ever agreeing with him that we would stay together no matter what. Both of us felt unsure about whether we would be attracted to each other when her new form settled in. The answer loomed foggy for us both. How could we know?

Fred and I had been on countless adventures together and had envisioned many different experiences over the course of our marriage. For some time, we'd made plans to hike the Pacific Crest Trail. We'd also considered buying a house on the coast and renting or sharing it when we weren't using it ourselves. At one point, we had even dreamed of having a nanny accompany us on our travels when we had children so we could maintain our romance and work while the boys learned other languages effortlessly. It seemed odd to have this dilemma on our hands which appeared to be a fulcrum for our future, yet there was no way we could see to prepare for or even reliably predict any outcome through research. How could we parent responsibly not knowing what would happen? How could we move forward at all?

If ever acceptance has been hard-won and complete in my life, it was the acceptance around not knowing the future of my marriage. This acceptance did not arrive overnight like a package from FedEx, neatly taped and bundled. No, it was more like the process of felting—a mess of hairy wool spread between us that we poked and prodded at daily and finally saw shrink from overwhelming to just barely manageable. We poked at it each day at breakfast, the only time of day that we had the energy to face the unknown. Our family breakfasts sounded like this:

"Well, what do you think? Should we make plans to do something different?"

"I don't know."

"Yeah, me neither. I just can't imagine what this is going to be like."

"I know. Me, too."

"I got something hard in my cereal. It's yucky."

"Here, give it to me."

"Do you think you'll still want me?"

"I'd like to think so. But I don't know. Will you?"

"Wish I could say."

"Mom, there's a bug on my napkin."

"Hmm. Look at that."

"I'm not sure we're going to make it."

"Me neither, but no point in changing today."

"No, that wouldn't make sense."

"Sam's elbow is taking up the *whole* table."

"Honey, put your elbow here, on your side."

"Yeah, so . . . I guess we'll know when and if it makes sense to make a change."

"I guess. And we'll deal with it then."

"Well. At least today is out."

"Yep. What time will you be home for dinner?"

I didn't mention who might be saying what in the conversation above, because we switched roles regularly. The kids' input varied, but as certain as there was food before us, there was The Topic. At least the elephant was no longer invisible. We would stay together until it made sense not to. That was the agreement. In the meantime, I asked myself what it was I most wanted and then proceeded to free-write about it in my journals for the NVC Parent Peer Leadership Program.

Predictability, I wrote. That was what I needed. If I had predictability, then I could rest and focus on what I wanted to demonstrate: patience and unconditional love. But if I wished to love unconditionally, then what was the value of predictability? I should be able to love no matter what happened—that's what unconditional is about. This was tricky.

Maybe what I wanted was not predictability but trust. Yet, I could not expect to trust Fred to do any one thing or another— that would be depending on some strategy, person, or event outside myself. That was kind of like predictability. I wasn't so sure that predictability could really be a universal human need anyway, no matter how much I wanted it to be. As I understood it, universal needs could not be attached to circumstances.

Something about trust did resonate for me, though. Did I need to trust myself? Perhaps. I needed to know that I would be able to come back to a place of self-connection no matter what the situation was. But that put the burden of trust heavily on *me*, and I wasn't so sure I could trust myself under that kind of pressure. In the past few years, I had faced countless challenges and had not displayed the most consistent performance, inside or out.

What I really strived for was a sense of inner peace from which I could easily love unconditionally, regardless of circum-stances. Ahhhh. Maybe that sense of inner peace would spring from an understanding that there are infinite strategies to meet every need, whether I could currently recognize that fact or not. So trust was about cultivating a deep acceptance that amongst the infinite possibilities that could meet my needs, one of those possibilities would almost certainly be immensely beautiful and satisfying.

In this way, I came to see that trust is not about expect-ing others or myself to perform a certain way. Somehow, the notion of infinite possibility—though many would define this as God—seems less disputable and more clearly represented by the infinitude of the universe or the space within an atom. Surely, with such infinite possibilities, all of our critical needs could be met! Trust, a sense of peace in the abundant nature of the universe, was a need we could all recognize within us, and I dearly longed to have that need met now with so much uncertainty in my life.

At dinner one night in January, we told our boys, aged six and four, what we thought they needed to know. "I've never felt comfortable in my body," Fred told them. "It's always felt wrong, like it didn't belong to me. My experience being a boy never felt true, and I've been confused about this for as long as I can remember," he said.

"I'm going to make a change so that my body matches my true identity, my inner spirit that is female. I'm going to change on the outside from being a man into being a woman."

Both boys looked up at their father curiously, unsure of what to say.

"It has nothing to do with you at all, this stuff that's going on inside of me or my decision to make the change. And it won't change my loving you or the fact that I'm your father. It might change what you call me though. You could call me Maddy, like Jennifer Boylan's kids called her when she transitioned from male to female. Or I'm sure you could come up with something else that you like even better. What do you think?"

"We'd call you Maddy instead of Daddy?" asked Trin, licking the gravy off his spoon slowly.

"Yeah, or whatever feels right," said Fred.

"Maddy is okay," said Trin. Sam chased a pea around on his plate and didn't appear to be listening.

"Maddy," said Sam.

"You can take some time to think about it," said Fred.

It seemed almost ridiculous to give this highly condensed version to the two people outside of Fred who were most likely to be affected by the transition. And yet, there's such a thing as too much information with kids under the age of ten . . . especially when it has to do with the people they rely on to meet their basic needs. We didn't want to burden them with our processes any more than necessary.

Trinidad's face clouded for a moment.

"What's the matter, honey?" I asked.

"Well, this probably means that . . . Maddy won't wrestle with us or play rough so much," said Trinidad.

"Oh, no it won't," said Fred with a smile. "That I can assure you of." Trinidad brightened.

"Sam, what about you?" I asked. "Are you worried about this at all?"

Sam looked thoughtful for a moment then smiled. "No," he said.

Trinidad frowned again. "Is there something else bothering you?" asked Fred. We had dreaded this moment, what appeared to be the pivotal balancing point of our existence as a nuclear family. Everything would surely spin out from here, the cause of our disintegration no longer lurking invisibly in our midst. After tonight we would all know it, name it, and fear it.

"I'm afraid that I won't recognize you, Daddy," said Trinidad.

"Well, he will look different as a woman," I said.

"Yeah, so how will I know that he's still my dad when I see him tomorrow?" asked Trinidad, brows furrowed.

"Well, it won't happen overnight," said Fred. "It will take months, years even. I won't be wearing women's clothes all day long for some time. I'm still going to work as a man," he said.

"Oh!" said Trinidad, relaxing visibly. Then he smiled, relieved. "Oh, well that's good."

And that was all they said about it.

Seda

"I DON'T THINK that Heather is the right name," he said.

I can't say I was sorry to hear that; the name still struck a tone of dread in me, a felt memory of trying to peek around blinds that I didn't want to see behind.

"What do you think my name should be?"

"Sequoia?" I asked.

"Sequoia?" asked my she-husband. "Why Sequoia?"

"I don't know. It's . . . big."

Fred deflated. That had been the wrong thing to say.

"I mean . . . powerful," I corrected myself. He cocked his head.

"Maybe," he said.

The next day, Fred suggested a middle name to go with my offering. "How about 'Sequoia Dawn?'" he asked.

"That's pretty!" I said. And I meant it.

The naming wasn't over. Fred had made some friends on the internet. Much as I had reached out looking for the support of people in like circumstances, so had Fred sought mentors in the transition process. After looking at the profiles of dozens of transwomen on Lynn Conway's website,[1] he had connected with a transwoman who had worked as a pilot and now owned a few of her own businesses, successfully navigating her world as a terrifically skillful, six-foot-four woman.

This woman had offered Fred wonderful advice about love, work, and even fashion. I appreciated her experience, self-connection, and confidence in stark contrast to our worried fits and starts forward as a transfamily. Her accomplishments after transition also offered us hope that we would sustain ourselves as a family emotionally and economically beyond Fred's transition.

When Fred told his new friend about the name "Sequoia Dawn," she compressed it into a more comfortable moniker. "Se-Da!" she said. "I like it."

Fred liked her version so much that he smoothed the composite into one single word—Seda—that would name her existence as the woman she was always meant to be. She has never felt inclined to change it since.

Seeking Support

THE SLOW-MOVING effects of synthetic hormones could not possibly satisfy my partner's desire to live in a woman's body *now*. Daily, he watched his breasts from all angles, trying to determine whether they were actually growing. He wanted to be able to go out as "herself," but his flat chest and manly haircut posed a challenge.

I decided to help. I went online and looked at wigs. Splurging (and loving it!), I bought her a shoulder-length auburn bob made of human hair. It arrived within a week, and I admit to coveting it perhaps more than I should have. It looked smashing on Seda, too.

Then, I packed up the kids, and we headed to a nearby lingerie boutique to acquire breast enhancers for our newly developing woman. I pondered whether to bring the children along on this adventure, but the dilemma I faced was emblematic of our transition as a family. Yes, I was still resistant to Seda moving forward into her life as a woman, because doing so threatened our family unit as we knew it. At the same time, Seda had been my husband of nearly fifteen years, and I daily lived the vow of supporting her. As a stay-at-home mom, my life's work centered around serving my husband and children, and I was rarely without one or the other. How else was I to go breast shopping during business hours except with the kids? Within the scope provided by the Transfamily Spouse Yahoo group, our transition had normalized in my mind to some degree, and this accepting perspective was the one that I wanted to offer our children.

So, as a surprise for Seda, we set out to procure a "veal cutlet" style of silicone breast enhancer. According to my Transfamily Spouse sources, such enhancers could be comfortably slipped into a bra to enlarge whatever size breast Seda currently sported. The boys and I opened packages, poked, and prodded at the clear, jelly-like pancakes. The proprietor appeared and offered her help.

"You are looking for a particular style of enhancer?" she asked. "For yourself?"

I looked down. Yes, I could see her point.

"No," I said. "It's for a friend."

"Ah . . . " she said. I was thinking fast. Who was this friend and what were her circumstances? Why hadn't I thought of this before?

"If she's losing a breast," said the proprietor carefully, "then you may choose whatever style you think she would like and exchange it if it isn't working for her later."

"I see," I said. "That's nice, that you have the exchange policy."

"Only for a woman," she said, looking at me intently over the top of her reading glasses. "Sometimes it is necessary. But we don't exchange as a rule, because sometimes these are purchased . . . with *other* intentions." She nodded slowly at me that I might catch her drift. She was speaking of my husband, of course.

So I lied.

"Yes . . . I'm sure my *friend* will appreciate these. It's just what she's looking for, I think. We'll know for certain later when she's further into recovery and can use them."

The kids were feeling up the silky sleepwear and didn't seem to notice their mother's blushing stumble from integrity. How *could* I walk in better alignment with my values? This woman's policy explicitly discriminated against transwomen. I was not going to admit to buying breast enhancers specifically for a transwoman because we lived on one salary, and if these $60 falsies didn't work for my husband's purposes, I wanted the exchange policy to apply to me, too.

I was scared. The shopkeeper's response to the needs of transwomen became a frightening example of how this population—how *we*—could be treated in coming months and years. We weren't even out of the closet yet, and the world already passed judgment. I kept my receipt.

A week later, I set up a date for Seda and I to go out walking together as a couple of women. At night. We all have to start somewhere on the path to honest living. I decided we would give it a go in the dark. I asked my friend Tina to watch the children for us while we went out for a stroll. She had watched our boys on the day that Seda told me she needed to transition some months ago. Tina was one of precious few who now knew our story, and I felt grateful to have her in confidence.

The big evening finally arrived, and I applied Seda's makeup myself after she shaved twice. We affixed the wig and slipped the silicone cutlets into her new bra. Our children watched with wonder as their father transformed before their eyes for the first time. A new pair of femme eyeglasses with purple wire frames did much to soften and change the shape of her face. She looked like she could be Fred's sister.

Tina arrived. "You look beautiful!" she cried.

Arm in arm, with skirts swishing around our ankles, we stepped out the front door and into the wide world beyond. It was dark, and my husband's auburn hair glinted in the glow from streetlamps above. Our hearts raced as we walked slowly through the park, boot heels clicking while we talked with each other quietly. This was a clandestine affair. My chest felt tight and my head spun dizzily. Someone could bash us for being gay. Someone could bash us if they recognized that Seda was trans. Or we could be valued all the more in our community for our living, breathing courage and diversity. Every step we took into the dark echoed with possibility.

Telling Michelle

I STOPPED BY my friend Michelle's house to drop off pea seeds that she could plant in her garden as the earth began to warm. Michelle had dug a two hundred square foot plot for vegetables in a grassy area beside her apartment complex. I admired her ingenuity and commitment to learning how to garden in a less-than-welcoming environment. She was not afraid to start from scratch, ask for help, or even fail. Alongside her two children, each a year older than mine, Michelle cultivated both food and home in the midst of a sea of homogenous gray apartments. I was delighted by her spirit.

Michelle's face lit up when I came to the door. "Kristin!" she said with her wide, beaming smile. "How nice to see you! Come in!" I stepped into her living room where a five-year-old boy sat behind a fortress of multi-colored Legos. He looked up at me and grinned.

"Hey, Orion. Whatcha' building?"

"It's a castle," he said. "And here's a catapult to fire things at it!" Orion shot a Lego head against the plastic wall, and it bounced off.

"Cool. Doesn't do much damage though, does it?" I asked.

"No. But there's a giant, too, and that helps," he said, with a mischievous look in his eye.

"Really? Where?"

Orion stood up and pulled on black rubber boots then crashed his foot down onto the castle wall with his face screwed up into a scowl.

"Aaooh!" I said. "Giants! I'm out of here!"

I followed Michelle to the kitchen. She looked tired but smiled at her son. Michelle pulled a shriveled orange out of the fruit bowl on the kitchen table and made a face at the gray fuzz that covered one side of it. She took it to the compost bucket on the counter, raised the lid, and dropped it in.

"It's all Legos all the time these days," she said. "It drives our homestay student crazy. She's really good with the kids, but she doesn't like to step on Legos when she comes downstairs."

"Caltrops, Fred calls them."

"Caltrops?" Michelle asked.

"Yes, the nasty metal barbed things knights threw on the ground so horses would injure themselves in battle during the Middle Ages."

"Oh!" she said. "Yes, I guess they're like that. I think I've bruised my heel on those sharp little points before. Do you want some iced tea?" she asked, reaching for the fridge handle. "I warn you that we're out of ice."

"Sure," I said. "But I think it's just tea, then."

Michelle smirked. She took a glass from the shelf with one hand and filled it by opening the spigot on a jar wedged onto a refrigerator shelf.

"Honey?" she asked.

"Yes, dear?" I quipped.

"Silly!" she said, patting my shoulder and flashing me a broad smile with her perfect teeth.

"No, I'm fine with it unsweetened." I winked. Michelle handed me a full glass, condensation already forming on the outside. She took one, too, then gestured for me to sit beside her at the kitchen table. I did.

"How's the homestay thing going?" I asked. Michelle had recently become exceptionally creative with her budgeting and leased one of their two bedrooms to a young woman from China who attended the University of Oregon. A queen and a single bed pushed together filled most of the remaining bedroom with their family bed. This makeshift bed boasted more square footage than our king-size mattress, but her daughter was growing fast. I tried to imagine how they all fit, with the new student, into this tiny apartment together.

I also wondered how their family managed to live in public in their own home. Michelle's husband, David, was a rather eccentric and extroverted man who made it no secret that he enjoyed his wife in all ways. He would regularly put his hand on her rump from behind or make comments or jokes that implied he was ready for bed as soon as she was. In general, I found his banter with her endearing, but the last time I was over, he was walking around with his hands cupping imaginary breasts and squeezing them gently.

"I don't know how women get anything done considering that they have these wonderful, round, squishy breasts in front of them. If I had breasts, I would have to call in sick to work so I could stay home and play with them all day long." He made motions to bounce and fondle his air breasts, completely unaware that inside I felt ill watching his antics. My husband was in the process of growing very real breasts. This was not a laughing matter to me at all. I left the room.

"The student's name is Min Yi," Michelle said. "And it's going very well." Michelle reached into the fruit bowl again and proffered a banana. I shook my head to decline. She peeled it for herself, broke off the pale yellow tip, and popped it delicately into her mouth.

"You cook for her, too, right?" I asked.

"Yes," she said, chewing. "We provide two meals a day, and she's on her own for the third. She doesn't always eat with us though. Sometimes she goes out with her friends."

"That's nice, that she has friends already," I said, sipping my tea. "I imagine it would be really hard to come across the ocean to a new home, new foods, and a language you're not used to. Having friends always makes things so much better. I don't think I ever realized how much better until I had kids."

"I know what you mean," said Michelle. She and I had relied on each other regularly from the time our babies were born. After Trinidad came home with us from the hospital, we discovered that Michelle had organized a meal train so we didn't have to cook for a week. When I had not fully recovered in that time from two serious tears on my inner labia, Michelle called our network of friends and arranged for them to bring meals for yet another week.

I was in awe of the generosity and abundance that friendship provided and, at the same time, it was very difficult for me to receive it gracefully. At the time, I cried and protested, but Michelle stood her ground insisting that help was needed. Her lesson was a valuable one—I had never before allowed my friends to give me so much. After that, I found myself giving effortlessly and abundantly to others, as if they were my own family.

I smiled warmly at Michelle, grateful for her teaching.

"Kristin, you brought me some peas?" she asked.

"I did," I said, reaching into my purse to pull out a wrinkled brown paper bag. "I bought these in bulk and figured you could use what I didn't. It's so hard to gauge exactly how many you need."

"That's wonderful," she said. "I so appreciate you sharing."

"I brought you edible pod and shelling peas, but they'll both need a climbing structure. Fred is supposed to put ours in this weekend, but I couldn't wait. I planted yesterday. I guess that's hopeful!" I said.

"How is Fred?" she asked.

"He's doing fine," I said, tentatively.

Her voice dropped. "I mean, did he ever get over . . . wanting to be a woman?"

We hadn't talked about it for over two years because Michelle was the first friend that I'd told, and she'd made it very clear that she saw Seda's yearning as a sickness and aberrant from God's plan. I was terrified to tell her the truth, but I knew I couldn't lie either.

"Actually, no Michelle, he didn't," I said. "He was in therapy for the last couple of years and healed the stuff that needed to be healed from his childhood. He tried. He really tried to find a way through it. But there's no way. He's going to transition now to living as a woman."

"Kristin, what?" she asked, her eyes wide.

I nodded and took a deep breath. "My husband's name is Seda now, and *she* is taking female hormones and dressing as a woman when she's around the house. She'll transition to live as a woman full-time in public sometime in the next year or so."

Michelle turned pale. "What about the kids?" she asked.

"Well, they're still *our* kids," I said. "We're going to raise them as best we know how."

"But they're not going to have a father," she said. "And you'll have to get a divorce. Kristin, that's just awful. Fred is such a nice man. How can he do this?" She shook her head and dug her thumbnail into the banana peel so it split on the table.

"Well, at least she's still alive, Michelle. She thought about committing suicide but didn't want to leave the kids with that memory."

"That's so weird to me, that you call him a she," she said, almost to herself.

"It's her truth, and I'm going to honor it," I said.

"So he's still going to be an active parent then? As a . . . woman?" She said the word as if it tasted bitter in her mouth.

"Yes, she is," I said. "God gave those boys two parents for a reason. And one reason is so that I can keep my sanity," I said.

"I can't imagine what you're going through," she said, tears welling in her eyes. "I'm so sorry. Nobody should ever have to do this. I don't understand. It's just not right."

"Well, it is what it is. Lord knows that we've both tried to make it any other way. And I have to say that so far, she seems pretty happy about it all. That's some relief to me."

"Oh my gosh," Michelle said. "That's just so unfair that she should be happy while the rest of you suffer."

"Well, the kids have taken it pretty well," I said. "They don't seem to mind."

"They don't?"

"Nope. I think they like Seda better. She's more available to them."

"That's weird," said Michelle.

"I don't know how you want to tell your kids," I said. "I can give you more information or be here to help or tell them myself if you want."

Michelle looked at me, stricken. "Kristin, I can't tell them that. It's not natural, and it's not God's way. I don't want them to think that that's normal at all." I ran my fingers lightly along the table's beveled edge then finished my tea and set the glass down softly. Michelle watched me in silence.

"I'm sorry," she said.

I leaned forward and spoke in almost a whisper. "Michelle, if you don't tell them then I will have to lie to them about how Fred is doing. The boys will have to lie. Why do you think I haven't brought them with me to visit for a while? I've been afraid to tell you. But I won't lie, and I won't ask them to."

"Kristin, I can't. I don't know what else to say. I don't want my kids to know. We can still be friends, but our families can't get together for as long as this is going on. David's just going to flip. He is not going to like this," she said.

I couldn't breathe. It was predictable, yes, but still it seemed impossible. Was the fabric of friendship and community so easily rent? I shook my head. Tears came to my eyes. What else could I say?

"I have to go." I stood up and collected my purse.

"All right. I love you, Kristin," said Michelle. She reached out to hug me, and I complied mechanically then pulled away and turned toward the door. I touched Orion's hair gently as I passed him in the living room.

"Goodbye!" he called.

"Goodbye," I said. Michelle still stood outside as I pulled my car around and drove past her apartment. She looked sad. Michelle raised a hand tentatively and waved, smiling bravely. Did she just need time? Did the whole family need time to adjust to the news? Sadness welled within me, but perhaps it was unwarranted. Emotions and convictions could change, and I had little energy left for unnecessary tears. I would give her time.

A City Job

SEDA HAD BEEN working out of our home as a residential house designer for over a year. Her business had boomed but was slowing a little. She worried that over the course of transition, she would have trouble focusing enough to succeed, and she feared that contractors and potential clientele would be put off by her appearance as she made the shift. How would she function professionally as a private contractor without the support of a team through such a vulnerable time? She found herself surfing the help wanted ads for similar employment in a setting that offered more predictability, support, and healthcare benefits for herself and our family.

Seda discovered a job posting for a residential plans examiner for the City of Eugene. There were hundreds of applicants and countless qualified in a tight job market. Somehow, she managed to land the job and found herself working for the government during the first steps in her transition.

Seda was hired as a man. She did not plan to tell co-workers about her intentions to transition for at least a year, until her probationary period was over. Daily, she tore off her male attire as soon as she walked through the door after work. I lovingly nicknamed this ritual, "The Clark Kunt Maneuver." It would all be worth it, she assured me, and I hoped she was right.

Everything worked according to plan for about a month. The hormones that Seda took didn't affect her ability to concentrate or show up for work in any negative way. In fact, they generally rendered her the best possible version of herself. Estrogen helped Seda to feel more focused and comfortable in her body, less distracted by unwanted fantasies, and more in touch with her feelings. The kids had already responded to this latter shift favorably, and I imagined that Seda's work persona was all the easier to connect with as well.

She did not, however, count on the challenges that electrolysis would pose. In order to receive treatments that effectively disintegrated her hair follicles, Seda had to show up for her electrolysis appointments with about four-days growth on her face. This meant that she couldn't shave on a Friday or a Monday for those appointments set on a Monday afternoon.

As if showing up to a new job looking scruffy wasn't bad enough, the treatments themselves made her look worse. Seda came home from these appointments with her chin and upper lip fiercely red and swollen. She smiled weakly as her face seeped yellow serum beneath the ice pack that she held to the clear cut her technician had given her. We later learned that this strategy of deeply clearing a small area at a time would not only remove the hair, but also leave a faint scar. The ramifications of Seda's early transition are in some ways still visible. At the time, we both tried to accept the horrors with a stiff upper lip.

While Seda's appearance concerned the boys and me, it was even harder to explain at work. In general, people didn't ask much about it. Fortunately for us, it is not considered good manners to ask why someone's face is hideously swollen—particularly if they are new at work.

In addition, for maximum effectiveness, the treatments needed to take place weekly and that required a certain amount of accommodation from Seda's work schedule. This combination yielded a situation at work that could be best described as awkward. I can only imagine how mysterious poor Seda (still Fred at work) seemed to others in the office. Who says that working for a bureaucracy is dull?

We both felt nervous about Seda's new job. We couldn't imagine a better employment option to carry her through transition, but we were terrified about the possibility of her losing it. If our family could stabilize economically, then we would be in a much better position to handle the ups and downs emotionally and socially as she shifted genders. Our ability to stay connected as a family likely hinged on her keeping this job with the City—decent pay and benefits, predictable schedule, holidays, and paid vacations. Without it, our already topsy-turvy world threatened to become a terminal case of vertigo.

Heart-Stopping

AT HOME, OUR lives began to settle as winter melted around us, and my efforts in the yard became visible. The garlic I had planted with so many tears in the autumn shot through its blanket of leaf mulch in countless spikes of brilliant green. The tiny bulbs rooted themselves into the dark earth below in preparation for the summer drought to come, in preparation for death and renewal. We think of garlic as so many things—the promise of good food, good health, and a plant yet to be born, which will form another whole head of garlic from a single clove . . . miraculous!

But there is something else quite magical about garlic. The moments in time when I plant garlic in autumn and harvest it in mid-summer stand out in my mind like bookends around the story of winter. What was my state of mind when I set the bulbs into the ground? How was my heart at harvest? The best of medicine, garlic bears a story and the strong flavor of a winter endured.

Our garden sprang to life as the days stretched longer, and our children bounded out of doors barefoot or with rubber boots on. Ducks landed in the pond, frogs sang, and the neighborhood cats sparred at dawn. Seda and I took our gardening gloves and clippers from the basket and headed out to dig up opportunistic blackberry vines then give a final mulch to fruit-bearing bushes and trees. We had gardened together for years.

"You're the captain, I'm the crew," she'd say. "I'm as good as you instruct me to be!"

Gardening was not Seda's thing exactly, but she was always happy to support me in making our yard the cornucopia it was for us all. We worked together while we talked of the past, the present, and, when we dared, the mystery of our future. We talked about whether Seda would prefer to be with a man or a woman when it was all over: inconclusive. We talked about how we might support each other if we found ourselves separating next year, the year after, or in thirty years. Seamlessly, we weeded, mulched, dug, and transplanted. Our dance had been perfected over time, and our habits kept us moving like clockwork tending to our green space whether we were right next to each other or on opposite sides of the yard.

Seda put away a ladder on the east corridor while I headed for the henhouse. Opening the narrow white door, I exhaled sharply through my nose. "Whoa, girls," I said of the stench. "Time for a change."

I grabbed a short-handled shovel and emptied the hen house bedding into a nearby wheelbarrow. The matted, ammonia-scented straw would later decompose in layers with spring weeds and coffee grounds from our local coffee shop. This magical concoction would transform over the course of months into the compost that fed our garden beds.

I suddenly stopped, an inexplicable sense of alarm welling up in my chest. I swung the door shut. "Seda!" I called across the yard. "Are you all right?"

Seda leaned one hand on the picnic table at the back of our house. She sank slowly down to the bench. "I'm not sure," she said.

She and I were so closely wired that when something went wrong, I knew immediately, as bees afield know when their hive is being attacked and then fly to defend it. I crossed the garden in a flash to stand beside her. Seda looked distant.

"What's going on?" I demanded.

"I don't know," she said. "I just feel . . . weird. Like . . . not really in my body. Everything is really . . . slow motion." Space fell between her words, and I had the sense that there was space between us, as if she had allowed her inner self to dangle on a tether somewhere outside my reach.

"Does something hurt? Are you okay?" I asked anxiously.

"I don't know. It's . . . not right," she said.

"Come on. We're going to the emergency room," I said. I had no doubt that help was needed and fast, though I didn't know what for. I sent the children next door and drove Seda to urgent care while she insisted she was probably okay.

At check in, Seda's heart rate measured much lower than normal, fifty beats per minute, though she had improved markedly by that time. I suspect that her heart rate had fallen to a dangerous low in the garden, and whatever had caused the drop had somewhat resolved on our drive over. She improved further as we waited for a doctor to join us. Seda had left the house in a work shirt and Carhartt pants, so she presented easily as a man. She had not yet made her foray into urgent care as a transperson, so the doctor would see us as the world outside still saw us: a married, thirty-something couple dressed in garden garb.

When the doctor arrived, he reviewed Seda's charts. "Hmmm," he said. "Your heart rate was very low. Are you on any medication?"

"No," Seda said shyly, looking at her feet. My mouth opened and closed. I caught her eye and glared sharply before she dropped her gaze.

"Yes, he is, doctor," I said, taking the role of the unhappy messenger. I did not ask for this position, and I certainly did not want to report our story to a total stranger, but there we were, and my spouse's life depended on it.

"He is taking female hormones for gender dysphoria." My statement rang into the air like the bark of a dog, confined and declaring injustice in the world. The words fell sharply around us, striking hard on the stainless steel and glass surfaces of the hospital exam room. They echoed the misfortune of it all and decried the circumstance that called on me to deliver the truth.

After a long moment, the doctor raised the back of his pen to his lips and rubbed it in the corner of his mouth. Something like the edge of a smile emerged and his eyes softened. "Well," he said. "That's another matter. I suppose you're on testosterone blockers, too?"

Seda nodded. "Spironolactone, 50 mg. once a day," she said.

The doctor stood up straighter. "There's the problem," he said. "Spironolactone is primarily a heart medication that they have discovered has a side effect of blocking the release of testosterone into the bloodstream. Too much, and your heart will slow down. Sounds like we need to adjust the dosage."

Seda nodded again, sheepishly. My stomach pressed upward toward my throat, and I stood trembling. This was exactly what I feared! We had lived such a healthy lifestyle for so long, seeing medical doctors once every decade or so, and now Seda was taking hard-core synthetic hormones and testosterone blockers full time, regardless of potential side effects. We'd had this conversation. Was there a way around it? No. Not unless we accepted her suicide as a potential side effect of that route. Would she die younger because of all of these medications? Possibly. But, not as soon as without them. My jaw tightened, and I breathed through my nose. It wasn't fair.

I could not see a way around it. I felt trapped into supporting Seda in a way that would likely kill her in the end. Oh yeah. The end. Like any of us could escape that. I smiled a little. My stomach relaxed, and a heavy sadness met the irony that now pursed my lips. A sense of humor was the only out, really. What was I to do? She was the captain, and I was the crew.

Brunch with Doug and Janet

AFTER A MONTH of living as Seda on the sly, my partner—wife or husband, I knew not how to think of her—was ready to make her debut into the wider world. She and I were finally ready to go out together in broad daylight. I had slowly and quietly collected enough women's clothes in Seda's size that she had a few complete outfits to choose from.

It is worth noting that one of the difficulties of early male to female transition is in dressing the newly identified woman. She cannot, with any sort of ease and acceptance, take a handful of dresses or skirts into a fitting room while sporting a raw-looking beard, men's haircut, and masculine attire. It's frowned upon. The two of us already had enough sensitivities around the experience that we decided it made more sense to leave the shopping to me . . . at least for the moment.

Seda's face had begun to respond after a few months of hormones and hair-removal treatments, and she looked slightly more feminine. Thankfully, we left electrolysis behind for the time being when we got lucky with a coupon and promotional gift from a laser boutique that guaranteed the whole beard off in a year for only $1,200. While this treatment effectively eliminated most of her beard, the growing number of gray hairs would still have to be removed later by electrolysis, a route we came to realize was slower, more painful, and more expensive, though necessary for light-colored hairs. It was a relief for Seda to witness the change of her physique in the mirror. Her confidence grew, and she found a glimmer of beauty in her own reflection.

Our friends Doug and Janet Smith invited us to a pre-Mother's Day brunch at a swanky restaurant on the bottom floor of the Valley River Inn. We had opted to celebrate Mother's Day before the crowd gathered in May so that we could have the easiest possible entry into public outings with our new identities.

Going out cemented the shift in our relationship as nothing else could. While we struggled painstakingly to create ourselves anew from the inside, the world defined us by outward appearances at a glance and moved on. We were a woman with a woman-in-man's clothes, or a woman with another woman (poor dear), decidedly queer on either count. I wish I had felt more comfortable with my own definition of us before taking in that reflection. But how could I? We couldn't wait forever. The outer reflection we obtained by moving into community would inform the next piece of our inner work; both worlds seamlessly intertwined.

If nothing else, this period of time taught me that identity is a co-created experience. If I had previously believed that Seda could simply be a woman in a man's body, I now understood otherwise. Our world treats us differently when it sees us differently. For Seda, being seen as a homely woman was preferable to being seen as a man. Her dearest truth at least was apparent. For me, the effect was quite the opposite; I was seen as something I believed I was not: a lesbian. I am challenged to describe what it feels like to be seen this way; it must be experienced.

Consider the story of the ugly duckling who is fortunate, in the end, to appear beautifully and only as himself amidst other swans. The confusion the duckling felt on the inside did not stop him from becoming beautiful on the outside, nor did it keep him from finding other birds of similar feather. If Seda had continued to live in a man's body, the ugly duckling story could never have resembled hers, and she would never have achieved her place in sisterhood, never received the particular set of gifts and trials that belong to and shape a woman. If she could never pass as a woman, she would never fully realize her place as a swan and find her peace. Two external variables— Seda's physical shift and whether it merged fully with the expected gender territory—would play a large part in determining Seda's inner landscape as a woman; acceptance both inner and outer. Safety.

And now, the dilemma was mine. Holding the hand of my partner, I no longer represented a housewife living the American dream. At best, my identity was questioned by onlookers, and my own questions then stood out in graphic relief, shadowing all that had been familiar. I was the confused and ugly duckling in my own mind with no clue of how I might find myself beautiful again. I had never seen so clearly that the story of the ugly duckling is about courage, faith, and perspective. How desperately I wanted all three!

After much deliberation, Seda and I were dressed for our big outing in skirts and blouses. She shaved twice and applied full but conservative makeup then clipped on earrings. The cutlet breasts gave her a much-needed lift, and even with her longish boy haircut, she did present as decidedly female. Seda looked like a conservative dyke on a girly sort of day.

We arrived at our destination, parked the car, linked arms, and bravely searched for the restaurant on foot. Double doors stood open wide to a busy room on the ground floor. Seda and I entered smiling with feigned confidence. Perfectly coiffed couples milled around purposefully, and a large poster hanging on the wall welcomed us: A Weekend to Remember!

"It looks like this is not our place," I said softly to Seda.

"Looks like it!" said a perky blonde woman beside us, with either cheer or amusement. "This is a Mormon marriage workshop. Where are you two trying to go?"

"Out to lunch," I said, wondering if they'd rather have us stay to deliver a keynote address.

"Down that hall," she told us with a smile. It was indeed a weekend we would all remember.

Seda and I walked several yards in silence before bursting into laughter. How did our first foray into the public eye manage to land us *there*?

We located the restaurant, found our friends, and took seats under an awning by the river. What a welcome reprieve! The brunch party understood and silently nodded its approval of Seda's appearance. The men seated there had approached me on the sly before our date to ask if Seda would prefer them to wear their kilts as a sign of support. This suggestion came from men of a generation fifteen years older than our own, and the creativity and consideration had been appreciated even though I'd gently declined their offer. It is difficult for straight folk to imagine how best to support the emerging queer.[1] It's such a different paradigm, and the shift seems to be less in what one *does* to support someone queer and more about how one *sees* them. With this shift in perspective, the social norm opens to encompass us all.

Brunch was delicious, and we stuffed ourselves. Every time we got up to refill our plates, I broke out in a sweat. Faking my best relaxed smile, I trained my peripheral vision on every waiter and guest within twenty feet who might be eyeing my partner doubtfully. I could only think that if there had been cause for concern among them, their acting skills were at least as good as mine. After two more glasses of champagne, I no longer cared. For almost three hours, we enjoyed normal adult conversation about non-trans topics with Doug, Janet, and their two other friends. For almost three hours, we successfully entered the public realm wearing the identities that we had formerly only kept in private.

You would think I'd have felt a sense of homecoming, but I did not. Instead, I felt like I was building a suspension bridge without a safety net, a bridge from one world to another. I felt an appropriate sense of urgency around construction—there are transpeople in the world, and I was married to one of them. Transpeople deserve to be seen and valued for their inherent worth and ability to contribute, as we all are.

A bridge was needed to connect the two worlds and provide everyone safe passage. As far as I could tell, we were stepping out for the first time and crossing the bridge correctly. But this business of building a bridge while simultaneously crossing it, swinging wildly in the wind, was something I just had to get used to until construction was over. Somebody had to build the bridge and, this time, the job was ours.

Telling Mom

"MOM, THERE'S SOMETHING I need to tell you." The line was quiet.

"Okay." Her voice tightened.

I took a breath. "This is hard to tell you, but I have to. Fred is going through some changes. Remember when I told you he was exploring his past and getting therapy, trying to understand who he was?" I paused. It was so hard to say. "He did that because he was . . . he wanted to wear women's clothes. He has for as long as he can remember, but somehow he didn't see it as a problem—he didn't see it as something that would change him out of being a man, or a husband or a father—until just in the last year." There was no sound at all. I sat at the kitchen table looking out into the wilds of our backyard. Everything there was still.

"Uh-huh," said Mom in a strangled version of her this-can't-be-so voice. That's all she said. I continued.

"So, he's been really working on this, trying to figure it out because his life as a man means so much to him. *We* mean so much to him. He would do anything for me, you know that."

I suddenly wondered if she did know that because, despite how perfectly matched I felt Fred and I were, my mother had never really adored my husband. Sometimes, she had become angry with him and said that I just couldn't see Fred's faults because I was in love with him. I always felt aggravated when she talked about him that way, using her soft voice as if she accepted what she could not change, while being no less irritated about her son-in-law's failure to impress. I was her daughter and "deserved the best." But she didn't understand how valuable it had been for me this past decade to have a husband who was gentle, caring, and provided for our family. Nor did she see how precious peace and harmony could be to a person who grew up in a fair amount of chaos and violence.

"He's been in therapy for a few years now, and he's been diagnosed as being transgender. That means he was born in a boy's body but has a girl's brain. He identifies as being a woman. So. He's a she. My . . . husband is a woman."

It was weird at first to talk with my mother about Seda as Fred. I'd begun to get used to referring to that person as *she* and *her*. But there was no way that I could think of her as anything but my husband, Fred, right now on one of the most important phone calls in my life. I gave myself permission to formally shift back in time and speak of the man I married as if he still existed.

"Kris, are you sure?" she asked.

"Yes, I'm afraid we're both quite sure at this point. We just haven't told anyone yet, because we wanted to be *really* sure first. It's pretty scary, but right now, the scariest part is telling you."

"Well, honey, I love you. But what does this mean? Does this mean you're getting a divorce?" she asked.

"No, not right now anyway. We're doing okay for the moment, kind of taking each day as it comes."

"But, does this mean Fred will . . . want a man? Will he want to be with a man?" she asked. Her voice was small and charged with electricity. I guessed that my mother felt the same sense of betrayal in this news that I had years ago. I heard Seda in the next room holding her breath, moving quietly, as she tried not to listen.

"I don't know," I said. "We don't know. We're not sure. That's really a question of sexual orientation, and usually that's not tied to gender identity—whether you feel like you're male or female. But I think we'll need some time to see where Fred stands on that. And me, too. He's still my . . . my partner, spouse, whatever. We don't really know what to even call each other. But we're still in love. I think I'm heterosexual, but I do really love this person I married, Mom. I don't want to give it up until I'm sure that's the right thing to do."

I lost my footing suddenly and slipped from the stance of the cool educator into the role of daughter who was watching a mirage of the death of her husband. Should I be grieving this, or was everything okay? Everything was *not* okay, and my mother knew this because she was my mother. It was really not okay. I started to cry.

"Kris, I don't know what to tell you," she said. "He can't just hold it together so you can all be a family? At least till the kids grow up? He can't do that?"

"I know," I said, tears dripping off my nose. I sniffed raggedly and wiped my face with the back of my hand. Outside, Rosie chased a squirrel back and forth through the yard and up the tall willow tree. It ran around and around the trunk. I cried harder, shaking, and tried to do it quietly but when I took breaths, I gulped great lungfuls of air as if I'd been held under water. A high-pitched moan escaped my lips. My mother's anger turned palpable.

"This is stupid, Kris. He should just stay a man while the kids are growing. He can do that. This is not all about him."

"I know. I know it seems like that, Mom," I said. I sat up in my chair, took a deep breath, and looked up at the ceiling. I heard my husband talking softly to Trinidad as he asked the boys to put on their boots to go outside. "I wish he could."

"He's just going to have to figure this out, Kris. He's going to have to grow up!" Something inside me flared. Impulsively, I rebelled against my mother's desire to fix my life for me. This equal and opposite reaction propelled me back into the driver's seat.

"I get what you're thinking, Mom," I said. "I thought that, too, but I was wrong. I thought that he could be a guy if he really wanted to, but I didn't realize that would be like me pretending I was gay if I was not—and that may come to pass as something we have to deal with. We just have to take things one step at a time." I heard the front door softly open and shut as Seda and the boys went out.

"Well, I think this is ridiculous," she said. "And you and the kids can come down here to live any time you want to. That's why we got the farm. So you would have a place to go if ever you needed to."

"Thanks, Mom," I said. "We're all fine for now. We're making this work while we try to figure it out."

"Do his parents know about this?" she asked.

"Yes, they do. He told his mother yesterday."

"Well, what did she say?"

"She was surprised and confused, but she took it pretty well, all things considered." I had sat beside Fred on our king size bed while he made that call, watched him staring at the floor while he said things to his mother that he'd been terrified to say all his life.

"It seems like we should have known," said his mother at one point.

"Yeah, it does," said Fred. "I wore DeeDee's bra under my clothes for almost a year when I was about thirteen and nobody said anything. I guess I kind of wanted to get caught."

"Huh," said his mother. "I don't know what to say. I just never had any idea."

"Geez, they had one kid die and one get incapacitated," said my mother. "Now this. I don't know how she does it."

"Well, what can they do?" I asked. "It's Fred's thing to deal with. He told her, and she said that she saw him as a child of God—you know how they're Christian Scientists—and she said he didn't have any gender at all, as far as she was concerned. So he could do whatever he felt he needed to do, and she would still love him and be his mom."

"Hmm," said my mother.

"I thought that was pretty sweet, really," I said.

"I love you," my mother said quietly. "And I'm sorry you have to go through this." Tears welled in my eyes again.

"Thanks, Mom," I said. "I'll call you soon."

"Okay, honey," she said. "Goodbye."

The job was done. I sat back and felt the weight lifted from my chest. I started to cry again, but this time with relief. She finally knew. One of my biggest fears ever, conquered. Living with a transgender husband was almost as hard as lying daily to my mother. And now I only had to do the first.

Snapshots 2006

I discreetly study Seda out of the corner of my eye every morning as we eat breakfast, and I try to see her as the woman she sees herself as. This is not easy. I have to imagine away the beard stubble and the face of the man I fell in love with almost fifteen years ago. I screw up my courage and almost arrive at the place where I can see my . . . wife? Then it all falls apart, and I see the tired-looking face of the father of my children who wishes it would be easier for all of us.

We take Seda to get her hair cut and ears pierced after work one day. This is a much-awaited milestone. As Seda happily bicycles home alone, the boys and I drive across town to pick up a bee-hive (our second) in which I collected a swarm earlier that day. The entrance to the hive is duct taped closed, but I worry that we will hit a pothole or get into a car accident releasing 20,000 bees into the station wagon with the three of us. I know how to sweat. I've gotten good at it.

Seda announces to her managers at work that she is a woman. Her employers make a plan for this transition, and to our relief administration is explicitly supportive. We did not expect to make this announcement so soon, but Seda is no longer willing to lead a double life and the raw, shaggy appearance before and after electrolysis is too difficult to otherwise explain.

I prepare to tell our neighborhood what is going on and, despite the fact that they all appear to be queer-friendly, I find that I am utterly terrified that we may lose our closest community. To my relief, they are understanding. To my surprise, one woman tells me that she wishes it were her husband who wanted to transition. She'd always identified as a lesbian but fell in love and had children with a man. I wish I could wrap it all up neatly in a box and give it to her.

Seda's interest in sex drops markedly. This development fills me with anxiety as I realize that most of my attraction to her is embedded in the mutual escalation of our excitement around one another. If she is no longer attracted to me or interested in sex, that part of our relationship will be over, and I will not even get to be a lesbian! I can hardly believe my marriage has come to this.

I make pancakes or waffles every Sunday morning. I no longer measure the ingredients. I am not attached to how they turn out. If the result is heavy or flat, the next round will be better. If the batter is exquisite, I am appreciative beyond measure. I consider writing an un-cookbook about the Zen of cooking without recipes. There is no place for failure.

I am drawn to birthing and even consider becoming a surrogate mother. I order the paperwork and comb through it imagining myself carrying and relinquishing a child that belongs to someone else. I realize that mine is a future without any certainty of family as I've known it. I wonder if I am trying to buy time.

One morning, I walk into the bathroom and gasp. Seda is getting out of the shower, and her chest is completely bare. For some reason, I had never before realized how much hair had grown there and what an anchor that hair was to the memory of the man I'd married. I cannot speak, but back away stifling quiet howls of pain. Seda is shocked by my reaction but feels terrible for me. The shave was unavoidable; she thought I knew it was coming. I want her to put it all back, but I know this is impossible. How could I stop or change any of it, ever?

I miss having a man in my bed. Sex is sometimes fun with a woman, but I still want to be entered and filled with all that is male, something Seda will no longer pretend at. One night I begin to cry as Seda and I make love. My tears fall fast through the entire coupling and at the end, I collapse sobbing on her chest. I know that my husband is gone. I grab the camera and photograph what is left of his face from all angles. He looks ashen and drained. I am photographing the dead.

My mother comes around to accepting and supporting my choice to stay with Seda. We visit her in California, but Seda stays in bed all weekend with a migraine. My mother tries to help by cleaning out her closet and offering Seda clothes. In fact, Mom gets a little giddy at the prospect of taking part in making Seda into a woman. She also tells me that under no circumstances am I to tell my grandfather. He has been through enough.

I write poetry regularly now; in tears, I drop to my knees in the hardware store by the caulk to write and pray—all one work in a tiny spiral notebook. I am creating. I no longer worry about what other people think of my tears or my frenzied writing.

Birthing Love Song

This is just
the journey of birth,
the labor that brings life
into light.
It is a natural process
unfolding.
Stay with it.
Breathe.
Do not be afraid.
There are mothers and
lovers here before
you.
There are those who
will come after, each
to hunker down into her own
labor,
spilling her blood,
the sheer sensation of stretching open wide
and open wide
to let life through.
This is the sacred center of
love unwinding.
Breathe through it.
The contraction expands,
tightening to release.
And this I know:
you will have enough strength

Housewife

in you to do this work.
Enough courage.
You will have just enough.
You will forget everything you ever
knew about birthing,
about love.
You will forget your
nakedness.
In the heart of all sensation, you
will forget even
yourself
and your breath will be carried
forward from your ancestors
through you
to the next generation.
You will know nothing and
it will be more in that moment
than you have ever
known.
Breathe into it.
And remember:
there is no promise that you
will ever birth or love
again.
Let that inform your attention.
Labor in love,
not fear.
Trust in the pain to
guide you.
It takes time.
Savor it and hold
it gently, this work,
even when it screams.
And it will change you.

The Forest Garden

I CLEARED BLACKBERRY briars from the back half of our lot. Thick leather gloves protected my hands, but thorns bit into the bare flesh of my arms. I grew leaner and tan through the long spring afternoons as I pulled trailing vine after vine from the three dimensional labyrinth that had devoured the pond and willow bush before our arrival. Lengthening and strengthening muscles, I reformed my body as I bent to my work. I poured my energy into the land beneath our home as if quietly renewing my vows. Sometimes, I worked past dark, leaving the children to sloppily make peanut butter sandwiches on our kitchen table in lieu of dinner. I felt desperate to bring forth fruit from this feral place.

I dug out clay and planted edible perennials into beds of compost and leaf mulch. Strawberries would feed us across years, as would the canes of loganberries and boysenberries that we trellised along the eastern fence line. I carried broken chunks of concrete or "suburbanite" from one end of our property to the other and built a twenty-foot dry stack planter with it so that my raspberry canes would not get their feet wet.

The dog followed close at my heels. Wild mallards swam in the pond beside me while I placed stone after stone. The neighborhood children climbed our tall willow tree and swayed with their faces in the slanting sun as they called to one another over fences; some crafted a boat on which they punted across our pond with a long bamboo pole; others caught snakes. The backyard pulsed with life and I took my place in it, working at a frenzied pace while our Willamette Valley was consumed by blossom and green.

I planted dozens of fruit and nut bearing trees and bushes, both native and exotic—almond, heartnut, plum, medlar, apple, aronia, filbert, serviceberry, and seaberry among them. With a pick mattock, I dug out the previous occupant's ornamental trees, iris, and lily bulbs—too many flowers and not enough food. We had integrated chickens, rabbits, and bees into our permaculture paradise. I wanted this effort to sustain our family in times of trouble. I refused to starve. I built this garden to last.

Sam's Wisdom

ONE DAY AT breakfast, the boys and I discussed what we found difficult in life. Trinidad said he had trouble with reading. Sam, at age four, wished he had an easier time on his skateboard. I turned from the stove where I had been stirring oatmeal.

"I bet it often seems like kids are the only people learning things, and that adults have it down. I'll bet you think I've got it all together and don't ever have a hard time figuring out how to do something, but that's not the case. I'm here to tell you, I have a tough time, too. Every day."

I considered the emotional challenges I faced, my struggle to stay present, the way I longed for the freedom of a broader perspective. What words could I use to share these challenges with a child?

Sam regarded me quietly. "I know, Mom," he said. "Like turning off the washing machine . . . when you're inside it."

Meeting Jack

I MET A MAN at the farm upriver. It was June, the end of straw-berry season, and the fruits of summer grew plump on the vine. I joined a group of winter gardeners to plan and share seeds in preparation for the far-off chill of autumn. We sat on bales of straw in the morning light and shared our best understanding of winter crops. We explored how to sprout stubborn carrots, har-vest broccoli in tiny florets rather than whole heads, and sow ever-bearing beds of potatoes. Over the heads of this perma-culture community, both new and wonderful to me, I saw him— the tenant farmer imported from Great Britain—and my path took a sharp turn on the spot.

Jack was tall and rough hewn with bronze skin that blushed at the neck from too much sun. Long suspenders held up his frayed Carhartt pants that had years before taken on the cocoa hue of our Willamette Valley clay. His fingers bore coffee-col-ored creases and thin lines of earth showed through behind short fingernails. These were hands that knew the dirt. He waved them broadly as he spoke, sometimes allowing an arm to hang in the air with an open-ended question mark or gesticu-lation of wonder. I tried not to stare, afraid he would notice me studying him, afraid he would wonder at the meaning of that. Later, he told me that he actively avoided looking at me, and every time he did steal a glance, I was looking away.

A corner of Jack's shirt hung loose outside of his trousers, the bottom carelessly left unbuttoned. There was an air of importance about this oversight. It said, "We have mouths to feed, seeds to save, so little time to prepare ourselves for droughts to come. What are the buttons of a shirt but vanity in the face of this?" Already, the romantic in me was stirred. The wind lifted his thin cotton shirttail, and I found myself glancing sidelong to catch a view of what lay underneath.

At the end of our session, I waited in line to get myself a sample of overwintering cilantro, the first developed in our region. Jack described the seed at length, his words resounding richly— full and robust. His fingers brushed my own as he showed me how to fold a makeshift envelope out of a page from an outdated seed catalogue. The hairs at the back of my neck stood on end. He was standing so close that I could smell him: male sweat, curry, sweet onions, and patchouli. I could scarcely breathe. After he shook tiny, black seeds into my folded packet, I turned my feet mechanically to go, though my heart had stopped there.

I had forgotten—or perhaps I'd never known—what it was to appreciate a man.

Part Four

Together Apart

I WAS TRANSFIXED by the tall, dusty Englishman. We exchanged several emails each day, and I summoned the courage to ask him to go walking with me. I sat back in my chair at the computer desk to ponder this turn of events, Jack's last email glowing from the ether.

How was it that the attentions I offered this man felt right even though I was still married to Seda? There were no printed guidelines for how to behave when one suddenly found oneself attached to a transgender spouse, and I wanted to better understand my options. Curiosity moved me, but I did not feel ready to step away from the stability I had in my marriage, home, and family life.

At that point, Seda and I had already departed from the beaten path as a typical American family, or perhaps it just went on without us. Not only did the papa want to wear the mama's clothes but, after some misgivings, the mama had used good preschool ethics and decided on an open closet policy. In American culture, such ethics are hotly debated.

The vast majority of couples who experience one member in transition end the romance in short order, divide the assets, and then see each other in court to determine custody of the children. Most often, the transgender partner is seen as being in the wrong while the other partner is cast as an innocent victim. I am aware that to this point in our story, my character may seem heroic because I worked with the odds rather than against them, maintaining (more often than not) an open heart and mind. I also refused to take on a victim mentality and that self-empowerment, I am told, sets me up as either saintly or off my rocker.

The fact remains that Seda had no more choice in being transgender than I had in being married to someone who turned out to be. Arguably, we both could have picked up on some singular clues and abandoned denial a decade earlier, but neither of us wanted to do that when we had so much in common. Seda and I enjoyed each other's company immensely. We worked, played, and dreamed together. We had actively cultivated denial for good reason—we wanted to be together as a couple, and her being transgender would not have allowed that.

On the other hand, Seda may never have had the spaciousness, courage, and skillset to explore who she truly is if she hadn't had a secure partner. She may have continued to bottle her confusion in depression and substance abuse as she had before we met. Given the many years of marital bliss we were gifted, Seda and I now share responsibility in having entertained denial for so long. It has been tempting at times to blame her for our struggles because they arose from her being trans, but I could not agree to calling her a villain. She has not been in choice about the confusion that welled inside her.

Because gender dysphoria (GD) is not yet part of our societal norm (though, thankfully, this is beginning to change), a person with GD might be seen as being guilty of transgenderism, as if it were a choice. Why would we see them as guilty when announcing their dilemma? Gender dysphoria is complicated and muddled in comparison to a culture of strict gender binaries (male/female) such as we have. The transgender person is the one responsible for bringing their incongruity to light, when life would be much easier for everyone around them if they did not. To make matters worse, their credibility is questioned and their condition is often marginalized because popular culture has not yet jumped on the brain research being done around gender.

Gender dysphoria has been a regular variation since the beginning of recorded time and those experiencing it often had distinctive and respected roles in society. In other parts of the world today, that is still the case; however, patriarchal inter-pretations of the Torah and the New Testament that serve the ruling class (pointed out in a compelling argument by Judith S. Antonelli)[1] have anchored popular culture to a construct of strict binary genders, deeming any variation abnormal.

Gender dysphoria is also confused with homosexuality, which seems bizarre to those who understand that gender iden-tity is about which gender you identify with internally, not about with whom you want to have sex. Gender and sexual orientation are tangled more in our popular view of them today than they actually are in biology. Despite the fact that sexual orientation (a person's sexual preference) develops separately from gender identity (self-identified sense of whether one is male, female, both, or neither), our culture sexualizes gender from a young age in the stereotypical binary gender roles[2] of male and female: Pre-pubescent girls model high-cut bikinis and low-riding capris on billboards. Young men with sculpted muscles and zero body fat sell sex through cologne and denim jean ads. It seems that conventional wisdom deems the sole purpose of gender to be in service to sexuality.

I believe that our heteronormative bent is the real reason that gender variance is so often confused with homosexual-ity. When sex is sold on billboards through cosmetics, clothes, and cologne, we can largely count on it depicting a *heterosex-ual* orientation. If we see the purpose of gender as a necessary piece to complete the puzzle of heterosexuality and therefore procreation, then we see gender through this heteronorma-tive lens. Accordingly, to express a gender that doesn't match the sex one was assigned at birth is typically interpreted in our culture as expressing oneself as gay, because if a boy wants to dress like a girl, this translates in a heteronormative culture as a boy who is trying to show he likes boys (because anyone who looks like a girl is expected to like boys), when in fact, people do not try to conform to our heteronormative world by changing genders. It just doesn't work that way. As a nation, we are largely confused.

With gender strictly dichotomized and sexualized, it can be terrifying for people in our culture to encounter a person whose gender presentation is ambiguous. Confusion around sexual orientation and a fear of male violence seem to be at the root of concern around transwomen in public bathrooms. The question may be posed, "Is my wife going into a public restroom to squat half-naked beside someone who looks like a woman but has a penis?"

The worry in this question arises from assuming that the person with a penis is a heterosexual male who is trying to appear otherwise in order to more effectively prey upon women. This fear is fueled by cultural assumptions about male predation and a lack of understanding about transgenderism in general (see Prologue).

If safety is the real concern, a transwoman is much less safe presenting female while walking into a men's room. Additionally, cisgender (gender corresponds with assigned sex) women are more likely to feel fearful of a transman who passes as a cisgender male when he turns up to use the women's room in compliance with state laws that require people to use restrooms according to their gender assigned at birth. It is my hope that such ludicrous laws will be short-lived. Some people are threatened by ambiguous gender expression because their identities, which could be seen as personal safety nets built on cultural norms (binaries/heteronormativity) and religious beliefs, are shaken foundationally.

Men, especially, have a history of reacting to such ambiguity with anger and violence because the ambiguity does not fit with how they understand the world, and their sense of belonging, privilege, and inherent value is no longer clear when gender roles go undefined. Such angry responses are categorized as transphobic, and countless transpeople worldwide lose their lives to this violence annually. Seda and I have always been aware of the risks she takes by living as a transwoman, but we've had little choice in her taking them.

Explaining my home and family life to others had become a labor of love, as with each telling I waded through my own thoughts and feelings about the transition while also navigating the potential shock and awe of my audience. Telling Jack was no exception.

Most of the story had come out over email, but hiking up the back side of Mount Pisgah, we shared our predicaments with one another in real time, grounded by earth, sun, air, and water. Gazing out over the winding rivers and green fields of the Willamette Valley, we acknowledged the almost eerie sense of familiarity that already existed between us. We were both passionate about stewarding the earth and children and felt clear almost immediately that it was work we would share for some time.

I knew then that my ever-decreasing sex life with Seda had reached its end. Over the course of that day with Jack, I formally declared it so, realizing I was heterosexual through and through. I still saw what was sacred in Seda and appreciated the love that we had tested over time. The scope of my care now extended to include the parts of her and me that no longer fit together, and in a flash I felt acceptance about it all.

By contrast, the attraction that I felt for Jack awakened my body, mind, and spirit as one. I felt relieved and clearly knew that it was time to move on, even as the grief of ending my romantic relationship with Seda formally descended. Ironically, I had feared this moment of clarity above all else. I imagined that losing my grip on our marriage would break me in ways that I could never recover from. As the moment arrived, a gentle trick of the universe made the transition almost effortless; I surmised that my grief had largely been spent in the previous years when I tried to imagine my husband as a woman.

The truth was, our marriage had been over for some time. The man I shared vows with and my role in that union had died with the identity of the man that I'd married. My efforts to remain with Seda had been legitimate and valuable; she was and would always be my parenting partner. She was also a sister of sorts to the man I married, worthy of a special friendship. We had and would likely always maintain a keen interest in one another's well-being. We were family. But that was all. My husband had long been dead. The burden of fearing our separation lifted, and I felt light and alive for the first time in years. If I was ready to live again, it was not just for loving another. I was ready at last to embark on the next chapter of our story, neither together nor apart.

Jack worried about the feelings he had for me, because they opposed the personal vow of chastity that he had made on his own spiritual path. His letters to me were filled with wise words of warning from the likes of Rilke: " . . . beauty's nothing but/ the start of terror we can hardly bear,/ and we adore it because of the serene scorn/ it could kill us with. Every angel's terrifying." I saw the truth in all of his words, and I did not turn away. I had adjusted my eyes to the darkness. I had adjusted my eyes to the light.

Why was it that Jack and I were coming together now? What was his role in my world, and mine in his? He professed a sort of faith that Spirit would guide us. I didn't know what to make of any of it, but surprisingly found myself looking optimistically into the future. I imagined more than just my happy, healthy children there. I began to envision myself as joyful and productive. It had been so long since I'd experienced that kind of hope that it felt entirely innocent and new. My letters to Jack brimmed with faith in my own heart to reflect the divine.

"That only which we have within can we see without. If we meet no gods, it is because we harbor none. If there is grandeur in you, you will find grandeur in porters and sweeps," wrote Ralph Waldo Emerson.

"We are the porters and sweeps," I told Jack. "Reflecting light back and forth, one to another, working the earth side by side."

While I was giddy with what Jack called "the timbre of our unfolding," Seda sadly watched me step away from our shared bed. She understood that I was moving into my own integrity while she was still ambivalent about whether she was hetero or bisexual. Her attraction to me was born out of love more than any visceral tug to one sex or the other. She didn't know what the future would hold for her, and she didn't want to keep me from having the heterosexual relationship that I'd committed myself to in marrying her. At the same time, she grieved for the end of what precious intimacy we had shared. Even as her transition had catalyzed our separation, Seda was the last one to hold onto our union.

As I blessed and released the death of my marriage, I felt sadness for Seda more than anything. I had wanted so much to make it work regardless of my sexual orientation. My spouse was still herself after all—isn't that the only thing that matters? "You marry the person, not the body," successful couples from the Transfamily Spouse Yahoo Group touted enthusiastically. These were not the only examples of how people dealt with the gender transition of a partner, but they were the ones I sought to emulate.

As Seda became more comfortable in her gender identity, I lost interest in her as a romantic partner. That was the rub. A clear shift in our chemistry had taken place, and I realized that I had become deeply content with our friendship, though I was no longer attracted to her as a mate. I felt embarrassed and sad about this. I saw that I had failed our marriage by being attached to the material facts and chemistry surrounding our bodies. Frankly, I was aghast at this proof of my shallow commitment to our vows. Yet, our dilemma was not clearly addressed by the clause, "in sickness and in health." There was no recommendation at the altar for how to steer the course of one's marriage in the event of gender dysphoria.

I aimed to take the high road and committed myself to kindness and compassion for us both. When others disagreed with my strategy, they usually chose to distance themselves rather than discuss their thoughts with me. My biological father told his mother that the only sensible thing for me to do was to divorce and banish Seda. He never spoke to me about that or much else ever again. His mother, despite being of a different generation, accepted our news without batting an eye.

Michelle, my conservative Christian friend, took a most unusual tack: while Seda's disorder clearly fell in the category of "sickness" in God's plan, He surely did not intend me to stay married to her despite that niggling little clause in our marriage contract about sickness and health. Changing genders was weird, after all. So weird that she thought all children should be protected from it, hers and mine included. Apparently the high road was whatever I could live with. My choice.

I had put every effort into making sex with Seda work. One of my posts to a friend on the Transfamily Spouse site showed how game I was to explore our sexual future together. "You said that your sweetie's erections were infrequent at best but you still have great sex anyway . . . I'm so excited to hear this!" I wrote. "I really consider myself uninformed, but I hope you'll straighten me out; is it possible for her to have an orgasm without an erection?" Yes, my mentor told me, but it would be milder, deeper, and slower coming.

The nuts and bolts were in place to continue our exploration, but I suddenly became clear that I no longer wanted to try. More had changed for me than just the way our bodies worked together—my gut attraction to Seda had simply failed. The presence of Jack in my world had shined a light on this fact.

Seda was, in her own way, happy for me. She loved me so much, and she could not help but share my jubilance as I rattled off the story of Jack and I walking together. She was delighted to see me shining, and she wanted more of it.

A writer herself, I knew Seda would appreciate the eloquence of Jack's and my platonic love letters to one another. It seems rather callous in retrospect to have shown them to her, but one tenet of our relationship was full disclosure. The only flaw we'd ever encountered in this plan had been the acknowledgment of Seda's transgender tendencies. That single omission had proven to be like the near-fatal spinning needle in Sleeping Beauty's castle. We had no desire to duplicate the experience, so we prized full transparency above all in our communication. But perhaps adjustments would need to be made here, too, as we moved forward together as individuals. The degree of our intimacy was indeed changing, and Seda's peek into our correspondence made that clear to me.

When Seda read the letters, she became suddenly sober.

"What's wrong?" I asked.

"Well, he's falling in love with you," she said with a sigh. "And watching him fall in love with you is not so very different from remembering how I fell in love with you myself."

I felt instantly abashed, and the awareness of what I had, and what Seda did not, stood out to me in heartbreaking chiaroscuro. I would not share this way again.

Later that week, I took the children camping on the Pacific coast. It was my first family outing without Seda. I left her at home in bed with a migraine, likely estrogen-induced. Two days into the trip, I realized it was Seda's and my fifteenth anniversary. I called her to observe the date formally. We would never again celebrate our anniversary as we had before. I noticed that I was not sad about that; my mind was now focused on the open road before me.

As the boys and I played tag, picked berries, roasted hot dogs, and hiked the hillsides, I could not think of anything but Jack. I couldn't eat, and I couldn't sleep. Was this distraction from parenting healthy? How could it be avoided? I struggled to stay present with the beauty of my children, but I found myself exhausted. My boys, at five and seven, never stopped moving. I followed them a mile and a half down the trail to a grandmother spruce tree, hundreds of years old, and I sat beneath her where the earth was worn away by passing pilgrims. I wrapped my arms around her damp brown trunk and prayed that we would all find peace and be happy again someday.

I could not imagine what the future held for me or for my family. My head whirled with possibilities, white noise, and the ocean calling to me. We spent the afternoon in a protected cove and chased the tide in and out. I danced with my shadow in the surf. The boys ran barefoot over clay cliffs, and I walked behind them soundlessly, pale feet pressing into the cool, damp earth. My senses vibrated with the intense acuity of falling in love, and my hyperawareness of this experience was only dwarfed by my view of the expansive steel-colored sea. I felt so grateful for its presence.

Stepping Away

AFTER ONLY TWO encounters and a few weeks of intensive writing shared with one another, Jack pulled the Hanged Man's card from the tarot deck twice and decided that the universe was guiding him to withdraw from our relationship. I was broken-hearted but let him go only to find a note from him in my inbox within the week, chagrined that he had allowed me no options as he stepped away from what he called our "supernova." I wrote him back with what I had learned.

Brother Jack,

I am surprised to hear from you, and grateful. You did not leave me options, but I might have requested them. Having guessed at your needs, I chose not to. Still, I wished for the chance to slow from light speed and explore the universe in tandem instead of seeking our universe within one another. I have a deep sense that this is where the real work in us lies. I am unhappy indeed if, in my intensity, I have destroyed the prospect of all that may have been gained.

I value our meeting beyond words. Before your coming, I had been hanging here ripe, uncomfortable, and completely unaware of what I needed to do in my relationship with Seda. The habits of care I had cultivated were no longer serving me, and without your shake I might have fallen in a way that was ultimately more painful for all of us here in Collierland. You will take your own lessons from it, but do not take the hand of remorse on my part.

After sitting stunned with your words yesterday morning, I realized how comfortable I am now in my relationship with Seda. Not without sadness or some fear, but completely in my integrity. I looked to my garlic beds (secretly, I think I'd not wanted to pull them in case you ever came over; it was some assurance that I can grow *something*) and saw that it was time to harvest. Hands to earth, I thought of this transition between us, my transition with Seda, and Seda's transition within herself, knowing that all outcomes are a mystery. Head by head, the garlic lay in rows to dry in the morning sun.

I planted that garlic last autumn aware that my life as I'd known it was crumbling. I planted it with no hope of harvest, unsure of whether I'd be here to see it grow to maturity. I planted and loved, and yesterday I found that the rich bitter fruit is of a variety I would never have expected. Delicious. One head was mysteriously blue. Next fall, the metamorphosis will continue.

Do you remember that my New Year's resolution last January was to shift with lightning speed from the perception of challenge to the awareness of opportunity? Drinking poison as wine. What on earth did I think I was asking for? Nonetheless, I am delighted with this life I have chosen.

So what now? Beats me. Can I pester you with gardening questions? Will you come out to see our

place some time? To cultivate our friendship and not
feel my heart jumping to respond, I'd like to see you
once every one to four weeks. How does that sound?

   k

And with that, Jack returned with apologies for the curveball
of melodrama he'd thrown our way. The letters that followed
between us now landed in the file marked "Post Nova" but my
experience of him was no less brilliant and inspiring. Despite
my request for less frequency in our connection, Jack and I continued to write one another daily and see each other a few times
a week.

Jack's first visit to our home proved a greater challenge for
his nerves than for Seda's. My former husband found herself
quite charmed by Jack, attracted to him even. A poly relationship never emerged as a possibility for us because I feared I
would be jealous if insecurely attached. I had experienced this in
the past and had not demonstrated my best self in the circumstances. I had some acceptance around this weakness, for better
or for worse, and had no desire to put energy into correcting the
trend at that time. Seda concurred, and so Jack was integrated as
a family friend and my intimate of sorts.

If there was a lack of clarity around the sexual nature of my
relationship with Jack (to myself and the world at large), I felt
relief to know that spending time with him had at least contributed to clear boundaries in my relationship with Seda. She
had moved her bed out to the living room futon, and I kept the
tiny bedroom as my own. I no longer perched myself on her lap
in the mornings while we planned our days together. She and I
settled into an easy and comfortable friendship that echoed our
marital partnership in many ways. It was a transition that felt
authentically rooted in my feelings for her. In this, I found some
small degree of peace.

Eclipse

I THREW MYSELF into tending the garden, flowing with the vision of permaculture that Jack subscribed to. "Gloom and doom is upon us! Let's grow an orchard and some greens!" was the subversive, ubiquitous slogan. Every seed swapping potluck gathered our burgeoning community—old hippies and new, hicks, and fringe-dwellers alike—to cheerlead for the cause of saving ourselves, our families, and the planet. Every sensibility in me agreed with the politics of the matter. A few monster companies controlled over 90 percent of the seed genetics in the world, said Jack; if we were to survive, we must save seed and share it in community.

I set new seeds and starts in the ground by day as the children pruned tunnels through their wild scape between the pond and blueberry hill. A neighbor boy got stuck twenty-five feet up in the willow tree one afternoon, naked, at the same time that his mother needed him for a dentist appointment. Trinidad caught snakes and released them again, often with fresh Band-Aids applied to wounds from cats or birds. Sometimes we'd see them, ragged bandages intact, months later. I built beds and planted brassicas enough to last the winter as well as carrots, even though I trusted that my dog, Rosie, would dig and eat them before they got to be the size of my thumb. I just kept trying.

Seda supported us financially and was there for me whenever I asked. It was clear, though, that her preference was to spend time alone, immersed in the study of trans issues. Over the past couple of years, my mind had focused full time with Seda's on the trans arena we found ourselves in. We'd researched hormones, both natural and synthetic, and their dosages and potential side effects. We'd studied plastic surgery and gender confirmation surgery, and then we'd daydreamed countless hours about how we could fund it. We'd read others' stories of breast implants, social struggles, prejudice, and the violence encountered by transpeople and their families.

There was so much to learn. Seda's research had revealed that injectable estrogen in once a week doses had a high chance of causing migraines—hence her tendency to vomit for two days straight after injecting. She had then switched to oral estrogen and, even so, debilitating migraines came on average once every six weeks and lasted for two to three days at a time. After she'd spent a weekend recovering in bed, Seda spent the next weekend catching up on the things she hadn't done the weekend before. She was ready to actively participate in parenting again the following weekend, and I was often fighting bitterness by then. Despite my intentions of patient kindness, I was a lousy nurse and felt most desperate for a break from the kids when it seemed that one was near at hand. Seda's being in the house but unavailable was hard on us all and made for a bumpy domestic partnership at best when the migraines came on. I became more and more self-reliant to avoid disappointment.

At the time I met Jack, my focus was already beginning to shift from trans issues toward sustainability in a larger sense. I had learned that having my hands in the dirt was a grounding experience for me and for our children. I saw how we thrived on living simply, growing our own food, and eating it. I recognized that moving into health would require more than just an integration of Seda's proper gender, but also an interconnectedness with each other and the earth. I wanted to live and share with our family a more wholesome lifestyle, where we actively engaged in growing and feeding our bodies and spirits. The boys and I spent time outdoors together, cooked together, played together, and read aloud to one another. When I realized one day that for more than fifteen minutes my thoughts had not touched on trans issues affecting my life, I cried with relief. The weight of our shared burden had begun to lift for me. My life beyond transition was emerging.

As I moved forward with a vision of permaculture that included the diverse experience of our family, I strived to accept the fact that Seda was not done with her part of intense transgender exploration. It was difficult to be patient with Seda's process. I had waited and given space to my husband as he once delved into childhood trauma and unearthed the resentment of forty years of darkness. I had allowed that anger to raise its ugly head and thrash blindly until the victim my husband thought himself to be finally died and a new, more powerful person took his place. I had watched with fear and confusion as Seda struggled to determine whether her transgender identity would require a full shift to living as a woman, and thus displace our marriage as we'd known it. And even if the work itself was Seda's, even if she fully deserved my utmost sympathy, I was tired.

During Seda's process over the past few years, I studied my own path in relation to Seda's and, most importantly, I parented our children largely alone. I was ready to move forward now, into life and light, and if Seda could not yet join us, I would trust her to follow when she was ready. My daily work embodied our family as a unit, and I believed that my efforts in pursuing what was wholesome would balance Seda's inward, self-centered odyssey.

Seda was going through puberty again, this time growing a woman from the inside out. Finally, the latent teenage girl who had worn her sister's bra under her flannel shirt in rural Wyoming could develop the graces of womanhood for herself. Seda practiced the walk, the talk and, God knows, the makeup artistry. At times, I clenched my jaw to keep from commenting and turned away when Seda put on a lilting new femme voice contortion or w⸗ 3 a bit heavy-handed in the application of rouge.

It was time for me to step away and let her grow on her own. In the meantime, I cooked and fed her exquisite and colorful meals from the garden. In the end, I believed that the beauty and inherent health of the earth would inform her journey, and we would meet again as people more similar to each other than different.

One afternoon as the sun went down, I discovered that I was in need of compost. Jack suggested that the boys and I come around and get some from the farm where he lived. I jumped at the opportunity to see him and doubted that Seda would miss us. Bundling the children, I packed some snacks and headed off on a pastoral adventure. There was to be a lunar eclipse in two hours.

Jack and I loaded the steer manure compost onto a blue tarp in the back of my '82 Volvo station wagon. That car was a workhorse and would vacuum out in no time to be ready for the next camping trip.

After we closed the hatch, Jack and I scrambled up a massive pile of leaf mulch to find seats for the heavenly show. Trin and Sam chose to climb a neighboring mountain of leaves and ran up and down the side several times before collapsing, clammy and winded, as the sun set. Nestling my shoulder against Jack's, we spoke quietly of sustainability, growing herbs, and crafting medicine. We talked about the importance of modeling food cultivation and wildcrafting around the children as a means of initiation. We danced carefully around the topic of our future, but despite our utmost care and caution, words about global change inevitably collapsed down to the intimately personal. Exactly where did our relationship fit into our permaculture community? Who were we as a couple, as a family?

"I am not sexually available," Jack had growled darkly during our first walk together. "I cannot be your lover." I later learned that Jack had taken on a monkish lifestyle after perceiving himself sexually inadequate to engage in an intimate relationship. Whether his physical failing was, as he saw it, a sign from God to become chaste, or simply a bigger, more embarrassing challenge than he felt equipped to cope with, only he can know.

I tried to accept and understand his words but thus far had not been successful. Hadn't he surrendered himself to courtly romance in countless letters, our mutual care and passion alight and alive on the screen? And how could I characterize the Friday nights I'd spent supping with him as he prepared every part of a sumptuous meal without the smallest bit of assistance from me so that I could just sit, read poetry, talk, and listen—an uncommon indulgence for a mother of two young boys. He touched my hands, my arms, and my face with delicate, searching fingers that warmed us both. He prized me like a rare bird and lived in fear that he would have to release me. We both did.

I boldly envisioned a future where Jack would live with our family, helping Seda and me with the education of our boys. I pictured his love of the land sinking its roots into my own garden where he claimed to be learning from me the skills I had intuitively collected in cultivation of tilth. I learned from him about diversity—the unfathomable variety of winter pears, apples, spicy brassicas, and pale parsnips from Slavic countries that needed to be grown out to preserve their heritage seeds.

Jack gardened across the internet and fertile farmland alike. He collected information and seeds, ambassador to the old ways in the twenty-first century. He wrote about this work as I wrote daily about the happenings in my life, great and small. We had so much in common. Wasn't it possible that his path could join with my path permanently?

My goals seemed humble. I wished to parent and love consciously while maintaining a garden that renewed itself— chicken and rabbit manure feeding plants that fed people, rabbits, and chickens. Fruits, vegetables, nuts, legumes, and even grains now rose from our loamy plot that had once lain compacted, dried, and cracking in the sun. I had in mind an urban farmstead that would feed my growing family, the resourceful Jack included, and I nurtured this vision largely alone.

The voicing of my plans, my hopes, and my dreams always summoned a shadow to fall across Jack's open features. I thought that perhaps it was fear alone, and it would pass. While Seda and I had always been completely upfront with one another in all ways, I dug deep into my heart for the patience and creativity to meet the challenge of Jack's withholding. I decided the best course was to give him space that allowed for healing, and then if Jack's care for me grew enough, I imagined he would seek help or the treatment needed to feel comfortable with his sexuality again. This could take time.

I loved Jack the way I had come to love Seda: whole-heartedly, and with trust in his inherent goodness and value. When Jack complained of being broken or damaged goods, I saw otherwise, fixing my gaze on the purity of his soul and then noting every way that his actions supported the picture I held of his divine strength and capability. This was a practice in faith, which for me is a way of seeing.

Such vision, held jointly by Seda and me, had served the two of us as human beings far beyond our roles as husband and wife. We had come to see the unique beauty in one another as more valuable than our ties in matrimony. Our commitment, ultimately, was to support the actualization of ourselves and each other. We did not discriminate in this but operated in service to the whole, and that whole extended beyond our union and family into the community and world at large. My love for Jack, like my love for Seda, thus centered more on hope than expectation.

And so I sat with quiet faith that the greater good would be served while the moon hung deathly white in a violet sky. Darkness crept across the pale face of the moon, and a hush fell over the boys as well. Fields of corn whispered secrets back and forth amongst themselves. The scent of honey wafted up from hives set between plum trees below. Bats arced full tilt in frenzied rings around us like bits of onyx tossed into the jeweled twilight. Jack took my hand in his when the moon fell into total darkness, and we sat together waiting for the light.

Our Family in Community

"THIS WEEKEND, I would very much like to visit my friend Jonathon by Dorena Lake," said Jack. "Would you and the boys like to come? We could make an outing of it." He grinned broadly, showing crowded teeth. I loved the angular expression of each and every tooth, despite Jack's warnings to not look too closely.

"I would love to," I said and began planning a picnic lunch that would hold us over for the day.

The weather was fine as we drove south, both boys laughing and pointing out the windows. We pulled up at the farm before the sun rose to high noon. Evergreen trees dressed the slopes dropping down from all sides to a tiny valley where the farm nestled, bustling with activity in preparation for the chill of autumn. Jonathon greeted us amiably. A patched work shirt hanging from strong, lean arms, he waved us out to the raspberry field where we plucked juicy red berries from the vine. "These are the last of the season," said Jonathon. "We've got to get them all in."

Wasps alighted around our ankles in the dewy, tall summer grass between rows as we talked of pollinators and beekeeping. Jonathon had lost two hives to bears in the past year. It was a challenge I had not encountered in the city. We discussed replacement hives and the more natural, smaller-combed varieties I had been investigating. Jack cast his merry eyes over the tops of the raspberry canes. From the other side of the bush, I could hear his throaty grumble, "I had a feeling two such pillars of wisdom would find no shortage of things to talk about."

"Sorry!" I laughed. "I suppose you'd like to get a word in now and then!" He came around to my side of the bush and pulled me up to him. I pressed my face into his broad chest and breathed in his maleness—sweat, fresh air, and a hint of curry—also something sweet that I could never put my finger on. I drank his scent and never tired of it. *Is this what a man smells like?* I wondered.

"It is my utmost pleasure," he announced, "to connect two people who are so very dear to me. Just being here to listen to the two of you banter on is an honor and a gift." He traced my temple with a finger and swept aside a lock of silvering auburn hair. "You are so beautiful, Kristin Collier," he said, lowering his voice. "I can hardly bear to look at you sometimes, you know. It's like looking at the sun." He wrapped his arms around me and rested his chin on the top of my head.

Trin ran up excitedly. "Mama, look! I caught a snake!" he cried. A thick silver-brown gopher snake writhed in his hands, and he gazed upon it with the purest admiration.

"Ah . . . " I said, torn. Stepping away from Jack's embrace reluctantly, I turned to share this special moment with Trinidad. Jack squeezed my arm with one of his broad hands.

"Go, Mama," he said gently, smiling down as he turned me toward my son. "You don't want to miss this."

It was true, and I was grateful to Jack for embracing my role as a mother. It seemed that my interactions with the boys never took me from his heart. Rather, my mothering of them endeared me to him, so touched was he by the manifestation of my maternal energy. It was a piece of me he longed to know more deeply, a part of life he had not yet participated in enough. Jack released me but continued to stroke my shoulders from behind as I marveled at Trinidad's find.

Later, hot and with fingers stained sticky red from raspberries, we dove into the river that coursed through the eastern edge of Jonathon's farm. The water shocked us, cold but refreshing, and the boys splashed and played for over an hour. Jack showed them how he got to be the toe-racing champion of the western world in his day, sitting at the top of the water and paddling backward with his hands so that only his toes stuck up before him.

Lying on the grassy bank in the sun, Jack shared stories of his childhood diving competitions, including one story in which he split his swim trunks right up the back, causing him to exit the pool quickly with the torn remainder clutched at his groin. The boys laughed heartily at this and wanted more tales of Jack's days of rugby and boarding school in England. Stretching ourselves out in the open air to dry, we talked awhile and then lay quiet in the stillness to listen to the river's song. The tender flesh of purple plums gave way beneath our teeth, and we sucked their sweet juices as the sun sank slowly toward the treetops. Jack and I held hands in the golden light of the afternoon and marveled at the exquisite beauty of family, friends, and community. In that moment in time, we were not tangled in the mystery. In that moment, we were content.

After pressing apples into cider, I brought my picnic contribution up to the farmhouse as dusk began to fall. Opening plastic and glass containers, I doled out tuna fish sandwiches to all. The boys descended upon theirs, half-famished with the hunger of a day spent entirely out of doors. Jack took a quarter of a sandwich into his mouth in one bite and chewed slowly with a look of bliss.

Authoritatively, he turned to the boys and said in his upper-crust British accent, "Your mother makes some really kick-ass tuna sandwiches." I laughed and the boys nodded enthusiastically. Tuna sandwiches were not a gold medal natural food achievement in my opinion, but I enjoyed sharing them with an appreciative audience. In a roomful of hippies and people who professed to live squeaky-clean lives, I discovered that I had companions in the creature comforts of my childhood. I wondered why I hadn't thought to bring finger Jell-O.

Jonathon's daughter emerged from a back bedroom. She held in her arms a tiny baby, less than a month old. Her little girl cried inconsolably. "I can't figure out what's wrong," she said to her father, shaking her head sadly.

She was a young mother, just seventeen, and her father looked with concern at his granddaughter. Jonathon did not have a wife, and his daughter's mother was not present in their lives. The two of them exchanged looks of bewilderment.

"Let me have a go at it," said Jack. He took the baby into his arms, her tiny fists flailing. "Mmmmmm," he hummed softly, resting the baby face down over one arm. He walked the floor back and forth whispering to her as she quieted and began sucking ferociously on the back of her hand. In another ten minutes, she dropped off to sleep. Jack did not set her down, but continued his quiet march back and forth, one foot in fatherland and the other stepping in and out of my conversation with Jonathon.

As the full moon rose and shone crisp and white through the picture window into the dimly lit living room, I saw the man I'd fallen in love with. This was a man I could parent with, I thought, and for one unearthly flash, I saw the vision of a baby in his arms that we had made together. The image troubled and excited me as we drove the windy road home in silence under a starry sky.

Coming Out

AT THE END of August, the boys and I planned to attend Family Camp once more, this time with Seda in tow. She had come out at work to management months before, and together they had made a plan for a smooth transition in the office. In the week following camp, Seda would return to work as a woman after fellow employees had been educated and alerted to the change. Seda and I agreed to make her official out date on the first day of Family Camp, August 12, 2007. From that day forward, Seda would present and live as a woman in all ways and in all places. We thought that the Parent Peer Leadership Program's Family Camp in Napa Valley would be a warm and receptive space for Seda to transition in. We anxiously awaited the big day.

In the week before departure, Seda made an appointment to appear in court so she could be granted her official name change by a circuit judge, thus completing her legal gender transition. We expected this formality to close without a hitch, so the boys and I dressed ourselves in our Sunday best to join Seda as she formally departed from her male-gendered past. When we arrived at the courthouse, it slowly dawned on me that no one there appeared to be in the mood for or even capable of celebration.

I stood quietly behind Seda, looking around me at the hundreds of people standing in line to get court orders or receive verdicts that held no joy for them. None of these people looked hopeful. Some were already in tears. Many set their jaws in anger, tapping a foot, looking at the clock, or shouting into their cell phones. Children clung worriedly to their parents' legs. I gathered my own boys to me in an instinctive effort to protect them. Seda looked distant but held her head high. We stood in line for almost an hour before Seda was assigned a room and a judge.

In that time, I came to understand where we were. Our family had docked in the land of broken dreams. Yes, this was the final stop before Seda could set sail on a new adventure in which she could legally be herself. Yes, it was necessary to smash the old dream publicly before embarking on her new, more salient course. I just hadn't anticipated how I would feel about taking the precious notions, hopes, and plans of our shared journey and destroying them before the public eye.

Thankfully, our marriage would remain intact on paper because of a grandfather clause that honored our contract even though Seda's gender had shifted during the course of our marriage. We needed the marriage certificate to ensure my health insurance through Seda's work and the ease of joint taxes. Same sex marriages were not recognized by the state of Oregon at that time. Still, Seda's name change would denote a public acknowledgment of her gender shift and then the dusty dreams of our formerly heterosexual, romantic marriage would become public record as a fragile memory.

Grieving Fred's death would have been easier than this in some ways. At least in death, one may enshroud the past in mystical optimism that frames its finest angles. One may take out nostalgic pictures of their union and say, "Those were the good old days!" But when it turns out that one partner is not who either person thought they were . . . what do you do with those memories? They are so delicate, ethereal almost, yet brittle and easily crumbled.

What is the integrity of a dream that was dreamt by a persona who never existed? I can say persona now, but then I only knew my husband to have been the person I married, and while a person is always that same person deep down, the trappings of one's gender role in relationship have a great deal to do with the shared dreams, alchemy, and identity of a couple.

My faith in the good of all began to waver. My own dreams, our dreams, stood before the court, exposed as a sham, a lie, a nothing. And here beside me were the children who were birthed because we both believed in this lie. What gift was the truth to them?

Thank God they knew nothing of my inner monologue. Trin and Sam poked each other and made faces at their reflections in the highly polished floor out of boredom. I did not fare so well. As I realized the magnitude of this public outing, my tears fell silently at first, then faster until I excused myself to sob inconsolably in the ladies' bathroom. At some point, I gave up on the idea of composing myself again and returned with a quiet, steady flow of tears to witness the judge signing and handing Seda a release to be herself in every legal sense.

I walked her out of the courthouse in my best dress and gave her a hug on the front steps. I did not tell her the reason for my tears. I did not talk at all, but Seda understood. Her eyes reached out to me beseechingly. Could she possibly help me in any way? Could she assure me that everything would be all right with us as it was in the deepest sense with her now? No. It broke her heart to see this. Hands shoved deep in her pockets, she shook her head sadly and consented to leave me there with the boys. I smiled through my tears and waved her off, back to work. We both had responsibilities to attend to and our own realities to adjust. Life would go on.

I was grateful to have the close companionship of some wise and loyal women for solace. One was an old friend who, unlike Michelle, had embraced Seda's transition, easily integrating it with her conservative Christian lifestyle as a calling from God to love and accept all people regardless of form. My two friends overseas listened with patience and care as I wound my weary way down the path I'd been gifted. One neighbor became a stalwart friend and assured me that when it was time to leave the relationship, I would know. I would. I saw her do it with her husband, in fact, and my experience since has supported her words. Confusion is not the ideal footing for decision-making, and clarity is worth waiting for. So much of my vitality in the past several years had been squandered in the realm of confusion!

Finally, the universe gifted me a new friend who showed up with a mutual friend at a monthly NVC workshop I taught. Susan asked pointed questions and debated the philosophy of Compassionate Communication fervently, trying to assess whether and how it could support her in a conflict she had experienced in her community.

"What about *that* little Buddha?" Jack asked me as we left the meeting.

Susan called me the next day for support, and I gave it. Within the week, I called her for empathy myself. I found her presence and spiritual path to be in alignment with my own in such a way that I will likely spend the rest of my life being grateful for the resonance between us. Our discussions are the closest thing to church that I have ever regularly attended. To say more may be to stumble onto sacred ground, so I will leave my account at that.

On our last evening in Eugene before leaving for camp, I gathered close women friends and neighbors for a coming out event. Each friend brought a special thought, quote, or gift for Seda as she transitioned to take up her role in our community as the woman she was. Our neighbor Terry brought her new baby who was passed around until she landed in Seda's arms, where she slept for the rest of the evening. We lit candles and shared our insights and inspirations in the golden light of the kitchen over chocolate cake. I wrote this poem for Seda:

Welcome Seda
(with love from Kristin)

Women are made of
water
pouring their hearts into
bodies of sand,
settling into earth
at dawn.

Women are made of
shrapnel
eating fear like friendly fire,
fixing fair havens in
foxholes to rear
young.

Women are made of
crosses-to-bear
solemn pilgrims seeking
beauty over and
over with less and less
to carry.

Women are made of
wind
bending into trees and
over mountains
stretching thin and wild
like ghosts.

Welcome,
Seda,
to our circle.

Seda sat shining in our midst with Terry's baby sleeping peacefully in her arms. For over a decade, my friends had been her friends, and she had maintained alliances with only one or two men inconsistently. Over those years, I had wished Seda would get her own friends and her own circle. Finally, on this night of Seda's transition, I let go of that wish and offered my circle to her wholeheartedly.

See this beautiful woman? She is amazing in the million ways I thought I would count on for a lifetime, in one of the sweetest partnerships ever to be had. That is no longer to be mine. But look what a treasure she is in our circle of women! Her courage, love, responsibility, talents, and kindness are such a resource for us all. We are stronger for that. I release her from being my own so she may be ours. That is some consolation to me.

My nervousness began to shift into a deeper sense of pride and awe. I began to focus on the gift of Seda's arrival rather than the risks of her coming out. The transition of our family held blessings for community.

In Napa Valley, Seda stepped out of the car into public as herself, never again to appear as male in public or private. She met a group of people eager to support her in her transition and in her process. Over the next week, Seda and I worked with our fears about the shift in our world back at home and shed many tears honoring our love for and commitment to one another as parenting partners.

We broke bread with other campers doing their own work. One, a young man living in the Bay Area, was transgender female to male, and he was sometimes joined by his long-term partner. They, too, found themselves defining and redefining relationship across the years of transition. The companionship, support, and inspiration of Family Camp carried us like no other set of wings as we made our way back to Eugene, Jack, and life as we knew it.

During the week that followed, Seda experienced no direct conflicts when she came out at work. Instead, she returned to heartfelt cards, well-wishes, and occasional requests for clarification of our circumstances. Only one or two people in the whole department appeared disconcerted, and that was only apparent in their silence. For weeks, we breathed deeply, preparing ourselves for the possibility of harassment or conflict in the office or in town as Seda went about her business as a woman. It rarely happened. Whether that was because we actively saw the best in people or because we were lucky, I'll never know.

Seda's greatest pet peeve (common to many transgender people) was being referred to as *he* despite women's attire and accessories. I threatened to bead her a pink necklace that announced in tiny block letters, "It's a *she*!" Seda kept a sense of humor about the whole thing and spent her mornings in prayer and meditation forgiving any small oversight or unkindness she felt she had received. Her role was now defined and clear, our romantic separation complete in the public eye. Finally, Seda was living her life as a woman.

I Write

AS JACK INSPIRED me to write, I filled every crack and space in my day with more ways of doing it. I started a blog, and the many subjects of my days collided there. I wrote of honeybees, my heart's confusion, celebrations with the boys, poetry, and last night's dinner. Everything became sacred and meaningful, and I witnessed it all, drawing up coherent stories as one draws a net from the sea to collect a thousand swimming fish that thought themselves to be free. I spent hours at the computer, barely stripping off my garden gloves to put my hands to the keyboard, bending over it standing, half-poised to run to the kitchen where a child might need help finding the yoghurt.

I wondered how writers managed. How did they parent and live so that their work vibrated with their experience and still have time to capture it? Did they never sleep? Sleep was important to me, and my dream life continued to inform my waking hours. Images translated into words and erupted from my fingertips onto the screen or into spiral bound notebooks I kept on the kitchen counter.

I showed up at poetry readings and shared my work with Jack beside me. Each day, we stepped deeper into a relationship that we both knew was not likely to last; neither of us could give up hope.

One afternoon, I had been pitching leaves into a wheelbarrow and spreading them among my garden beds for hours when

I saw Jack winding his way up the street. A sideways grin on his face and his eyes filling with tears, he took my pitchfork and looked at me for a long moment before speaking.

"You are so lovely and pure," he said, pressing his lips together to hold back tears. I felt a little irritated, as I often do when people call me that. He was not seeing me whole. I remained quiet.

"You said something very wise yesterday, and I don't know why I didn't see it before," he said. "You told me that friends do not discuss the fact that their relationship is only friendship. There is no need to because there is never any question. So I can see how this monk has been a point of confusion for you," he said, blushing in reference to himself. There it was again. Jack putting his very finger on the problem but never moving to solve it. And again, I experienced relief that he understood, but frustration that this understanding would be more of a box to put us in than a vehicle to move us forward. I sighed.

Perhaps the only way I could manage to set foot outside of our box was to write of my experience, slow it down, transition upon transition. If I lost faith in those around me, I needed more than ever to find it in myself. So much in my world had fallen, and the chaos sometimes dizzied me. I remembered the way that a forest regrows itself, from the bottom to the top. Weeds cover the ground willy-nilly after a fire or excavation and they hold the soil in place for grasses then bushes to take root. Only after that do the long-lived trees come to stand their ground so the forest can have some sense of stillness across decades, even centuries. How I longed to see such stillness in my world again.

Flash Flood, March 2008

this pale dream is laid open a thousand
miles wide, all
sagebrush and sand stretched
thin under
blue.

if i could sniff a storm coming, i'd
hightail for tall places,
wrap my coat around me twice,
thank my inner weather
vane.

i wonder how they'd clock me if i
could run so fast as
that—pushing wind to
gravity, two breaths before
the flood,
cracking sky to
let me in.

A Close Shave

DESPITE THE SOUL stretching I valued so deeply, I seriously wondered if the frustration in my partnership with Jack was sustainable. The interminable good will that Seda and I experienced in our relationship had been fed daily by our actions. The security of our faith in one another was bolstered by the outward expression of care across years. Over a decade of kindness anchored me through the tremendous effort it took to maintain connection through our transformation of roles. Jack and I had no such history to draw from. As Jack continued to claim that our friendship was not intimate, I struggled to receive comfort and joy from the relationship we had. It seemed we were breaking up over and over without ever admitting that we'd been together.

Perhaps I was afraid to be alone. I had not been without an intimate partner since the age of eighteen. Was my suffering in stepping away from Jack about finally being without a partner for the first time since my marriage ended? I cried so hard and long one day that I used all the cloth handkerchiefs in the house. I left them on the laundry room floor, and overnight a mouse chewed holes through every one. I held them up the following day and peered through the open spaces into the light. Someone or something wished me to see through my grief and move on. I dearly hoped that I was on the road to learning how.

Excerpt from a letter to Jack
March 30, 2008

Only a week after being ill and unable to eat for four days, I was sick again through Sunday—feverish, aching, exhausted, visionary. Something had moved in me. I felt the urge to rise and cook a colorful meal: potatoes, carrots, and broccoli with a tahini-miso-garlic sauce, a bit of round steak from a local cow.

While cooking, I felt at moments light-headed and watched the knife with care. I saw the reflection of my hair in the kitchen window. Long and dark, it did not belong there anymore. My hair no longer suited me. I wished it gone. I considered this carefully. What if I was homely without hair? It is arguably my prettiest feature. Well, so? It would be nice to know if I was unattractive without it. And what if others treated me differently? How would I respond? Much to learn, nothing to lose. After all, what would be the risk of such a small change in comparison to what Seda has gone through in shifting her presentation? Would it make me somehow less of who I am if others saw me differently in a way I didn't enjoy? In a state of total trust and power reflecting the moment, I shaved my long hair off.

Thank God for the inspiration. It was a joy to see myself naked and unadorned. I showered after and felt completely healed of that dread sickness, fully curious, joyful, and grounded.

And still the learning settles.

The big topic for my exploration lately has been this: Do we create our path, or do we follow it? Well, a balance always—no, an interplay, dynamic in every way, very different from balance, actually.

Tonight, in bed with the boys, linked to something Trinidad said (if only I could remember what!), it struck me like a meteor, complete heaven-to-earth wham-bang. What do I most want? *To grow my capacity for love and the expression of it, supporting others who seek to do the same.*

Do I give up the notion of creating happiness beyond my wildest imaginings? Of course not. Stretching my capacity for love will necessarily grow my capacity for imagination. If I choose the above as my purpose (as I think I have since dawning on this planet, though unconsciously), I will also experience an equal and extraordinary degree of pain. There are enough wise people before me that have pointed to this truth, and I know it well within. So, here I am, stepping consciously into my singular, purposeful path for the first time. The outer and inner enfolded as one.

Nice haircut.

No one who saw my bald head today looked particularly shocked. In fact, I had the sense that they were only seeing more of me than they had before. I most enjoyed my friend Maggy's response.

"What have you done to your beautiful hair?" she asked with a sigh.

"I did not do it for beauty," I told her, though it is an aesthetic that pleases me just now.

"Well," she said. "When do you ever?" She was only half smiling.

And one more thing: I find forgiveness for all of the pain between us in every line of poetry I write that is inspired by our work together, Jack. Channeling this is such an honor. It's the key to return from my personal underworld, bearing gifts of peacefulness and presence—at least for a time—in a quality I've never known before.

Blogging the Journey

I HAD DINNER with Michelle that spring for the first time in months. She still didn't feel comfortable telling her children about Seda, but I had decided to remove that topic from the table in order to maintain our friendship. I felt very confused about how to manage this, but my focus in the moment was more on my grief with Jack than Seda, anyway.

"Kristin," said Michelle. "I don't remember you being so upset when your marriage ended. Why is that?"

"I don't know," I told her. "You're right. That's weird. Maybe it's because the break was so slow, across years. And then it was over as something new began with Jack. This is the first time it's all really over. I'm not sure."

Later that night, I discussed the possibility of my somewhat delayed grief process with Seda. She could see my point about having gleefully shifted my attention to Jack. He was so romantic and met so many of the needs that were unmet in my relationship with her at the time.

"It was a gift, though," Seda told me. "Even if it was hard for me then and is hard for you now. I think it's better that we are no longer romantically together. We weren't doing very well with that anyway."

"I know," I said.

"But," said Seda, "I don't understand how you can get

together with Michelle when she can't accept me as I am. Do you have any idea how painful that is for me?"

"I'm sorry, Seda. I'm just trying to keep my friendship alive and trust her in her process. I'm hoping it will change. She says that David is having a really tough time with the idea."

"Yeah, I can see why," she said. "That's what's so frustrating! This whole right wing, Christian thing of turning your back on someone because you can't understand them. Because you judge what they are doing as wrong, quoting some passage from the Bible. Is that what Jesus would do? There are also passages that suggest that male and female can coexist in one. You can basically pull Biblical passages to support whatever argument you want. But what's bothering me right now is that I don't have support from you, Kristin. When you continue your relationship with Michelle despite her lack of acceptance, you are silently agreeing to discrimination and exclusion. I have a really hard time with that."

Seda began to cry. I sighed. This was so hard! I didn't want to lose my friend, but I could see Seda's point made sense, too. Over the years to come, I wrestled with this, finding myself on either side of the fence at different times based on the quality of compassion I felt. Sometimes, I thought, *Life is short! Let Michelle learn at her own pace, and let me not discriminate against her for that.* Still, I wished she could make an effort to see that the friend she had in my husband still existed; Seda had many of Fred's qualities and more.

"She hasn't given me a chance," Seda would say.

But I wondered if Michelle would ever get past her own grief. "In a world where there are so few truly good men," she told me once, "he was one of the best I knew."

It seemed that everywhere I turned, I was being asked to let go of something—marriage, dreams, identity, friendships, and now this unsustainable romance with Jack. Some days I felt ready to fold. With the intensity I once applied to researching gender transition and permaculture, I blogged about it. I hoped that focusing on my heart would help it quiet or move through its storms more quickly.

BLOG POST

Paying Homage

Grief comes to me in waves, and in its waters I visit the sacred. The sensation of that tide's approach becomes more distinct to me as I grow older. It has a sound, a pressure rising, a hue that rushes before it into my day, across breakfast dishes and spilled milk. I feel it coming like a storm, and I find myself in choice to take cover or open my heart to it whole.

Today, in the opening, I discovered a fear I have harbored. Is the letting go of what is no longer mine, the acceptance of what has ended, somehow permission for that precious experience to dissipate, to be lost?

Lovingly, I tried to make space for that fear and the temptation to hold tight to the vessel I cared for while I watched it spring leaks and sink before my eyes. As the object of my care went under, I found myself swimming deeper and deeper, following the beauty as it descended. I witnessed my world falling inward to the tide of love rising in me, feeling that ecstatic presence that binds me, unthinking, to the divine as the vessel finally slipped from my grasp.

I saw that the letting go is a taking in, a drinking deeply, integrating what has been beautiful so that we may be beautiful. What we release with love nourishes us. We are changed. We grow. Letting go is the sensation of fully recognizing the manifestation of what is holy so that we may pay homage to the source itself.

Weekly, I continued to chronicle my heart's journey in the blog as I slowly transitioned out of relationship with Jack. I received feedback from friends that my experiences resonated with theirs, so I continued to publish my inner landscape as I explored it in hopes of contributing to others. I felt courageous in sharing my process with the world, as I had never dared to when Seda went through early transition. What would the repercussions be?

People might say I was wrong, silly, or that I did it out of ego or a need for attention. I accepted that I might get these reflections. I knew, too, that Jack might read and comment. I did not wish for that but imagined it could happen. I trusted that whatever came would shape us both in the ways we most needed. I walked an honest line for the first time in my life. The pendulum had swung away from hiding, and now I laid our path bare before the world, having faith in its kindness.

Being completely honest is a daunting but valuable practice. As a teacher of NVC, I was accustomed to being observed in public. Friends and acquaintances who had taken my classes often looked to me as a model in parenting and relationships, and I made every effort to walk my talk. Blogging neatly dovetailed writing with my practice of NVC, offering real time examples of NVC in action.

I did not worry about looking pretty or correct. I welcomed messy, because I knew from listening to people in my workshops that messy is one of the most predictable facets of parenting or sharing a home with others. As individuals, we unwittingly get in the way of each other's plans, giving rise to incessant conflict.

I wanted to demonstrate how one *learns* to make peace, from the ground up. I hoped that my example would give others the courage to face their biggest emotions with an open heart and work with them as best they knew how. I wanted to inspire people to at least be honest with themselves, and then hopefully to be truthful with each other and the world.

If I had learned anything from Seda's transition thus far, it was that hiding hurts the most. I wanted to offer a different model. Parenting, too, can land us with feelings of embarrassment, shame, and isolation. Often we are fearful to tell our stories or reach out for help when we need it most. I wanted to show that it could be done, and that there is greater safety and relief in visibility, even if it is messy. Perhaps such transparency is not for every individual, but collectively I think we need it and, ultimately, it is up to individuals to lead the way.

In May of 2008, I had concluded in my blog post that letting go allowed for taking in more deeply. A month later, I reflected on that process again in my blog:

BLOG POST

(Un)attached

A wise friend recently told me that she would like to open herself to enlightenment, no matter what earthly experience such a growing required. Have I asked for soul realization so clearly? No. I have been afraid to ask, because the price might be too high for me to bear. Too high? Such as? The death of a child or a loved one. My own incapacitation, the loss of my home or garden. The loss of my value as a teacher and mentor. Possibly so much more.

Why am I afraid to lose these elements in my life? Because the pain could be unbearable. Yes, and why? Because the pain is connected to my identities in this plane, to who I am. It could kill me. Hmmm. Who am I? The mother. The lover. The teacher. The gardener. The housewife. Yet, these are not at all who I am. These are the roles I play, all the singularly defined perceptions that my ego is so eager to grasp. But none are who I am.

Oh. They're not, are they? I am smiling now. For I am something undefined in this world. Something colorful and infinite in size and shape, my spirit forever unfolding into what I had not yet imagined. I am in awe to bear witness.

Me is without edges. I am a hue of the All, vibrating with a resonance that sends me spirit-bound into everything I see, touch, feel, and know. There is no role nor identity in this me that is in any way real, there is no risk of losing me and no pain associated with being part of infinite mind and love.

I know it, and I feel it. I can walk it. My attachment to you is no more than my attachment to me, which gives me a new perspective on un-attachment entirely. For that piece of me that seeks some hide-bound connection with what I have cared for is most drawn to the exquisite and finite beauty of what should be, could be, and might have been. It knows the symphony of sorrow, the tragedy of love unrequited, the match that nearly struck a fire to light heaven itself.

Nearly. The word speaks to a framework of limitations. That's a tip-off. The worldly dramas that catch at my heartstrings and play scenes in my mind are all drawing hard on me in my roles. As a gardener, a mother, a writer, or a friend, it doesn't make sense that the primary relationship I have worked so hard at could have failed. The notion of failure itself is heart-rending.

But if I am not these roles at all, if I am only my essence unattached to everything, then . . . what? What does separation mean to me? No more than a bird's first flight. If only I could allow myself to be guided by instinct alone, trusting that my deepest sense of self would carry me effortlessly from fear into flight. That would be freedom.

It took me a good few minutes to make that kind of commitment to myself, to let go of my roles and identities and experience what it is I am more fully. Interestingly, I notice that the same cornerstones I experience in my practice of empathy are guides to finding the real me in this moment: full focus, genuine curiosity, and the sole intention of (self) connection. I have been practicing with the tools. Only the willingness to trust and to fly were in question.

All day, I have checked in. Is it me? Is my response to this conflict me? The color combination I chose to wear to the party? My biceps that a friend is so impressed with? The competence Seda applauds in my achievement? My worries about the kids' abilities to navigate socially? No. Not a one. I have been smiling so hard all day that my face hurts.

Un-attachment is a taking in. But the work, once integrated, cannot be labeled or categorized in any way. No sentimental token survives the fires that forge these changes. And the rest—memories of earthly words and deeds that appeared beautiful in their joy or pain—I am now willing to lose or forget as the wind blows. I was terrified to let these go before; they were exquisite in their own humanity, so full of meaning. Now, I see that this beauty held me because it appealed to the beauty I found in my own identity and limitations.

I am open to being ugly now. Open to forgetting what happened yesterday and letting go my worries for tomorrow. I am me in my heart either way. The world will or will not understand me. That won't change who I am for a moment. And that is my new affair: I am discovering what it is to be me at one with all.

Music with Ben

ON A SUNNY spring afternoon while I was weeding the front yard, a neighbor walked by and paused to discuss rabbits with me. "I know you have that one bunny," she said. "Do you ever think about getting another?"

"Yes, we'd like that," I told her. "Chai is kind of lonely, but I haven't had time to look for a friend for him yet."

"I have a sweet girl rabbit that I would be happy to give you," said my neighbor. "She deserves more attention than I'm giving her. You can have her right now if you want!"

I set down my trowel and gloves and accompanied her up the block to her house where we loaded the rabbit with her cage onto a wheelbarrow. The neighbor across the street, also a friend, called to us over her fence. "Hey, while you're at it, I have a piano I'd like to find a home for. You interested?"

I had always wanted a piano. When I was young, my family could not afford to rent an instrument, so I didn't play in the school band. I watched my friends with envy as they studied piano, flute, and clarinet, and I asked them to teach me. I practiced on their instruments long after they'd gone to bed when I slept over. Now, someone was offering me a piano of my own! I couldn't believe my luck. Here was a chance to learn something painlessly and joyfully for a change. I decided maybe it was time for me to realize some of my closeted dreams the way that Seda had come to live hers.

I agreed to take it and for a small sum, the piano was mine. A troupe of four strong-armed friends lifted the delicate, honey-colored Betsy Ross Spinet and carried her to a pickup truck that rolled her slowly home to me. In the living room, I lovingly stroked her curved keys and shared my dreams in whispers. I decided to call a music teacher so the boys and I could learn to play as soon as possible.

I knew who I wanted—my former neighbor and friend Ben Blakeman who was a music teacher as well as a sailor. I had spoken to him on several occasions about the possibility of the boys and me taking lessons together. I called to tell him we were ready.

"Great!" he said. "Who in your house is playing music right now?"

"No one," I admitted.

"Well, we've got to change that. Kids do what they see their parents doing, you know? You take lessons first, and the boys will follow." His plan made sense, so I took my first lesson at his studio the next week.

I had known Ben as a neighbor and acquaintance for years. His wife was our family doctor. The two of them lived simply, gardened, and took pleasure in building community. I found Ben endearingly affable, extroverted, and eccentric in ways that surprised and amused me. His rubber Birkenstock garden clogs in robin's egg blue, sunshine yellow, lime green, and tangerine always caught my eye. In the winter, he wore these clogs with hemp shorts, a T-shirt, and brightly colored knee-high socks. In the summer, same outfit sans socks. You couldn't miss him. I had no idea then how Ben's colors—inside and out—would grow on me and shape my world in years to come. I just knew it was finally time to make the connection I'd always dreamed of and bring music into our household.

Ben had shared with me early on that music was his passion. It wasn't hard to imagine this; he talked with his hands as if he was conducting the symphony of his life. When Ben told a story, he articulated emphatic statements with sweeping gestures, his whole body leaning into the point he was trying to make. Not long after I started studying with him, Jack told me he'd seen my music teacher talking to someone out in front of his house "waving his arms like a lunatic."

Jack respected Ben and believed he was a fanatical genius touched by God. I was beginning to believe that myself. Not everyone resonated with the quality of energy Ben expressed. Many people rolled their eyes when I mentioned him. If they knew him, they either enjoyed and appreciated him or could not find the exit fast enough. People who were familiar with his musical gifts generally respected and admired his talents and passion regardless of their feelings about him as a person. I never considered looking further for a music teacher. Something about Ben just fit for me and our family.

I quickly discovered that Ben's teaching encompassed far more than just piano lessons. We began our time together with a shared drumming session, he and I finding a rhythm, a shared beat to connect with. Then he asked me to play how I felt using any instruments or parts of my body I chose. Because I had little command over the piano, I usually used my voice to find melodies and tones that resonated. Ben began this exercise with a guided meditation and then sat across the room on his orange loveseat watching me intently between the open lid and stocky body of his Mason Hamlin grand piano.

The liberty to express myself musically in a private studio where no one asked anything else of me proved to be the ultimate high. My heart and mind opened up to find the lost melodies of decades past, unearthing them from beneath phantom piles of plastic Easter eggs, dandelion greens, and discarded women's clothing. I did not know what I sang of. I only sang . . . low, haunting legato, sharp staccato inquiries, and lullabies of longing. I closed my eyes while the melodies emerged from my feet, my belly, my hands, and I worked them in my mouth, my face, and my throat until they found some story of their own and emerged with a beginning, middle, and end, some magical thread binding them through me to Spirit.

I felt surprised and amazed at what emerged even as I strangely deemed myself responsible for delivery. At the end of these songs, I kept my eyes closed and sat still in the silence that followed. Then I would open my eyes shyly to see Ben watching me intently from across the room. He nodded and waited a moment before asking the question that he posed every week.

"Did you find what you were looking for?"

"Yes," I usually said.

"How could you tell?" he inquired.

Then I would describe to him the sensations I felt as the song rose into my throat, how I moved with it and it with me, how the melody changed and developed as I set it free. He would watch me quietly. This was a rare state for Ben; we sat in the stillness together as if in a chapel, breathing in the last of the sacred before turning to the piano as a technical instrument. Sometimes, Ben pulled out the recording equipment and asked me to sing my song again so we could capture it digitally. More than one of these tunes I later fleshed into songs in collaboration with Ben, who provided harmonies and notation.

Ben's piano, a squat, dark beast with a voice like Nina Simone, stood waiting to be played. Ben smiled and turned me to her, pointing to his broad penciled scrawl in the stave book. "Let's see how this is coming," he would say, and I'd practice my Beethoven, Bach, and Bartok. In a flurry, Ben pushed me forward and then dove into music theory as I barely kept pace through every explanation.

Ben's excitement and enthusiasm were contagious, but at times I would shake my head hard and say, "No! Wait . . . I need time to take this in." Ben would sit back then and from the set of his jaw, I knew how hard it was for him to pause and trust my process. He did honor it, almost every time, and we grew familiar with each other's intensity, turning and tacking lightly with one another when sailing directly into the wind proved only to slow our progress. Working with Ben became an exercise in intuition, and learning music proved much more artful than I had imagined.

Ben honored the expression of my spirit in music. "You know what you know, and it's much more than you think," he said. The words landed with me as more than just a compliment. They were water-witching words, pointing to a well that I had only prayed could exist. I admired his vision as a teacher, and I hoped to cultivate my own ability to see that depth of potential in others. Imagine the thirst that could be quenched in this world! I watched Ben carefully as my teacher and as a teacher in general, fascinated by his ability to see what could be and to integrate the creative with skill building.

Each week, my hour with Ben ended as suddenly as it began. The sailboat clock on the wall indicated at the top of the dial that our time was up. Honoring the predictable, finite hour space that the clock measured reminded me of picking flowers and putting them in a vase on the mantle when I really wanted to live in the meadow in which they grew. I packed up my notebooks and hurried out the door because Ben scheduled lessons back to back, and someone was always waiting. I paused on the porch for several minutes, composing myself and letting our session fall into place. I stretched to meet Ben every time and he stretched to meet me. I was learning.

In my third week of lessons, I could play a simple arrangement of Beethoven's "Ode to Joy." Ben told me that he was proud of me, and that I should take it home and play with it.

"Play with it?" I asked.

"Yes," he said. "Play with it. Make it yours. Improvise."

"Can I do that?" I asked. "It's the first song I've ever learned."

"Of course you can! That's what you do when you've learned a song. You play with it, put some of yourself in. Come show me next week."

I did, of course. And then within the month, I found myself composing from the heart, propped up at the piano bench while fighting the flu, feverish and exhausted but compelled by something like madness to write down the notes to a song of parting that I had welling inside of me for Jack. Ben and I recorded it on his Mason Hamlin months later, and the negative space in that song haunts me still.

Jack's Split

IN THE END, a bitterly amusing irony visited us all. Jack, my charming and romantically chaste monk, found himself bedazzled by a beautiful local goat farmer. Sarah, twice as wholesome a mother as I'd ever hoped to be, was also an artisan cheese-maker and had just been sent as our regional delegate to the International Slow Food Conference in Italy. I marveled at this impossibly comic twist. If I had been daft in choosing Jack as an unconsummated lover, apparently I was in good company.

I took to Sarah quickly and sensed that my relationship with her would prove to be more long lasting and meaningful than mine with Jack had been. I asked if she felt that what they had was special and if they would like to grow the relationship. Sarah nodded her head sadly, hating the fact that this would bring me pain. With tears in my eyes and a twisted sense of the darkest mirth, I smiled and walked away from Jack for good.

Jack

You said yours was a path of suffering and mine
was not. I remained obediently behind,
traced the outline of your footsteps for ages, read
over and over the pages you'd written me until
they became plain prose.
My heart settled into a duller martyrdom, some lonely
penance on a crowded street, one more nameless cross to bear.
When Jesus said he died for our sins, I did not hear it
present tense, that every day it is our sin
to ravage the holy.

Water for Life

ON OUR LAST project together, Jack helped me lay irrigation over the grounds of my urban farm. We collected black plastic tubing from other farmers' refuse and bought a few new parts in town. On a rainy day in early June, Jack showed me how to punch holes in the pipes and connect the collars that would hold the skinny black plastic tubes which leaked water through pinprick holes. Jack helped me start the irrigation project and then ran off with the goat farmer when she came to deliver my milk.

I continued on in the rain alone, kneeling in the mud to cut and press plastic bits together like Tinker Toys. The Waldorf model of our neighborhood home descended into chaos as the children, left to their own devices while I concentrated on what seemed to be a quarter mile of plastic tubing, turned the Cherry Popping Daddies up full volume and invited the neighborhood kids over to their party. I saw that everything they could think to eat had been pulled from the refrigerator and piled onto the kitchen table. They built Lego creations and danced wildly around the house with their friends. It seemed a sort of Bacchus revival in lively contrast to the death and rebirth I felt taking place in our garden as I released Jack and set out the irrigation system.

Trinidad wandered out to the back deck and regarded me between showers. When I looked up at him, he smiled. "A horse smells like it is, Mom," he said. I reckoned that was so.

Jack later brought me a Wolf apple tree. He dropped it off with this post-romantic statement: "Here is a productive tree with apples suited for storing or preserving. Each will weigh a pound or more to make processing easier and more efficient. It's a very special variety. I bought one for you to have on this side of the hill and one for me to have on the other. Perhaps we will each be called upon to feed our neighbors someday, and I will feel good knowing that you have my other Wolf apple with you." He smiled in that special way that I knew was only mine. And Sarah's. And whoever else was yet to come.

Two years later, the Wolf apple tree produced one enormous apple and then died inexplicably the next spring. The same summer, after watching my water bill rise rather than fall, I shut down the inefficient web of plastic and attached a sprinkler to the end of my hose. The following year, I tore out the irrigation completely as I was tired of tripping over black plastic that I wasn't using.

Part Five

Turning Tides

AFTER SIX WEEKS of piano lessons with Ben, I agreed to take voice lessons in trade for gardening sessions. I had always wanted to learn how to sing, and Ben and Katherine had been looking for ways to make their garden more beautiful and productive.

The following weekend, the two of them sat down with me to plan their future garden. They wanted to plant everything one could find in the produce section and more. I dutifully jotted down several lists and began to draw plans of where the plants might like to go. I told them I would be back the following weekend with a complete proposal.

When I returned for our next session, Katherine's seat at the table was empty. "She said she had something else to do," said Ben, chagrined. "I told her you would want her here."

I chewed my lip thoughtfully. Katherine's yard abutted Ben's—they owned two houses and appeared to live next door to each other with garden paths that connected the two yards. Ben lived at least partly in his small wooden yurt beside the music studio where he worked. The yurt and studio were settled behind the house he rented out to college students, while Katherine lived in their main house next door. I assumed they joined one another for meals there and to sleep.

"Hmmm," I said, unsure of how to proceed without at least her blessing on the plan.

"Yeah, I'm sorry about that," he said, scraping dirt from his trowel onto a rock.

"Maybe we could just work on my side."

"I guess so," I said, looking at the tall stand of thistles, grass, and vetch that climbed the back fence line.

It would take some hours to tame the wilds on Ben's side of the divide. Katherine's yard, by contrast, had been partly cultivated the year before. I pointed to the tall arbor of bicycle frames welded together.

"I made that," said Ben proudly. "A bunch of old frames they were throwing out at the bike shop." I smiled. He was a bike enthusiast in all ways.

Ben and I pulled on our gloves and began tearing out marsh marigolds, blackberry, thistle, and mullein, working our way down to the roots with trowels he'd purchased on my recommendation. Ben and I weeded around the perimeter of the old apple tree and planned to lay the first beds at the back of his lot.

Katherine did not come to the next garden session, or the one after. I did not see her once while we pulled weeds and laid cardboard as the foundation for the new garden beds on Ben's side of their property. Ben and I deposited piles of heavy, wet leaves in mounds that were three feet wide and varied in length on the cardboard template, and these formed the base beds of his new garden.

One afternoon, Katherine called me at home. We greeted each other cheerfully while I finished rinsing the dishes then dried my hands. "Did Ben tell you why I haven't been in the garden?" she asked.

I gave the smoked Gouda and corn chowder a stir. "He said you had other things going on."

"Well, that's true," she said. "But I've planned those things and been away from the house because I have not been speaking to him for the last two weeks. I told him we needed a break. We had a huge fight, and I have to tell you, he has a real anger management problem. This time, it was just too much."

"Oh, I'm so sorry," I said, sitting down heavily on the wooden bench beside my kitchen table. I looked out the back window onto the garden where the garlic tops had shot up tall and green. I knew Ben was a passionate man, and I wasn't completely surprised to hear this, but I felt disappointed when I thought of their relationship struggling. Katherine and Ben made such a unique couple, and I wanted it to work out for them. I wanted to help them plan their garden together.

"It's okay," she said. "Honestly, I think I'm done with this marriage anyway. I've tried to leave two other times, and he talked me out of it. I'm ready for it to be over now, but I've agreed to go to counseling with him. I don't think it's going to help."

"Gosh, Katherine, I'm so sorry to hear that," I repeated, tracing the grain of the blonde wood on our tabletop with my finger. The light-colored finish was worn thin in places and the pale, soft pine emerged from beneath. The surface of the table was dotted with chips and dents—all memories.

"No, really, it's no worry," she said. "We've pretty much fought since the beginning. I'm not even exactly sure why we got married. Maybe we reminded each other of relatives or something. I think we've both been doing penance. I'm pretty much over it at this point."

Two scrub jays squawked angrily at each other on the plum tree before one dived across the yard and swooped up to pirate sunflower seeds from our bird feeder. I watched as he hung onto the wooden landing with both feet and swung hard back and forth, stuffing his bill with the black-hulled seed.

"Actually, you want to hear something amazing?" she asked. I could hear the smile in her voice. "I just reconnected with my first love from high school, and it's been so awesome! He's really funny and sweet. I've been rereading all these old love letters from him I'd saved. It's great. You should hear them— what a crack up! I think I ought to just get on with my life and maybe get back together with him." Her voice lowered. "I was kind of hoping that you and Ben would hit it off."

My mouth dropped open, aghast. I smelled something smoky, and I knew it was the soup burning, but I couldn't bring myself to move.

"Any chance of that?" she asked. "I know he admires you so much. He told me he thought you were a great catch. He did. Sure would make my life easier," she said. "I could just go my own way, and we could all be happy. Interested?"

"No," I said. "That's not my intention, Katherine. Ben is my music teacher. He's a great teacher, but that's all I want from him. I really don't want to consider him in any other role."

"Okay," she said. "But I'm just saying, you might want to think about it. He's really one of a kind—creative, environmentally conscious, committed to living a small footprint, and talented! I've met few people who are as talented as Ben. If he'd only do something with it. You two could make music together. Not many guys out there like that. I think you would be a great couple. You have a lot in common. You should consider it, Kristin. If anyone could help him straighten out his anger issues, it would be you."

"No," I said. "No, but thanks. Not going to happen. I wish you all the best in getting it sorted out, though." My stomach twisted into knots. How could she even suggest? I got up mechanically and tried to stir the chowder, scraping the bottom of the pot absentmindedly where it had blackened. It would be smoky corn chowder tonight. I probably just needed to transfer it into a new pot. My jaw clenched, and I inhaled the charred but sweet aroma through my nose.

"I guess I'll go through with the counseling," she said with a sigh. "But I really don't want to be with him anymore. We haven't been sharing a bed for a while. He lives in his yurt out there, and that's fine with me."

"I guess you have to decide," I said. "Work on it in counseling or be done."

"Yeah. I guess we'll do the counseling. It's our last try. Then I'm completely finished and can leave it behind without feeling guilty."

I didn't know what to say. I really hadn't expected such a call. I wondered if Ben knew. I couldn't bear the idea of our next music lesson, the unspoken standing awkwardly in the room. I decided to call him myself.

"Hey, Ben," I said.

"Kristin! Hi."

"Hi. Listen, Katherine called me yesterday and told me that you guys were on the rocks."

"Yeah, it's true, but I wouldn't have told you that because it doesn't concern you."

"Right," I said. "And I know we've been friends over the years, and neighbors, but I just want to be totally clear that what I need from you right now is to only be my music teacher. You're really good at that, and that's what I need."

"Of course," he said. I could almost hear him blushing. "Yeah, she told me that she'd called you and what she said, and I'm so sorry, Kristin. That was very unprofessional." He lowered his voice. "I was pretty mad about it, actually. You're my student, and she has no business bringing you into any other relationship without consent."

"Good," I said. "I'm glad you feel that way. And even though we've talked about the possibility of you teaching me to sail someday, and I know it would be fun, I'm just going to say no to that right now. Sorry, but I can't. I want to be crystal clear about our relationship because your music lessons are that important to me."

"That's fine," he said. "I totally understand."

"Great!" I said. "I'll see you Tuesday."

I hoped the call would put an end to that creeping feeling of discomfort that I'd had about Ben since receiving Katherine's call. I sat quietly for a few minutes checking in with myself. While some of my uneasiness had ebbed away since Ben and I spoke, I could feel the suggestion of desire winding ever more tightly around me, like vigorous vines of morning glory gaining purchase on my heart. I *was* seeking a relationship, and I had said so to a number of friends, including Ben and Katherine. But a relationship with Ben was not what I was looking for. The last thing I wanted to do was to play a role in dismantling someone's marriage.

Weeks before Katherine and I had spoken, I'd scheduled Ben to tune our piano. He arrived one bright morning in June with a handful of tools in a black nylon bag and his laptop computer under one arm. I tried to keep the boys quiet while he struck one note at a time, reading glasses perched at the end of his nose, adjusting the tuning pins. The mid-morning sun streamed in and lit half the piano so that the wood shone yellow and dust in the air sparkled as the tiny hammers flew and sounded.

My job was nearly impossible. Children and quiet do not go well together in the early hours of the day. I finally set the kids up outside throwing rocks at a can to practice marksmanship while I made sandwiches and a salad for us to eat at the picnic table out back.

Ben finally stood up and slid his silver tuning forks back into their nylon bag then joined us where I'd laid the spread. After the boys finished eating and took their plates to the kitchen, Ben and I sat looking out over the yard, crunching carrots slowly and talking about our dreams in life, what we stood for. He admired my garden and how its essence was reflected in all aspects of my life. Ben shared my enthusiasm for growing food.

"I had a great garden before I was married," he said. "It seemed effortless back then. As you know, Katherine and I don't always want to plant the same things. She grew cherry tomatoes last year—about fourteen plants. Can you believe that? I don't know what we were supposed to do with all those tomatoes." He shook his head. "I like kale. But I just haven't managed to get it in. It's hard when you feel like you're doing it all alone," he said.

This resonated for me. Since Seda transitioned, she and I worked together in the garden less and less. While Seda encouraged me in my endeavor to grow as much of our food as possible, she was not personally motivated to help make it happen where the fingers met the dirt. I appreciated that she supported our family financially so I could stay home on our urban farm to model such a lifestyle for our children. I managed to catch Seda between projects now and then and drag her out to the garden on weekends, but our schedules did not often overlap; she was usually preoccupied with her trans-odyssey. My time with Jack had at least fueled me with the knowledge and motivation to proceed alone in supporting our family this way.

"I like gardening, but I also want to sail," said Ben. "I went to Micronesia twice about fifteen years ago, and I loved the culture. It's so laid back. People sit around and talk for hours while they're making food. The women get together everyday to mash the cassava root, and the kids sit there in the dirt practicing with tiny machetes. The kids come up with their own games while their mamas work and talk about the big news of the day—maybe somebody's chicken went missing or something. The guys go do guy things—wander around, talk, kill a chicken, and bring it to their current woman or their mother. Everything is matrilineal. The women control it all. The men just show up with something for supper. It's so relaxed. I love it."

I listened to Ben while I watched my own chickens strutting in their yard. Princess Buttercup stole a worm that dangled from the beak of Fiona Fluffbottom, then she turned and ran.

"You want to go back there?" I asked.

"Maybe," he said. "Or maybe I'll sail around the world. Explore. Live aboard a few years. I'm open. It would be nice to have someone to go with me, but Katherine doesn't want to do it."

"No?" I asked, skin prickling at the back of my neck.

"Nope," he said. "She's got her career, and she's not into sailing anyway. She bought me that boat, the Westerly Nomad, but she doesn't like to go anywhere in it. She gets upset when I talk about sailing."

"Well, I can see why," I said, standing to clear the dishes. "Sounds like she thinks you're going to leave her to do it."

"Yeah, I guess I am," he said.

"What then?" I asked, stacking plates on my arm.

"Don't know," he said. "You into traveling?"

I could see where this was going, and I knew it was a slippery slope. At the same time, Ben and I were old friends, and I felt I should be honest in a simple way. "I like to travel, but I also like to be home in the garden. Right now, I'm most concerned with sustainability so my travel needs to be sustainable. Like maybe I would go live in Central America and farm or something for a while. We have friends in Panama. I've always wanted to take the boys to a Spanish-speaking country, so they could get a handle on the language before they left home. What an asset that is, a second language."

I realized that I hadn't mentioned Seda in my plans, but the omission seemed natural enough. Seda and I shared the dream of getting our boys to a Spanish-speaking country while they were young. Like Katherine, Seda loved her work in Eugene and did not have any intention of leaving it for more than a few weeks' vacation. I hoped to be gone for at least two months or more likely, a year.

Over the past several years, I had settled into a primary care-taker role for the boys and had become comfortable and skill-ful in traveling with them. I could barely remember now what it was like to travel with Seda along, too. We hadn't taken a trip together as a family since the Family Camp where she launched her transition, and before that the trip to Wyoming before Sam could walk. Though we played different roles in the boys' lives, I knew Seda would do anything to offer the best to our children. She and I thought so much alike that I trusted she would sup-port any idea that I thought would benefit our family, and I had no intention of being cavalier with her trust.

Ben nodded and looked thoughtful. I felt my ears redden, and I was suddenly ill at ease. Had I phrased that in a way that it sounded like I was responding to an invitation? I had just been honest. And if I continued to be honest with myself, I felt a tingling sensation, something like excitement or perhaps possibility. I bit my lip uncertainly then made an effort to smile as I carried our plates off to the kitchen. Ben stood up, stretched his legs, and returned to the piano.

Throughout the summer, Ben and I continued our conversations as we wheeled several more tons of leaves into his backyard. We built a network of mounded garden beds, Ruth Stout style, laying a few inches of compost over the mounds and tucking seeds and starts into the newly formed beds. Over time, the leaves themselves would compost, creating a fluffy raised-bed garden, rich in organic matter, high in tilth.

On a warm August evening, the sun dipped below the horizon as we cast tiny, mahogany-colored seeds to earth then squatted side by side to rest and survey our work. Puffy clouds stood out in relief, pink and orange against a twilit blue-green sky. I brushed a lock of silvering hair out of my eyes as I marveled at the show. Ben looked over at me, I turned, and his gaze locked on mine. I blushed, studied my hands, and dislodged a seed, rolling it back and forth between my hands. Why did planting seed suddenly feel so intimate?

Ben and I found ourselves playing music out in the garden as it became a more beautiful and comfortable place to spend time. In lieu of a piano lesson one day, Ben introduced me to the ukulele under the old apple tree that stood in the garden's center. We sat on the ground on a blanket, and he placed his hand over mine from behind to guide my fingers to the correct frets. At the end of "You Are My Sunshine," I shook my hand to release the cramp. "Do you get many apples from this tree?" I asked, gazing overhead and seeing none in the branches.

He looked up into its gray-green leaves a moment and rubbed his bristly chin thoughtfully. "Nooo . . . I guess we don't anymore. Maybe a few each year. Why do you ask?"

"Just wondering. Have you ever thought about taking it out and putting in a new tree?" His face blanched and he turned away.

"I mean, you would get more apples," I said. "But if you like the tree, if you're attached to it for sentimental reasons . . . well, keep it!"

He nodded. Months later, I learned that he and Katherine had been married under that tree twelve years before. At the time of their wedding, it had been draped in morning glory, and she had convinced him to let the weed grow because the blossoms were so pretty. The fertile abundance of bindweed marked a point of decline in the tree's productivity. My words about its fruitlessness struck a chord in Ben, and he could only wonder at their source.

In early autumn, I invited Ben and Katherine to join me in drying tomatoes and canning applesauce one evening. They had expressed an interest in learning these urban homesteading skills, and I thought it safe enough to offer a lesson while they were together on speaking terms. Three pots bubbled and spat on the stovetop while dinner warmed in the oven—a kitchen working at full capacity with less than eight square feet of counter space. Ben dutifully chopped apples at the kitchen table for over an hour before Katherine arrived.

Trinidad and Sam brought out all of their latest projects for our guests' viewing— metalwork Trin had done with Seda over a small fire in the back yard, magic tricks, mazes, and a bug collection. The boys sought me at intervals to get snacks, Band-Aids, and help with tying knots or finding colored pencils. The flurry of activity made Katherine's head spin. After half an hour, she rested her face in her hands, red curly hair spilling out in all directions across my kitchen table.

"I don't know how you do it!" she moaned. "I have a head-ache just watching."

Ben and I smiled at each other with sympathetic under-standing. Katherine did not have children of her own and was accustomed to arranging her day according to only her comforts and interests. She worked long hours as a doctor, but that work demanded one-on-one partnership rather than the frenetic dance that spun me through my day. Ben had told me stories of the large family in which he grew up. Everyone talked, laughed, and worked together in creative, spontaneous chaos. Life at the Collier house felt very homey to him. He finished his chopping and asked what was next.

Katherine went home after only an hour, and Ben and I were the last ones awake in the house at one o'clock the next morn-ing, jarring the final quarts of applesauce. Seda, wearing ear-plugs, had long since fallen asleep on the futon after putting the boys to bed around ten.

A month later, Katherine and Ben stopped going to coun-seling. They both attended an NVC workshop I taught on the topic of requests. The couple appeared to be deeply focused on how they might bring this work of compassion more actively into their lives.

The next day, Katherine left for a business trip, and Ben asked if I wanted to go sailing with him that evening. I said no, as I always had before, to an outing with just the two of us. I felt myself slipping into intimacy against my best intentions, and I fought it. "It's not just me," he said. "I'm going with my friend Jason. We're taking his boat. He's a musician and a teacher, too. I think you'll like him. And look at this gorgeous day! One of the last this summer. Come on, Kristin! Take a break."

"I have to make pickles tonight," I told him. Seda had taken the boys on a camping trip and left me alone with the mammoth canning project. It would be easier for us all that way.

"We'll get in early, and I'll help," he assured me. "You trained me up last time." His smile and the crisp autumn afternoon seduced me. The green leaves of my neighbor's aspens bore a tinge of crimson, a harbinger of winter at the ready. I said I'd meet him in an hour.

The sun sank low as we drifted out of Jason's slip at Fern Ridge Lake. Gulls called to one another and balanced themselves against a steady breeze as they dipped back and forth across the shoreline. The silver lake rippled in the evening light and cast a thousand diamond reflections as we tacked out of the harbor. Jason expertly guided our craft out to open waters. The sails filled, and we headed for the southern end of the lake.

I watched with interest the effect that the wind and water had on Ben, soothing him into a meditative state as we drifted for nearly an hour. Jason played his guitar and we discussed NVC, education, and parenting. Ben sat quietly with one hand on the tiller while gazing over the lake to the west.

As twilight fell into deeper shades of blue, Ben turned the boat back toward harbor. The two men then taught me to steer, adjusting the mainsail this way and that to catch the wind. Our craft skimmed along the inky lake with a quiet hiss, cutting through gentle ripples from the offshore breeze. A fat quarter moon rose into the clear dark sky—the pickle moon, Ben called it. With one hand on the tiller, I pulled to the left and right, not understanding the geometry of steering at all, but moving by instinct alone.

"You've got it!" cried Jason.

"I think she does," said Ben with a grin, leaning back against the rail.

The wind lifted my hair away from my face; I inhaled deeply, praying to the first stars above that my intuition would similarly guide me with men, so I could effortlessly catch and keep the wind in my sails. The pounding of my heart drove my prayer into the heavens, a peak experience received in the same breath it was given. Six years before, I could never have fathomed that I'd make such a plea nor imagined the need for it.

That night, Ben stayed over awhile to help me make pickles as promised. We took turns choosing music and sharing our favorites as we divided dill weed, garlic, and mustard seed amongst the jars. We talked long into the night as I poured brine over fresh cucumbers then sealed the jars and boiled them. We regarded one another with longing, but we each returned to our empty beds with no words spoken to name that we'd considered otherwise.

When I arrived at my next music lesson, Ben sat by his desk gazing at his laptop screen in the semi-darkness. He looked up at me over the top of his reading glasses and grinned. "There's something I want to show yooouuu," he said. I peeked over his shoulder at the picture of a tiny sky blue boat flipped upside down on someone's patchy lawn.

"What is it?" I asked.

"A Snark!" he said. "A two- or three-person sailboat just right for learning to sail. That's what I learned on as a teen. We crashed Jimmy Bank's Snark with four of us aboard, and it broke up like a Styrofoam cooler in Lake Michigan. Fuuuuun!" he drawled, grinning broadly.

"For *me* to learn?" I asked, dubious.

"You, or one of your young galoots," he said with a smile. "They'll be ready for the open sea before you know it."

"I'm not sure I want a sailboat," I said.

"Well, I'll buy it, and then if the boys want to buy a share, they can," said Ben. Two hours later, music lesson abandoned, we unloaded the Snark into my backyard. Seda did not appear excited.

"How long is that staying?" she asked flatly.

"I don't know," I said. "Ben owns it now, but the kids might buy a share . . . his wife won't let him put another boat in the yard." I bit my lip and smiled apologetically. Trin and Sam jumped up and down, squealing with excitement. Within a week, Trinidad had raised sixty dollars to buy a third of the boat. He and Ben started plotting their maiden voyage.

A month later, Ben and I finished making our album together. It was a music project that I could send to family and friends for Christmas, including two original tracks of my own with Ben on piano. We listened to the final cut with my head on his shoulder, honoring months of shared efforts. After waltzing to one of my original compositions, "Lullaby for the Mothers," we parted and bowed. Katherine returned from her business trip one week later and handed Ben a postcard with a request that she'd formulated during my workshop: "Would you be willing to grant me a loving divorce?"

This time, Ben agreed.

Medicine Dream II

I AM IN A foreign country, maybe China, with Sam. There are terraces here and signs of the sort of civilization present three hundred years ago, but we are in the countryside. A kindly woman, our host, leads us to the tent where we will sleep. We stand in front of this tent smiling and looking around us at the expanse of green. Suddenly, a roaring sound begins and grows louder and louder. I look questioningly at our host, but I know already in my gut that this sound signals massive change.

"Yes, that's how it happens," explains our host. "First, there is a great wind, then the world (I understand her to mean all signs of civilization) will be flattened. Then we will build again." She is fearless, matter-of-fact. I nod, also fearless.

The wind begins to howl so that the sound fills the sky all around us as the woman walks away. I settle Sam into the tent and turn to leave. The wind becomes more powerful still, and I turn back to him, tenderly. I would like to be with him for this, but not out of fear. I want to share the experience with him. I return to the tent. I sit with my son as our shelter is torn from the ground and swept away with all other signs of civilization. We stand alone in the empty space on a grassy hilltop, and the sun now shines down on us. All is quiet and peaceful, and we know that soon the rebuilding will begin.

Something's Coming

I OPENED MY email from Ben with an attached song from West-side Story: "Something's Coming." I read the few sentences he'd sent—the split, the postcard, no mention of his feelings. It was brief. "Just thought you should know," he said. I listened to the song and shivered.

Ben asked me to join him for dinner. I had cooked for Ben a number of times at my house, and this time he wanted to cook for me. I stepped onto the porch of his music studio twisting my hands apprehensively, getting up the nerve to knock. I had stood on this bare wooden porch so many times before for music lessons, but this time was different. The door swung open, and there he stood, eyes shining, kitchen towel slung over one shoulder. "Hiiii," he said, pulling the word long, like caramel, sweet and knowing. My stomach dropped.

"Come in!" he stepped aside for me to enter. I crossed the threshold to see candles lit on a table for set for two with salami, cheese, a baguette, and a bottle of wine.

"The soup's almost done," he said.

"Soup?" I asked.

"Oh, yeah. Split pea," he nodded emphatically as if I was in for a treat. "That's my favorite."

I sat down at the table. "Can I get you a glass of wine?" he asked.

"Sure," I said.

Two glasses later, I leaned on the edge of the Mason Hamlin as Ben played how *he* felt. The piano resounded with harmonies sweet and trilling yet anchored to a deeper, percussive chord that pulsed sometimes quietly and sometimes loud enough to meet and hold the melody itself. The next morning, he sent me the song when he'd finished composing it, complete with lyrics. It was called, "Just a Matter of Time." I found it beautiful. And terrifying.

"I'm not at all sure this will work," I told him on the walk home that evening. "We're so different. You're a night owl, and I'm an early riser. Playing music and hanging out with your friends are the big rocks in your agenda each day. I'm at a different place in my life. You're sixteen years older and don't have kids. Me? I'm homeschooling two boys. Parenting is the focus of my days and most nights. You're happy to eat raw broccoli and day-old bagels. I admire your thrift in time and money, but I need more nutrition and variety."

Ben nodded patiently. "It sounds like you're not sure that us getting together is a good idea, Kristin," he said. "I see all those ways that we're different, but I also know that people never match up exactly. No one's ever perfect for each other. I'd rather celebrate our differences. I think where you are in your life is beautiful, and I like where I am, too."

The night was quiet except for the sound of our footsteps. The moon slipped below the horizon. It was almost midnight, and I hoped Seda had gotten the boys to bed all right. The path through the park was barely lit by the bleed of distant streetlights, and no one at all met us on foot. Everything was still as if poised for the next movement. Still and dark.

"I'm afraid to, Ben," I said. "If I go into this with you, it's going to be hard to get out. We'll both get hurt, and our friendship means a lot to me. Our partnership in music, you being my teacher . . . I don't want to mess it up. I don't."

"So much of what you're saying could be true, and then it might not be at all. There's a point, Kristin, where you have to

get off the sidelines—stop worrying, cheering, and predict-
ing—and just play the game to see how it's going to come out.
Stop watching it, you know, and just do it. That's all I'm saying.
You'll know when the time is right. I trust you."

Trust. That quality of attunement we had achieved in the
studio bound us together even now as we tried to align our heads
and hearts. I felt so close to him and yet so afraid. The maleness
of Ben rocked me almost physically where my partnership with
Seda had always been quiet and sedate. The chemistry between
Ben and me was so much different from that I'd experienced in
my marriage, though the growing warmth felt familiar. It had
been so long since I'd been with a man sexually, and I worried
that some of my resistance came from a fear of being hurt or
failing, as I had in my own way with Seda.

Was part of my anxiety about embracing my heterosexuality?
I'd had so few partners before Seda, and they hadn't lasted long.
I wondered if I'd entered into a relationship with her because
I subconsciously recognized the quiet safety that our common
gender had provided. If I really saw myself as heterosexual—
and so much so as to leave my wife—then shouldn't I take the
leap and discover what that meant?

Here I was drumming with Ben again, falling into sync with
his rhythm, watching as he humbly sought mine. Afraid of the
coda, afraid of what could come. Integrating our worlds would
take the better part of a miracle, but already I moved to the beat,
held him a little too long when we parted. I had agreed to play
along; where the improvisation led was now up to us both.

Finding Together

A FEW DAYS later, I found myself walking through the park to Ben's music studio for my lesson, this time with turkey sandwiches wrapped in my backpack as an offering for dinner. The January twilight dropped a brilliant lavender curtain behind the dark, leafless branches of oaks while skateboarders wheeled noisily past me on their way home from the skate bowl. I tossed the end of my scarf over one shoulder and plodded on in my heavy leather boots.

I had been mulling over Ben's determination that we wouldn't know whether we'd succeed or fail unless we actually tried to forge a union. He had a point. My reluctance had become a weight and barrier against the flow. I had to admit that events and energy had us rolling in the direction of romance. Ben's marriage was over, and Katherine had moved out of the house next to his. My situation with Seda and the boys required flexible nonconformity in a partner, and Ben had that in spades. Even if it didn't work out, how could I know that we wouldn't harmoniously find our way back to being teacher and student again?

With some relief, I decided to surrender to the flow, accepting my confusion and sometimes reservation as part of our process. I'd told Seda that I didn't know when I'd be home that night and asked if she could be on duty until whenever I returned. "As long as it's before I go to work tomorrow morning at 7:30," she'd said with a wink.

Seda had adjusted to the probability that I would be dating my music teacher. Like me, she'd been ready for Jack to move on when it was time, though she'd hated to see me grieve so. She respected Ben and had supported me fully in taking music lessons with him; she saw how I lit up as I learned to play the piano and sing. Seda valued creative pursuits, and she loved having music in the house, though she herself had never learned to play an instrument. Both Sam and Trin had begun taking lessons in the autumn, and now we had a second pianist and a budding drummer amongst us. Seda was thrilled with all of that, and when Ben played the piano, she could understand why I was falling for him.

"He's so passionate," she said.

As I walked through the park to Ben's studio, I felt grateful that Seda had become so much more competent and connected as a parent. Since her initial transition, the boys had gravitated to her more often for both help and affection because she had become emotionally available in ways their father had not been. Seda's parenting skills had expanded in breadth and depth, and she took more risks in her parenting, driving the boys to new places and keeping them to herself for longer periods of time than before.

My relationship with Jack had prompted Seda to step out of her comfort zone and become a more active parent. That was the first time in my life as a mother that I'd found myself motivated to ask for one evening a week without time restrictions, and I'd kept that cherished evening in place after Jack and I split up by spending it with girlfriends or alone writing. This was the first such evening that I would spend with Ben explicitly without a curfew. I shook my head in disbelief and strode forward down the path, our native frogs singing their January mating songs all around me, thousands of tiny voices echoing across the marsh in one holy roar.

Ben and I began our session together that evening in a three-car garage aboard his Westerly Nomad sailboat. We had been working on this boat for the past couple of months as my trade instead of doing work in the garden now that the weather had turned cold and wet. I lay on my back in the double berth tucked into the prow of Ben's robust little yacht. I knocked loudly on the ceiling.

"This one!" I called, holding the nut in place with a ratchet while Ben unscrewed the bolt from above. I took the nut and dropped it carefully into a bowl then knocked at the location of the next. I heard Ben's feet shuffling above me as he felt for the place where I'd moved.

"Here!" In just moments, Ben had unscrewed the bolt from above, and the nut was free to fall with a plink into the bowl beside its mate. When all six were finished, Ben joined me below to survey what other hardware needed to be removed before he sandblasted the boat for painting. We lay next to each other on our backs.

"Pretty roomy, right?" he asked.

"I guess so," I said.

"Yeah, this little boat could go anywhere. It sure could. See the portholes? I just spent some time putting in new ones that are operable. You can open them to let in the breeze. That'll be really important in the tropics. This boat was built for the English Channel. You wouldn't need them there."

"You're going to the tropics?" I asked.

"Sure!" he said. "Why not? I'm still hoping I can convince you to go. I have just the book for you. It's called *Sailing the Farm*, and it's all about sprouting and living sustainably on a sailboat. Every woman I've known has had the same complaint about sailing—you spend too much time at sea. Well, this way you can take the garden with you!"

I laughed. He knew me pretty well.

"Think of the education that your young galoots could get!" he cried. I saw how being with Ben opened some wonderful windows of opportunity.

"We could take the folding bikes!" Ben went on. I had seen the Dahon folding bikes that he had purchased to use when traveling by sailboat and train. Ben had once biked fifty miles from a train station to a wedding that took place in Vermont. I enjoyed Ben's sense of adventure. His most cherished possession was now his orange Tikit folding bike by Bike Friday. It snapped into and out of a folded position in less than a minute. Quite impressive.

"Yeah, that would be cool," I said, thinking of the Bike Friday triple tandem that could be put together from three folded units in less time than it took to park a car downtown. I'd always had a crush on that bike.

"Think of the fun we could have traveling and teaching. You could get a job easy, I know it," he said.

"Doing what?" I asked.

"Teaching English!" he said. "It's not that hard. You can get certified online. I have a friend who did it."

"Wow," I said. That would be a dramatic change in lifestyle, but the boys were becoming more independent. Who knew where they would be in a few years? They could really benefit from attending school abroad, I imagined.

"We could live with a pretty small footprint by staying in one place for a long time. It's called eco-tourism. That's a thing! I saw it on the internet. We could use the boat and bikes. Maybe we'd even live aboard. We might need a bigger boat for that," he said with a wink. "Not a lot of privacy between these two walls." He thumped the fiberglass and I blushed. We were talking about traveling abroad and we hadn't even kissed!

I shook my head and sat up carefully. Ben and I squeezed out of the prow and climbed up on deck. Being on the boat in this makeshift dry dock felt uncomfortable. Hoisted onto a trailer to make room for three keels, Ben's boat seemed so tall and unnatural perched high above ground. I felt oddly vulnerable to falling as I walked the length of her with bent knees toward the ladder at the back.

"Careful there," said Ben. "It's time for us to do some singing. Gonna have to warm up those pipes." He flirtatiously reached to squeeze my hand. I looked down quickly to watch my step, nerves pulsing. Falling overboard onto concrete, I thought, was no way to end our first date.

That night, after we'd sung countless jazz standards sitting side by side on the glossy black piano bench, Ben and I moved to the orange loveseat where we cuddled. "No Y tonight?" I asked.

"No Y," said Ben. "The guys can steam without me." He wrapped one long arm around my shoulders.

"Is it possible?" I asked, raising an eyebrow.

"Every once in awhile," he said, "I miss a night just to shake things up."

Ben smiled. For over a decade, he'd gone to the YMCA for a steam and sometimes a swim one hour before they closed. The same group of men met there, night after night, and they had their longstanding friendships and irritations amongst them. I was grateful that Ben had male friends and cohorts. Community and ritual did much for a person's mental health, and I had always felt concerned about my husband before transition because he had so few. Conversely, as a woman, Seda had a lunch date every day of the week. I had no worries about *her.*

"The kids are going to do okay without you for awhile?" he asked, looking down at me.

"They are," I said. "Seda has them for as long as I need tonight."

"As long as you need?" he asked. I nodded.

Ben straightened himself and turned to look at me, placing a hand on each of my shoulders.

"Kristin Collier," he said. "You are so amazing. Thank you for being in my life."

He tipped his head down until his mouth met mine. I felt myself shaking. I kissed him back, slowly, feeling the warmth of his lips between my own, his breath with mine. Ben took my face gently in his palms and kissed my cheeks and brow while I rested my hands at the back of his neck. The shaking subsided. Ben scooped me into his lap and held me, kissing my forehead.

"Are you cold?" he asked.

"No," I said. "Just a little nervous."

"I could turn on the heat," he said, "and open this thing up into a bed."

"This little loveseat is a bed?" I asked, incredulous.

"Yup, pretty clever, huh?"

"Yeah."

"Okay," he said, setting me down gently and jumping up to take the pillows off.

"Oh, I didn't mean yeah in *that* way," I said.

"Oh, well, we can stay on the couch," said Ben, sitting down beside me again.

"Okay," I said.

"I just thought we might be more comfortable on the bed. We could keep doing what we're doing. If we decided to make it a bed, that is. No pressure to do anything different or more."

"Mmmmhmmm," I said.

"What do you think?" he asked.

"I guess we could do the bed, but I don't want to get too hot and heavy."

"Kristin, I am in love with you as near as I can tell, and whatever you want to do, whatever pace works for you is fine with me."

I exhaled and then took a deep breath. "I think I might be in love with you, too!" I said. Suddenly, my body relaxed. Some fear that what I cherished would be risked for too little, for merely lust, dissipated and the warmth of trust and care took its place. Ben smiled at me.

"Let's just keep it a couch," he said.

"No, let's make it a bed," I told him. "But I'm not taking my pants off."

"Great!" said Ben. "I think that's a good idea. Keep your pants on."

That very nearly worked.

Remaking Family

BEN SLEPT AT my house the next night and the next, quickly becoming part of the family. He joined us for supper a few times a week and Sunday mornings for brunch. I got up first to mix the waffle or pancake batter and prepare the vegetables and stock for the soup we'd eat for dinner in the coming week. After cooking brunch, I assembled the soup, and then I was done in the kitchen for the day.

"Boys!" I called. "Time to come help with dinner! Chop-chop!" It was rare that my first invitation was accepted with enthusiasm.

"Trin. Sam." I went to stand beside them. I had to break the focus they had on their respective books. Sometimes, they sat together reading the same book, placing a finger at the bottom of the page to indicate they were done. Sam read much faster than Trin, which proved to be an opportunity for him to grow his patience while Trin became a more fluent reader.

"Yeah, Mom? What?" they asked in tandem, hearing me for the first time.

"Time to chop vegetables for dinner," I said.

"Ohhhh," they said, looking none too excited. I directed them to cutting boards and knives at the kitchen table. We talked while they chopped and I stirred, exchanging jokes and stories about neighbors, friends, and the squirrels and ducks that visited our yard. They also told me about the books they were reading, usually in greater detail than I could follow. Sometimes, we listened to books on tape when working on a big cooking project, but not while Ben was sleeping.

I had pressure-cooked a chicken in water earlier that morning with a spoonful of vinegar, quartered onions, celery, carrots, garlic, and herbs from the garden. As Trinidad and Sam put the last chopped bits of parsnip, potato, leek, and carrot into a large bowl that would later be plunged into the steaming, salty broth, I sat down to pick the chicken off the bone. Ben shuffled out of the bedroom rubbing his face.

"Good morning, sunshine," I said.

"Heyyyy. Good morning," he leaned over and kissed my lips then put one leg under him to sit on the wooden bench across the table from me.

"Can I get you a cup of tea?" I asked.

"Yeah, that would be nice," he said.

I washed my hands, filled the kettle, and put it on to boil. Ben reached for me. I tousled his hair and allowed him to pull me a little awkwardly onto his lap.

"Want to go back to bed instead?" he asked.

"No. I'm just finishing up this soup so I can put the waffles on. The bacon is already done."

"Oh, that can wait, can't it?" he asked kissing my neck playfully.

"Not really," I said, amused. "Armageddon may be declared if brunch is not on the table before 11:30."

"Armageddon? I can't think of a better place to be during Armageddon than in bed with you in my arms." He smiled broadly. "Come on," he prodded.

"Here, cut this up!" I said, passing him some parsley with a cutting board and knife as I rose.

"Baby, I'm just waking up."

"Well, it seems that you have quite a lot of energy for just waking up," I said. "I thought maybe you could put some of it to use."

"You're missing the point," he said. "You should come here and sit with me. Have tea, come back to bed, sit and talk, take a break. You shouldn't work so hard. You don't have to do it all."

"I don't if you help," I said, smiling sweetly.

"What about the kids? Can't they do this?" he asked.

"Nope, they did their part already," I said. "We're in the final stages. I do need to get going or else there may be a nuclear meltdown in a few minutes."

"Okay," he said. "I wish you'd take it easy more often, but you have to do what you think is best. After I'm done with this tea, I'll play the piano."

"That sounds lovely," I said. "The neighbor kids are here with the boys, and they want to stay for breakfast. I told them they could invite the rest of their family, too. We have enough food."

"Great," said Ben. "The more the merrier." Ben was always up for a party. He sat sipping his tea as the morning light slanted in across his broad wrists and forearm. Piano hands. Ben's dark hair lit with a halo at its edge, and he looked peaceful sitting at our table. He chuckled quietly about the squirrels chasing each other in the yard then told me that his students seemed to be feeling the change in the weather, too.

Ben was excited to do his student teaching in math in new and innovative ways. He integrated music into his math curriculum and wrote songs about lines, angles, and the order of operations. He said he took his students outside with a rope to do a hands-on lesson about angles and geometry in the January sun and then nearly lost them all to the onset of spring. I laughed.

"Sam, please come peel some mandarins, and Trin, can you and Justin go and tell his family that brunch will be ready in twenty minutes?" I asked.

"Yep, we can," said Trin and Justin, jostling to get past each other to be the first out the front door.

"Well, I guess it's time for a little music," said Ben. He tipped his cup and drained the last drops of tea before he handed it back to me. Ben stood up and brushed past in his loose fitting lilac-colored hemp shorts and a yellow T-shirt that proclaimed, "Eugene. We're here because we're not all there."

Ben settled down at my Betsy Ross Spinet and closed his eyes, setting his fingers gently on the keys. I stood in the hallway, peering around the corner in my jeans, black T-shirt, and apron. Always the apron, all the time. I'm sloppy in the kitchen from head to toe. Besides, if you wear an apron backward, it's a cape, and you're a domestic superhero. I lived in mine.

Ben leaned forward and pressed the keys gently with his whole hands, his arms, his body. His foot, acting as if it was a part of the instrument itself, rose up and pumped the pedal intuitively. Ben had the entire piano between his hands and feet. He guided and coaxed the music, deep and resonant, from within the golden body of our spinet. Ben's other knee bounced up and down as if reassuring the mass of metal and wood that it was safe to play, safe to sing. He offered up a rhythm, and the keys struck chords and notes that reached and found his graceful pumping. The music became him and he the music. Ben not only played how he felt; he played like the lover he was. I blushed.

The neighbor family stood on our porch and knocked at the door, but Ben did not stop. He rocked his entire body toward and away from the piano as the song spilled into the room and out onto the porch as they entered.

"Oh, isn't that nice," said Justin's mom, Sarah.

"Yes. I feel very grateful," I said. I had always wanted to have a little restaurant that served waffles twenty different ways and housed a grand piano in the corner so that someone could play jazz on Sunday mornings while people ate at small tables. Here, it seemed, was my chance to realize that dream.

Seda helped to gracefully make space for my relationship with Ben in our family. She continued to take the boys one night and a morning a week so I could stay over at Ben's house on the other side of the park. Ben liked to sleep in the simple wooden yurt he had built behind his music studio, and I joined him there. When I looked out of its round-topped, four and a half foot tall hobbit door in the morning, I saw Ben's garden filled with lush green kale, collards, and rainbow chard—the fruits of our partnership already growing around us.

After two nights of formal courtship, Ben had slept with me almost every night thereafter, whether at my place or his. I usually went to bed before he got home, but I always woke intuitively a few minutes before he pulled his bike into the garage, then I lay waiting for his kiss in the dark.

Seda had been sleeping in the living room for almost a year by then. She got up earlier than the rest of us and made coffee and breakfast in the kitchen, so it made sense that she would be the one to sleep in the public area as long as we had no other options. On the other hand, getting the house quiet and dark by her ten o'clock bedtime was almost always a challenge. This living arrangement had grown uncomfortable for us all. The house was small, and Seda's sleeping on the couch had turned into more of a long-term situation than we'd expected.

We started looking on Craigslist for an apartment for her. It only seemed fair that Seda's home would also have room for the children, and an apartment that size wasn't cheap. Nor could I imagine the boys being quiet enough for her to maintain the lease of an apartment within regulations. Money and energy that went into split housing for parents would be taken from the fund that provided soccer shoes, high quality food, and family leisure time together, not to mention the operation that Seda would eventually need to complete her medical gender transition. Then, there would be the business of Seda stocking her kitchen and cooking for herself and the boys after she got home from work. I couldn't imagine feeling comfortable with what came of that and instead envisioned the possibility of me catering to her household. But how could I do that if I was working to pay the mortgage? The whole idea seemed ludicrous. Our resources, both in skillsets and money, were efficiently distributed now, and we were both happy with the support we provided the children. If only we just had more room!

Seda entertained thoughts of designing an addition for our home. Our friend Bob offered to consult and help with the foundation of the addition and provided us with recycled building materials. Seda's brother Pete said he'd join us for an intensive day or two of construction, and Ben agreed to do the plumbing. Another friend gave us a deal on the installation of hardwood floors, and I already had a volunteer painting crew at the ready. Before long, this course appeared to be the most sensible route to make room for Seda and me to share parenting while preserving space for each of us to have other romantic partners. After serious reconsideration, there was no compelling reason for Seda and me to part ways. A separate wing seemed the next logical step, and we broke ground in June of 2009.

Seda continued to be my most steady partner, domestically speaking. She came home for dinner every night, and this remained a cornerstone of our family time together. Still, I found myself alone in the garden and kitchen more often than I enjoyed. I called friends on the phone when I grew lonely, but I missed having an integrated romantic and domestic partnership. I tried to be thankful for the needs met by Seda and Ben individually, but our new family plan never felt fully harmonious. My world with Ben revolved around sensuality, creativity, and play, while my life at home was grounded in raising children, working with the earth, and managing a household. I struggled to integrate the spheres and often felt disappointed and frustrated with my lack of success.

I chose to celebrate peace and ease wherever I found it. Seda's family had accepted and integrated Ben as part of our unconventional family package, for which I was grateful. Seda's mother, Mumsy as we called her, delighted in the fact that Sam was learning to play Bartok and Beethoven, and that people made music daily in our home. She had grown up playing piano and was excited that Sam's gift was so easily inspired and cultivated now that we had a serious musician in the house. When Mumsy visited that summer, we all enjoyed dinner together, Ben included. Mumsy fairly melted when Ben sat down at the piano to play some show tunes afterward. I was glad she could see the beauty in him that I saw.

Seda's brother Pete, sister-in-law Janet, and their children also embraced us. Seda's brother had taken some time to come around to the idea that he had a sister in Seda, but I have to say that he struggled with the transition about as gracefully as one could hope. Pete assured Seda that he loved her but took awhile to adjust to her new name and pronouns. I had the sense that he spent the first year or two in disbelief that such a thing could be, and I certainly could understand that. The first few times that Pete called her sis, Seda beamed angelically. It was like she'd gotten her brother back. Pete and Janet's kindness to me never wavered, and when we showed up for Christmas dinner as a fivesome they welcomed us all with open arms. I couldn't ask for more.

Ultimately, I sensed that others' acceptance of us hinged on our own comfort with this unique family configuration. In moments of doubt, I reminded myself not to look down, because normal was so far away that I had vertigo even thinking about it. I'm sure there were plenty of people who doubted and questioned, especially from afar, but when they got to know us, many actually expressed envy. When I led NVC workshops and mentioned my parenting partner, people would often approach me afterward.

"What's a parenting partner?" they would ask. "And how can I get one?"

I would smile. "Careful what you wish for," I said.

The Insurance Agent

SEDA AND I sat beside each other looking across a broad wooden desk at our insurance agent who kept her eyes on the form she was filling out in our stead to request a new life insurance policy. Every frank question she posed required an answer of inscrutable honesty.

"Have you, in the last six years, seen a doctor or psychologist?" she asked Seda.

"Well, yes, both," Seda answered.

"For?"

"Yes, Seda, what's on the books?" I asked.

"Depression, I think. Yes, that was it. Then the doctor for hormone therapy," she said.

The agent scribbled quickly, looking relieved.

"Will they take you off the preferred rates for having gender dysphoria?" I asked Seda.

"I don't think so. I don't know," she said. The agent declined comment. "It was never an official diagnosis, and the gender psych I see in Portland is on a cash-only basis. No paper trail."

"They probably won't even notice," I told her. "Unless they look at that little box that's now checked female. Then they'll probably wonder. The name change, you know. But, hey, no formal diagnosis. It's an at-home transition. Something in your Wheaties."

Our agent suppressed a giggle, and kept her eyes on the paperwork, unsure about our relationship and how she should respond to us.

"Come to think of it," I added, "it must have been the Fruit Loops. I thought I warned you about those." Seda and I laughed out loud.

"Have you been advised to have an operation?" came the question from behind the desk.

"Yes," said Seda demurely. Then she turned to me. "Is that the right answer?"

"NO," I told her.

"Oh," she said, and folded her hands in her lap. "Well, the Association of—but then no, I've not been *personally* advised by a doctor to have an operation."

She'd have one, of course. And by the time the policy was up, the physical exam itself could not argue with that little box marked female.

Not that it would matter if the attending physician did argue. She is who she is, though certainly not the man I married.

"Are you—will you . . . stay married?" the agent asked uncertainly.

"It looks good on paper, doesn't it?" I said.

"That's about the extent of it," said Seda.

"For as long as we share children and a sense of humor, maybe."

The ancient Chinese blessing-in-a-curse: may you live in interesting times.

Snapshots 2009

Seda designs and gets plans approved for a bedroom, office, and bathroom addition with a private entrance. We break ground together, but it is Trinidad who cannot rest. He is digging the footing for our new foundation as if it must be done within the week. His friends come to play, and he invites them to dig with him. They tire, and he offers them a break while he digs. I am touched and inspired by his driving will, and I learn to meditate while dumping tailings beside the pond, one breath at a time.

I run to Home Depot across town for just one more thing almost daily. Seda's lists are well-intentioned but incomplete. At Lowe's, the boys discover that plumbing elbows can be pressure fitted into elaborate weapons. It is rare that they can keep their new toys.

I discover that my Xtracycle can carry dimensional lumber if it is held away from the pedals by a pizza box on either side, and, lo and behold, there is a Little Caesar's next to Home Depot! This maneuver is so gratifyingly efficient that I celebrate everything except what they put in those pizzas.

Beer proves to be a legitimate building expense in the absence of a paid contractor.

The boys pound nails and drill holes, but they are best at demo-lition. Seda, Ben, and I raise the walls together one Sunday after brunch. I love learning to build, but someone has to feed the crew, and I'm the most experienced hand.

Ben does a lot of the plumbing for the job and sweats count-less copper joints aiming in all directions to power a sink and a two-person claw-foot tub. This tub and the composting toilet are the crowning glory of our new addition.

I grow starts for Ben's winter garden at his request. I clear beds and plant almost a hundred baby greens. Ben says he doesn't want to water. He's over the honeymoon, over the mystique. He did just fine without watering before I came along. I tell him I'd rather have known his thoughts on this before I grew the plants for him and cleared the beds. His friend tells him, "Ben, water the plants." Ben gets out the hose.

One night, in a state of particularly heated lovemaking, Ben and I set off the smoke alarm in his yurt. I would think it was a fluke if it hadn't happened twice more the following year. "I'm afraid that our relationship is based on sex," I tell him. He takes me in his arms and looks straight into my eyes. "No," he says patiently. "Our relationship is based on really great sex. There's a difference."

Ben completes his student teaching in math and then becomes a substitute teacher. He sets his clock for midnight to check the website for jobs, responding to calls at three, four, and five o'clock in the morning. He mourns not having a classroom of his own and a regular schedule. I suffer when I see him so frustrated.

Sam tells me out of the blue that he'd like me to pack him a lunch so he could eat it somewhere else . . . like school. We spontaneously jump the waiting list and get the boys into an alternative public school in town where many of our low-income educated counterparts send their children. Sam begins first grade and Trin starts third. It's a gentle transition from home-schooling, and the boys and I picnic and read aloud together under a tree after school before we bike home each day.

Inspired by Ben who rarely uses his vegetable oil powered car for anything, we rely more and more on our bicycles, revving up the biodiesel station wagon once a week or less for trips to the feed store or lumberyard.

In August, just before sunset, Ben finally gets the recumbent tandem bicycle working, and he hooks his six-foot long flatbed bike trailer to the end of it. Ben pulls up to our house proudly and puts Seda behind him to pedal while the boys and I cuddle up on the flatbed. We cruise the park and then get ice cream cones a couple of miles away. In the evening light, our big family laughs and eats by a fountain at the university. Anything seems possible.

Not Telling

AT THE END of June 2009, we got a phone call one morning from Mumsy. Her voice sounded tired. "Can I talk to Seda?" she asked. Alarm welled in me as I went to look for my parenting partner out back.

The sun was barely up, but Seda already stood at the building site of her new wing, dressed in her moss-colored Carhartt pants and a lilac cotton T-shirt. She stood upright and leaned back a little with her head cocked to one side, holding a stainless steel mug of steaming coffee in one hand and a measuring tape in the other. She bit her lip and wrinkled her nose thoughtfully while she scanned the subfloor that she and her brother Pete had installed the day before. A faded leather tool belt hung heavily from her straight waist, and she pushed a loose strand of hair from her eyes with the back of one forearm. Seda was still mastering the art of plaiting her long, dark hair, and, much to her irritation, the braid she had managed that morning hung lopsided and loose down her back. Seda looked up when she saw me coming, and her face broke into its charming, crooked-toothed smile. Then she saw my concern, and her brows knitted together in a look of confused curiosity.

"Mumsy," I said quietly as I handed her the phone.

I stood a minute and watched Seda as she unlatched her tool belt and let it slide from her waist with a clink. She swung the thick leather belt and its hammers around beside her as she sat down on the edge of the subfloor to her new suite. I turned and walked slowly back to the house where I took my place at the stove cooking breakfast. Looking up a moment later, I saw her shoulders slump. Seda laid the phone down gently beside her and continued to sit awhile. Finally, she stood up and came to meet me at the glass sliding door. Her eyes were red and glassy from crying. I had already guessed what happened.

"DeeDee passed," said Seda. It had been a few years now since Seda's beloved older sister had driven through a cold Wyoming night and fallen asleep at the wheel. The morning after, DeeDee's truck was found in a ditch, and her body lay broken amidst bent metal and shards of glass. DeeDee had been airlifted to a hospital in the next state and barely survived multiple intensive surgeries. Her spine had been broken in six places. She remained in a coma for over three months.

The process of regaining awareness took DeeDee years. She had lost all mobility and struggled to learn to talk and use her hands again to some degree. We visited within a year of her awakening, before she had yet spoken more than a few sentences. It was rare that DeeDee's voice was heard then, and she communicated primarily with pleading eyes. We did not know how much she understood about what went on around her. Sitting alone with her when Seda and Mumsy had gone to find an attendant, I spoke to DeeDee quietly for a while then sat in stillness.

"I want my Mommy," she'd said.

DeeDee had gone from care home to care home, fighting depression and resisting physical therapy, aware of what she had lost, and unable to recover the bulk of her mental and physical faculties. She visited with her four children, one of them a preschooler, but could offer little help or guidance. Her husband divorced her in relatively short order, and Mumsy took up vigil at her bedside for months until DeeDee stabilized, then Mumsy returned to visit her a few times a week, driving thirty minutes across state lines to keep the connection alive.

DeeDee's situation had broken the hearts of us all in so many ways. It was unexpected and tragic to see this brilliant woman, an archeologist who had trained horses, fought wildfires, logged the Black Hills, surveyed land, and mothered four children—sometimes without electricity and indoor plumbing—now rendered entirely dependent on the care of others. DeeDee was a fighter, always had been, but she wasn't sure what there was left to fight for.

When Seda realized how isolated, lonely, and depressed her big sister had become, she did the only thing she could think to do. She wrote letters. Seda began writing these letters in July of 2004, and she sent them weekly for almost five years. Seda wrote letters to DeeDee describing her transition. She wrote letters about our family life. She wrote letters to tell her big sister how much she loved her, and how much DeeDee's courage, creativity, and spirit had been a model for her in the tough years of Seda's childhood, back when DeeDee had lovingly nicknamed her Skunk.

These letters became a lifeline for DeeDee. She looked forward to them every week, and on the rare occasions that Seda missed a letter, DeeDee chided her sister. As Seda moved further and further through her transition, she looked more like DeeDee with her sharp, narrow nose and serious, clear blue eyes. Seda's fat redistributed in the course of taking estrogen, and as her face became more feminine, she took after her sister more than anyone else in the family.

DeeDee accepted Seda wholly as herself, and Mumsy learned of the inner workings of Seda's transition through the letters she read aloud to DeeDee. Now and then, Seda's sister picked up a pen and wrote back in shaky, childish script. She apologized for the way her letters ran up or down the page, but she always expressed her love and gratitude for Seda and the time she had taken to write.

DeeDee had fasted before, refusing to eat until she was on the threshold of death once more. This last time, Mumsy said, her organs did not bounce back. DeeDee had died in her sleep somewhat unexpectedly.

Mumsy had been actively mothering for the past several years, and her life cracked open wide and empty as she observed the passing of her beloved daughter. Losing Frank, the middle son, had been hard enough. Losing her youngest son, Fred, and gaining a daughter in Seda had not quite been a walk in the park. Mumsy had not complained, but the grief had asked much of her. She turned, as always, to God for inner strength, opening her heart and mind to the divine reality of ever-present Love.

Mumsy focused herself on DeeDee's funeral plans. Family was what she most needed now, she said. Precious family. Mumsy planned the memorial, and Seda agreed to come.

Seda took time off work, packed her bags, and caught a flight to Rapid City, South Dakota the following week, then drove to Wyoming in a rental car. She was scared to death. She hadn't seen many of the people from the small town of her youth since well before she'd transitioned, and she wasn't sure how much Mumsy had told them. Seda also hadn't seen DeeDee's kids for some time, and a few of them were grown and had chosen life partners of their own. Seda would be meeting extended family, neighbors, and friends who were trying to unify the past with the present in regards to DeeDee, and then here was Seda, another unexpected variable. She telephoned me from the same bed and breakfast where our family had stayed so many years before when Sam was still tiny and Seda was at the beginning of her transition.

"How's it going?" I asked.

"Well—it's interesting," she said, and I could hear her smiling an ironic smile. "It turns out that Mumsy didn't really tell folks about me transitioning, so I get to do that for myself."

"What?!" I said. "Seriously? But she's been so accepting of you, so supportive."

"Oh yeah," said Seda. "She still is. She sees me for who I am.

But apparently she didn't have a lot of confidence that others would be so open-minded."

"Geez," I said. "What *did* she tell them?"

"Well . . . not much, apparently," said Seda. "They got progress reports on the kids and how my job was going and how you were, but she didn't really tell the *whole* story, you know? She never actually said Seda, or she. In fact, she only said Fred. And they were glad enough to hear that I was doing well. So I guess she never really felt the need to tell them more."

"Wow. How is that going for you?" I asked, incredulous.

"It's actually okay," said Seda. "People are being pretty darn open and accepting of everything right now, but I do think they're a little surprised. The Bearlodge Writers' group folks were great about it once they realized what was going on. Some of the people from town have been trying to figure out what's up with Fred and where this new sister came from," she chuckled. "And the neighbors—well, they just have to make their peace with it, you know? The women have been great. Mark Smith's wife came right up and gave me a hug. Mark just stood there nodding and smiling with his face turning red. I wouldn't say it was *comfortable,* you know, but people are dealing with it pretty well."

"Hoooeey, you are brave," I told her.

"Yeah, well, what are you gonna do?" she asked. "We're all here for DeeDee. And she was one hell of a lady who went through one heck of a lot these last few years. There's so much grief about that. She's being remembered and honored for her whole life, too. There's a lot to celebrate. And one of the things to be celebrated is community that comes together to help no matter what the challenge is. They're showing up. They really are."

"I love Wyoming for that." I said, remembering the people who daily dismissed stereotypical gender roles to be sure the cows got fed and food made it onto the table. "I love how the folks there just get the job done, whether it's bringing in hay before the hailstorm or tending to a neighbor's chores because the neighbor's injured or out of town. I miss that can-do attitude."

"Yup. I'm thankful for that now," said Seda. "It's not a bad place at all. And DeeDee's kids have been great about me showing up as their new aunt. Their spouses, too. I'm so glad, because it feels good to give and get lots of hugs right now." She swallowed hard. "My sister was a special lady."

"I know," I said. "And so are you. She was proud to have you for a sister, Seda."

"Thanks, Kristin," said Seda. "You're the best."

"That's the pot calling the kettle black," I said, using one of Seda's favorite sayings. We laughed.

Granted, I had my own bugaboos when it came to telling certain people about our transition. I thought of Fred becoming Seda as *our* transition, because it did not pertain to just my husband. My friends and family in particular wanted to know how the boys and I would go on living—would we split households, get a divorce? Was I now a lesbian? Was Seda actually still sane and responsible as a parent? Was our home now going to be Transsexual Transylvania—a den of wild orgies and debauchery?

Okay, friends and family would never have asked that last question aloud, but I think it was the worst-case scenario at the back of their minds, even if it was subconscious. Given that folks who are trans were once typically called transsexuals (transitioning from one sex to another), people, especially the older generations, got caught up in the word *sex* and didn't get much further than that. Unwelcome images of men in fishnet stockings, bustiers, and heels danced in their heads, and these images did not jive with the Ozzy and Harriet hippie-fusion lifestyle that characterized our family.

So, it was no surprise that I had followed my mother's instructions and refrained from telling my grandfather what Seda was going through. We spoke with Grandpa only a few times a year, after all, so it hadn't seemed like it would be a major problem. I was doing what my mother told me to do, about *her* father, so I tried to believe it was right. At the same time, I found my conversations with Grandpa more and more unbearable.

How many ways would I have to lie before I got off the phone? I found myself dreading to hear his voice on the answering machine and wishing I hadn't received a gift that necessitated my calling to thank him. Lying was worse than not talking to him at all. This discomfort offered yet another lesson in compassion for Seda, as I recalled how she had lived the lie of being male for well over forty years before she finally stood up and said, "Enough." There is little honor in lying to those you love, and it's worse yet when the lying is meant to hide your true identity.

Just the year before, after Christmas, I'd resolved that the deception had to end, even if Mom was not on board. I'd decided that I would honor Grandpa's experience and wisdom; it was not my grandfather's first day at the rodeo, after all.

Grandpa and his family had survived the Great Depression in part because, as an eight-year-old, he was resourceful enough to think of a way to keep his family from freezing. My grandfather went down to the railroad tracks every morning as a boy and threw rocks at the coal cars of passing trains. The coal car boilerman would stop stoking the engine's fire long enough to angrily throw coal back at my grandfather until the boilerman realized that every time this exchange took place on the tracks, my young grandfather picked up every last bit of coal to take home to stoke his family's fire. After that, the boilerman scooped and dumped a bucketful of coal beside the tracks whenever he saw my grandfather running toward the passing train. My grandpa was a survivor, and I wanted to pay my respects to that.

I called him up after opening his Christmas package. "Grandpa," I said, "I want to thank you for the box of goodies. We had so much fun eating those nuts and candies on Christmas Eve."

"You're welcome, honey. I thought you could use them, you know? Those boys have got to be growing, right?"

"They are for sure," I said.

"Yes, I'll bet!" said Grandpa. "How are they doing in school?"

"Very well," I told him. We had always had this conversation through the years when I'd homeschooled. He worried about whether homeschool would prepare them adequately for the world, but he never demanded I do otherwise, and he still referred to what we did as school.

"Sam is reading Sherlock Holmes aloud to Trinidad right now," I said. "Trin is paying him by the page because he'd rather listen to it than read it himself."

Grandpa chuckled. "Well, I never," he said. "And how's Fred?"

"Well, I wanted to talk to you about that," I said. "Fred has gone through some changes in the past few years. It turns out that he always felt like he was a girl, not a boy, but he could hardly believe that himself—especially since he grew up on a ranch in Wyoming. Nobody else seemed to experience what he did, and he just hated himself. He felt . . . confused and alone. He didn't know what to do about it. He figured there was something wrong with him. He couldn't even say what he thought was wrong, because he was so ashamed. That's why he became a Marine, then a logger, and then an Alaskan fisherman—to try to be a man. A few years ago, Grandpa, he started getting a lot of therapy to come to terms with his depression and anxiety, and he finally decided that he could no longer live as a man because he felt like he was living a lie. He was diagnosed with gender dysphoria, and now he's transitioned into living life as a woman. I'm sorry I haven't told you before."

There was a moment of quiet. "Yeah, that happens," said my grandfather. I almost dropped the phone.

"It does." I said. "More often than we know."

"I suppose," he said. "Well, what about you and the kids? Are you going to get a divorce and live somewhere else?"

"No, not yet," I said. "Maybe we won't ever. I don't know. We're just playing it by ear, one day at a time. We're still best friends. She's the best thing that's ever happened to me."

"Hmm," he said. "Did you know about all this before?"

"No, not really," I said. Which was true if you included my long stint in denial.

"Well, does she want to be with a man?" he asked rather gruffly.

"We don't know that exactly either. We're just trying to figure it out, but we're building an addition onto the house so she'll have her own space, and I'll have mine. She's come out at work—she told them, and they've been great about it. Really supportive. It's a good job, that City job."

"Yeah, well, that's fine, honey. You just let me know if you need any help or anything. I'm sure sorry that happened."

"You know, Grandpa, it's not too bad. I mean . . . I feel more like my husband died than I got a divorce. I had a pretty amazing marriage, and not very many people can say that. I still have an awesome co-parent. One of the hardest parts is telling people. I was pretty afraid to tell you, but I think you took it really well."

"Yeah, it happens," he said. "Why, you hear about it on TV all the time, you see? What's important is that you and the kids are healthy and okay. That's what's really important. And you're figuring it out, you're making it work. I'm proud of you," he said.

"Wow. Thanks, Grandpa."

"I love you, honey. I'd better go."

"Sure. I love you, too. Talk to you later," I said.

It was almost too easy. Grandpa had been my last frontier, and all of my worry had been for nothing. I couldn't wait to tell my mom. I called her immediately.

"Kris," she said excitedly after I'd told her. "Wow. I was wrong. You know—I've never been so happy to be so wrong! Thank God! And you know what?" she asked.

"What?"

"I know I shouldn't say this, but I like Seda so much more than I liked Fred! Seda is funny and outgoing and honest. She's so much fun to hang out with. I like her style, and I admire her. I'm sorry you lost your marriage over it, but, honey, I think your husband is a much better person when she's herself."

"Yeah," I said. "That was kind of the idea, Mom. That was kind of the idea."

A Change in Tone

MOM NO LONGER offered me advice. As I explored my relationship with Ben, my mother watched and listened patiently. I had not dated very many people before settling down with Seda, so I hadn't relied on my mother in this way before. I will always appreciate what she said to me, and what she had the sense not to say as I built and dismantled romantic partnerships. Mom seemed to have garnered a measure of self-control throughout our transition as a family, and whether she suspended judgment or simply her tongue, I will always be grateful that she was quiet on the other end of the line while I sorted things out for myself. Not only did my mother give me the gifts of empathy, autonomy, and respect, but she also stood as an exemplary model of how to effectively parent adult children.

I must have put her to the test with the range of emotions I expressed about Ben. When he and I started dating in 2009, I bought an iPhone just after he got his. I set Ben's ringtone to Blues because it reminded me of the way he played the piano—four upward trills on the blues scale punctuated by a low note. Every time my phone rang, I knew it was Ben, because the piano warbled enticingly. It was the ringtone that called, "Oh . . . fun! Your lover's on the line!"

The notes in that ring tone traipsed up and down titillatingly. It reminded me of reaching toward climax with Ben's fingers playing across my body. The hair on my head stood on end to hear it, and my heart skipped a beat whenever the phone rang. I crossed the kitchen in a flash to answer, unaware that I had moved at all until I'd slid my finger across the screen to accept the call.

In general, I was happy to hear Ben's deep, velvety voice come through the phone; however, as our house addition progressed, Ben's discontent grew with his lack of regular employment, and the tension between us mounted. More challenges arose in our relationship, too.

"I don't know where I live!" he told me. "My house on the other side of the park is a mess, the garden is weedy, and it doesn't feel like my home anymore. But this isn't my home either! I don't have anything here. I can't just hang out when everybody's gone to bed. I can't have friends over. There's no place to put my clothes! I feel like I'm in no man's land." He frowned.

It was true—my little bedroom was barely big enough for a double bed and a dresser. And while I thought him lucky to have a space separate from our family's to entertain in, I could understand his need to merge the various aspects of his life. Over the months that followed, I bought a little nightstand and rearranged my clothes so there was room for Ben's, too, but by then he'd changed his mind and didn't want any clothes at my place.

I made every effort to bring Ben into my life fully, serve him and allow for reciprocity. I cooked his favorite foods, kept the children quiet in the morning so he could sleep in, left him love notes, and gave him much of my attention whenever he was around. I washed the walls of his studio, helped him sand and oil the yurt, painted his rental house, and planted his garden. I wanted to bring his space into my awareness so we could feel at home together in either one.

I wanted to share common and meaningful goals with my romantic partner, so that our combined efforts benefitted the places we called home. The fact that my values differed some from Ben's did not help. While I would spend hours shopping for, roasting, and seasoning nuts and seeds to showcase in entrées or salads, Ben was content to eat carrots and broccoli raw until something cooked was offered to him. I could understand why my efforts seemed senseless beside his perception of a simple lifestyle, but he was nonetheless happy to eat the food I'd prepared. I gathered my courage to ask him to contribute to the grocery budget, at least.

"You don't think I help out enough? I spent days on that addition. Remember the night we didn't pass inspection, and I helped Seda wire in all new GFCI outlets? You seem to forget these things."

"I really appreciate those things," I said. "And I tried to show it by cooking for you one or two times for every shift you put in. I know that wasn't enough then, but I have continued cooking for you at least a few times a week since, and I'm only asking you to contribute to the cost of what you consume. I'm happy to gift the preparation, but we could use some help with the expense."

Seda and I were still supporting the household on her salary alone. It wasn't easy, especially with weekly electrolysis and hormone prescriptions factored in. Seda had lost her job as a plans examiner due to budget cuts and was offered a lateral move by the union. She had taken a twenty-five percent pay decrease to remain employed as a parking enforcement officer.

"Why do you have to do all this measuring?" Ben demanded. "That isn't love. That's business."

"It may be business," I said. "But it's also part of a sustainable relationship." I persisted in my request, intentionally shelving my rising fear and embarrassment. I knew that what I offered Ben was a generous gift, and I did not want to be taken for any more than I wished to give. To proceed without the adjustment I was requesting would have been to go forward with a sense of bitter obligation. I did not wish to poison myself or my family with such negativity from a romantic relationship, so I did my best to remain matter-of-fact. Ben decided to contribute $75 a month to cover the cost of his cereal and groceries after I mapped out a complete budget showing what I thought to be his share.

That is not to say that Ben couldn't be generous in his own way. He gave me a folding bike that he wasn't using and took me out to dinner once a week on his night to cook. He wrote me poetry, songs, and cards on my birthday. He played music with me and gave Sam lessons, too. I was grateful for all of this.

I just couldn't shake my confusion about why his temper flared when I asked for help. Seda and I said yes to one another's requests almost every time. We trusted that we wouldn't have asked if we didn't really need the help, and we made it clear in the request if we did not. We always adjusted our attitudes so that we could accomplish the task without resentment. We focused on the needs we would meet by making the effort for one another rather than thinking about what we were missing. Some friends suggested that we operated this way because we were both gendered female, but I didn't like to think so. For me, it was an efficient use of energy both spiritually and physically. We operated as one unit with no regrets. It was no use comparing Seda with Ben. I just sought to understand and cultivate acceptance for what I could not change.

One afternoon, I asked Ben if he would be willing to vacuum the living room. I had never asked him to vacuum before, but my to-do list for the day pushed the edges of the paper. I brought the vacuum cleaner up from the garage and parked it on the living room carpet as I posed the question.

Ben stood up from the bench in the kitchen. "I was just getting ready to go," he said. Ben drank the rest of his tea, set down the mug, and looked around for his backpack.

"All right," I said turning away, tears welling in my eyes. It had taken so much courage to make that query. I questioned whether the gamble of requesting was worth the pain of being turned down.

"What's wrong?" asked Ben.

"Well, I just—I really need some help," I said. "It's hard for me to ask."

"I'm glad you asked," he said gently, taking me by the shoulders. I looked down, my lower lip quivering. "I just have other things to do right now. You do too much, Kristin. You should ask for help." I burst into tears, and he pulled me into an embrace.

"Why are you crying?" he asked.

"I know it seems . . . silly," I choked out between sobs against his shoulder. "It's just that—when I ask for help, I really need it. You don't say yes very often. It hurts to hear you say no like you don't appreciate that I do almost all of the housekeeping and rarely ask for help. When I get to the point of being worn out and needing something in the last lap, I have so little energy left to ask. Preparing myself for the likelihood that you'll say no takes more effort than just pushing through and finishing by myself with some resentment."

"Well, I can't help you every time you hit me up!" said Ben, bristling. "I have other things to do. And I think it's ridiculous that you would think of not asking because you're afraid I'm going to say no. That's not very NVC of you. It's a request! I can say no to it. If you just keep doing everything because you're afraid to hear a no, then you'll never get a break."

"If other people would do the household chores without me asking, that's another way I could get a break," I said.

"Yeah, that's a good idea," said Ben. "What about the boys? And Seda? They could help you out more."

I sighed. "Seda is working full time and building the addition on weekends. The boys are doing their schoolwork and helping me with cooking and laundry. I would love to have more participation from *you*."

"Well, I teach Sam music, and I play music around here. Is that nothing to you? Doesn't that contribute? Think of what that would cost you in dollars and cents!"

"Yes, it contributes," I said. "I'm grateful. It's just that the housekeeping is required for us to live comfortably and safely, and music is an added benefit—it's like dessert to me."

"Well, it's not like that for me," he said. "But you can keep asking for help." He grabbed his backpack and sweatshirt. "Maybe next time I can pitch in." He shouldered the pack, kissed me on the cheek, and strode out the front door.

I stood with the vacuum cleaner cord hanging loosely from my hand, tears dripping from my cheeks and nose. I sniffed loudly. Closing my eyes, I focused on the darkness and descended into the quiet stillness of my mind. I grieved for lost hope. The fact was that I desperately needed teamwork in the colossal chore of housekeeping for five, particularly since I spent so much time growing food and shopping wholesale to keep costs down. I breathed into that sadness and stayed with it for a while, sitting down on the rug and wrapping my arms around my knees. I rocked myself gently from side to side. Then, as if surfacing the water of a great lake, I took another breath and felt ready to make an effort to understand my lover. I guessed that Ben had a history of resentment around requests stemming from the time he grew up in New Jersey with two bossy older sisters. To come to a place of joyful giving, Ben might need time to step away from old patterns into choice and personal empowerment, whether I liked it or not. This was his story, his path, his life to lead.

I wanted to be in my own integrity and living NVC as best I understood it, making requests and not demands. After all, I was teaching NVC to parents! I ought to be practicing and benefitting from the process myself . . . but right now the carpet needed vacuuming so that I could stand to walk on it again. I leaned my back against the wall. Dropping the cord, I covered my face with my hands.

What was it I most desired in my relationship with Ben? Connection and ease. I had grown tired of giving Ben empathy and felt exhausted by his hair-triggers. I had compassion for the place my lover came from. I understood him, I thought, but at times I did not understand my own choice to continue part-nering with this man because, ultimately, I wanted to use my energy differently. How much did I want to put into my roman-tic relationship instead of into parenting, creating, or teaching? This was the bigger question.

My care and respect for Seda as a beloved sister continued to deepen by the day. As I searched for peace in my relation-ship with Ben, I became all the more grateful for what Seda and I effortlessly shared, including our practical partnership. While she did not often initiate household tasks, she did respond favorably whenever I asked for help. Every evening as I finished cooking supper, she and I discussed our days, and in this way we continued bonding around the hearth of our home just as we had once before as a couple.

Growing the Family

WHEN I RETURNED home from helping my mother with the lavender harvest on her farm in Northern California the summer of 2010, Seda helped me unload suitcases and bundles of lavender and St. John's Wort. The boys gathered their things and went into the house, leaving the two of us alone in the garage. Seda closed the door behind them and started bouncing up and down with glee. "Guess what happened while you were gone!" she sang.

"I give up." I smiled, flipping open a suitcase and sorting the clothes that needed laundering. I dropped shirts, shorts, and socks into a pile by the washing machine then grabbed the next suitcase. Seda perched on the edge of her stool.

"Can I help?" she asked.

"No," I said. "Just tell me your news!"

"Well, you remember Lark, the woman I met at Pride last spring? I told you about her—she was working the booth next to mine where I worked for the City."

"Hmmm. Not really," I said.

"Well, I guess that was a while ago. Yeah, I'm not surprised. Anyway, she invited me to a party at her house last weekend, and then we got together on Tuesday. Then again on Wednesday. Then on Thursday. And guess what?"

My eyebrows went up. "What?" I asked.

"I got laid," said Seda. She broke into a fit of giggles.

"You did?" I asked, suppressing a grin.

"I did!" said Seda, crossing and uncrossing her legs playfully. Sam opened the garage door and stuck his head in.

"Mom, have you seen my Harry Potter?"

"Which one?"

"Prisoner of Azkaban."

"You're reading that again?"

"Yes! I left it here when we went to Grandma Kasha's, and now I can't find it."

My eye caught a piece of the dust jacket peeking out from beneath a laundry basket.

"Here," I said, sliding out the book and handing it to Sam. "Where's your brother?"

"I don't know," said Sam. "Reading."

"Okay, thanks. Enjoy! I appreciated your help unloading."

"Sure thing," said Sam, ducking out.

"Well, how was it?" I asked, swinging back around to face Seda.

"It was great!" said Seda gleefully. "I've never been made love to as a woman before—well, not by somebody who has only ever known me as a woman. And who was attracted naturally to women. She even managed to treat my dangly bits like they're part of the woman I am!"

"Nice!" I said.

"Yeah, we've been having a really good time together. She's super smart and funny, and she's getting her Ph.D."

"Fantastic. When do we meet her?" I snapped the suitcases closed and slid them side by side onto a shelf.

"Well, she and her girlfriend invited us to a party at their place next weekend."

"Girlfriend?" I asked.

"Yeah! It's pretty cool. She's been with the same woman for over twenty years. They're polyamorous."

"Whoa," I said. "Sounds like a lot of work."

"They seem to have it pretty well down," said Seda, catching a pair of socks I'd tossed and dropping them in the laundry basket beside her.

"Well, that's good," I said. Seda smiled.

I felt excited about this opportunity that Lark presented. I had always wondered how I would feel if Seda hooked up with someone else. Even though I was comfortable leaving our marriage for my own lover, would I be jealous when it was her turn? Would I worry for the stability of our partnership and home? I was pleased to find that I did not.

I met Lark the next weekend at the party as planned. Ben had a gig that night and couldn't come. Seda, Lark, and I all sat on the porch together having a beer, and Seda got us talking about food preservation. Seda had guessed rightly that permaculture was a good place for us to start. Lark and her partner Leena had been pickling, jamming, and jarring up the surplus of their gardens for decades. We started to hash over guerrilla food saving techniques and quickly sized up each other's rank.

I was impressed with Lark and Leena's conservation efforts. They even kept a bucket under their kitchen faucet to catch drips that they could later use in washing or flushing. Solar panels created shade in their backyard for an adorable pair of wolfhounds. I was won over in an evening, and I assured Lark and Leena that Seda and Lark's partnership had my blessing.

Still, a few awkward moments did arise. One afternoon, Lark and Seda emerged from her wing of the house noticeably flushed. I was hustling between pots and pans at the stovetop, putting away bulk dry goods, and feeling unconcerned about what Seda was up to. Lark did not meet my eyes as she walked through the glass-sliding door and rarely looked up at me for the next half hour. I wasn't sure what was going on, but I handed them each a dish of potato salad and a carrot. As she ate, Lark relaxed and finally chimed in to tell stories with the rest of us.

Later, when I spent a few days at Lark's house teaching her and Leena to lacto-ferment vegetables from the garden, Lark told me that she and Seda had been making quite a racket in their lovemaking that afternoon, and she'd worried that I was put off or offended by the noise they'd made. "I thought that bed was going to break through the wall!" she exclaimed. Lark had worried that I would be jealous then or at some point later, and she did not relish the idea.

I laughed at her story because, happily, I had no feelings of jealousy whatsoever. I am aware that this may be in part due to the nature of Lark's relationship with Seda; they had no intention of being each other's sole partners from the beginning. In fact, Leena became a part of our extended family, and to this day we count the couple as part of our close community even though Lark and Seda did not last as lovers.

There was only one moment of distinct discomfort between Lark and me, and it came up as if from a dream while we preserved dilly beans together one autumn afternoon. While Lark scooped yoghurt into a jelly bag to strain out the whey, she shared with me Seda's general approach as a lover. That in itself did not shake me; I heard the story as if I hardly knew Seda at all. Indeed, I did not know her in this way. I had partnered with Fred and with Heather. Seda had barely emerged on the scene when I'd split, and I cherished her as a friend.

Lark got to a part in the story where she related that Seda had expressed shock about Lark's requested style of cunnilingus. Lark said that Seda was bewildered by her preference because the technique had been so different from what I had once enjoyed. Whoa! I thought. Back up a minute! It felt as if a tower of blocks had fallen unexpectedly inside of me. The effect was not devastating, just confusing and uncomfortable. I felt as though my husband had come back from the dead, spoken through Seda, and was now being quoted by Seda's girlfriend! I shook my head to dislodge the image. "Wait!" I told her. "That's too much. It feels weird, what you just said, because it's from my former husband, and I don't know what to make of it!" I wrinkled my nose.

I must have looked peaked because Lark's eyes widened and she took a step back. "Oh, okay! Sure. I get that," she said. Then I laughed. It was a strange situation, because I enjoy talking about sex and generally wish people did it more. Think of what we could learn from one another! But this business was another thing entirely. I felt like there was a ghost in the room, but maybe only half a ghost. That made it twice as eerie.

Over the course of the next few months, Seda explored lesbian sex and came to two conclusions: First, she was not really all that interested in sex. Second, she was probably a heterosexual female. And so we arrived at a new destination: Seda wanted a male lover—but not one with too big of a libido!

Seda and Lark continued seeing each other as Seda sorted this out. There are advantages to being polyamorous. One does not have the same sense of urgency in defining and imagining the future of a relationship. A union can unfurl and close at a leisurely pace, like a moonflower opening sweetly each twilight until it naturally fades on the stem.

For Seda's part, this was a slow and arduous process of self-discovery. It's hard to know exactly what you desire in a romantic partner when the siren song of hormones has fallen quietly behind you. I wonder if Seda really did want a man. As I write this, she hasn't had one yet. And as the years pass, she is less and less certain, wondering if she has become somewhat asexual. Perhaps menopause came fast on the heels of her second puberty! The idea of romance appeals to her, but Seda's sex drive is much diminished. I wonder if that is largely due to not having met the right person yet; time will tell.

When Seda and Lark were dating, I relished the opportunity to be a sounding board for Seda the way she had been for me. Across years, Seda had listened patiently without judgment as I waded through my first forays with men. Finally, it was my turn to watch Seda navigate the business of being a lover. We see the world anew with a love in our lives, our imaginations renovated with an additional room that we do not tire of sitting in for some time. Lark's celebrations and challenges became Seda's during those first two months as they spent more and more time together. Our children enjoyed Lark's enthusiasm for soccer as well as her vitality and playful banter. As our family expanded, its tapestry grew even more rich in color and depth.

Lark and Leena also welcomed Ben into their home. He tuned then played their piano during a Thanksgiving feast that they hosted, and their friendship has since endured. Our family became more unconventional by the day, but it seemed like a safe and cozy way to raise children, nonetheless, and that was my acid test beyond all else.

Our boys appeared to be very well-adjusted for their ages and excelled academically, socially, and in sports. I have had no reason to question their assessment that the transition was and is "no big deal" in their lives. People are always shocked to hear that the boys took the news of Seda's transition so easily.

"What do they tell their friends who ask about it?" people wonder.

This is something I ask the boys periodically, and their answers have always been the same. "Well, if they're asking specifically about that, we tell the truth. Otherwise, we generally don't talk about Maddy, because we've learned that people don't get it and want to know who she is. We call her our other mom, or if we're around people we won't ever see again, we sometimes call her our dad because what she is to us is never the thing we're actually trying to talk about anyway. So explaining what she is just gets in the way."

When the boys gave more detail to new friends who planned to visit our home, the friends usually just nodded, whether it made sense to them or not, but when our visitors met Seda, they liked her at once and any confusion melted away. When the boys were younger, we had girls from the neighborhood over quite a bit, and they had questions about the logistics of swapping sexual organs. I answered their questions as directly and succinctly as I could and always waited for phone calls from their parents, but they never came.

"The worst time," said Trinidad, "was when some adult in school asked me about it and how I felt and all, and I told them it was fine. They told me that they knew it was really not fine, and they wanted me to know that they were there if I wanted to talk about it. That was SO annoying," he said. "What makes people think they can just tell me how I feel? And it's not even true!"

When the boys had friends over, the friends were introduced to Ben as my boyfriend. Trin and Sam apparently didn't get much heat over that, maybe because Ben was willing to play "knock down" with a whole crew of them at once on our queen-size bed. This looked like general mayhem with Ben grabbing and tossing kids down on the mattress, or he would hold one sideways as a bat and knock down another as the ball. The kids in our household seemed to be much more interested in what adults did with them than they were in the adults' gender presentations. Of course, we knew that the boys' perspectives could change around puberty, but Seda and I had agreed that she should transition early in the boys' lives to avoid any confusion and anger that might arise when they were older and exploring their own gender identities. I am still grateful that we made that choice.

People sometimes wonder whether the kids have been bullied because of our unique family structure, and the answer is no. That is in part because we live in a liberal part of Oregon, and they were enrolled in an alternative elementary school from the beginning. They have since attended mainstream public middle and high schools and still have had no problems. I believe their safety and peace is largely due to the fact that no one in our family believes in bullies. We see every behavior as an attempt to meet a need, and we do our best to live in a paradigm of abundance and love rather than scarcity and fear. Seda and I made every effort to expect the best of people during her transition, and the children followed our lead and have encountered no anger, violence, or even teasing about the matter.

On the other hand, both of our boys regularly come home from school concerned about the emphasis placed on the anti-bullying campaign and the numerous surveys they are asked to fill out that leave them little or no room to report NOT having been bullied. They see these efforts by administration as fear mongering intended to prove that adults care and are making an effort to do something important, superhero style.

Our kids think this campaign does more to pit youth against one another than to bring them together. When a child is tagged a bully, rarely does anyone feel moved to seek understanding for their behavior. Students and staff alike already see the "bully" as other and it's hard for them to make amends for their actions. Instead, they are more likely to repeat maladaptive behaviors out of frustration, isolation, and chronically having their needs unmet. No one wants to be friends with a bully. And the behaviors considered to be bullying, according to the surveys, can include not wanting to play with someone or simply using the word "lame." By these standards, most kids are and have been bullied, so the miniature war on terror reigns.

The cultural climate at school is one of anxiety (which my kids tend to poke fun at with their friends) as teachers and administration attempt to search out and punish name-calling instead of placing their focus on compassionate communication and safety. Research has consistently shown that we must ask for the behavior we want rather than focusing on what we don't want, but the temptation to try to eradicate the behavior by overpowering it is too great. The campaign looks dramatic, and adults are more likely to feel important and powerful when they are policing people younger than themselves.

The anti-bully campaign is both misguided and often misinformed. Recently, Trinidad noted at the bottom of one such climate survey that the multiple choice question asking students to identify their sexual orientation as heterosexual (straight), homosexual (gay), bisexual, or transgender was in fact poorly written. "Transgender is *not* a sexual orientation," he informed them. And he would know.

I am proud that my kids have grown up feeling the empowerment of compassion and positive thinking. The opportunity to embrace this paradigm is one of the gifts that our situation has offered them, and another case in point that it's not what life gives you but how you use it that matters most.

Sharing the Load

"I GOT A new student—the one we met in the cafe last week," said Ben.

"That's great!" I said. "Did he just call you today?"

"Yeah. I scheduled him for lessons on Tuesday nights at seven."

"Tuesday? But that's one of our dinner-together nights," I said.

"I know. I was going to talk to you about that," said Ben. "I just didn't see a way around it. It's the only evening he's available."

"Couldn't you schedule him for a daytime? Or for earlier in the evening?" I asked. Seda didn't get off work until seven.

"No, there's just no way," said Ben.

"Work is love made visible," wrote Kahlil Gibran, and I knew that I wanted to work beside Ben. I wanted to make music together, sew a patch on some pants while he paid the bills, or weed the garden side by side. We struggled to find windows of time in which we could meet this way.

I sometimes worked in Ben's garden alone, but when we were together, we had different ways of weeding, watering, planting, and harvesting. As we tried to find common ground, frustration and a need to be heard cropped up as major themes in our relationship. Hours spent working out our conflicts—whole days at a time—exhausted me, and we split up, but only for a day or two before realizing how much we missed one another. Were we addicted to each other or actually in love?

I changed Ben's ring tone to Piano Riff after our first split. The heavy, dark pounding of keys reflected the irritation that our relationship was often burdened with, though the melody still held that promise of the blues and a cathartic passage to heaven through suffering. Ben and I usually did connect more deeply after being at odds with one another. The homecoming tears, both humble and passionate, washed away what was broken in the storm, and we found peace for a month or two before discontent gathered like a dark cloud once more.

I was fairly certain that I was a happy person by nature, yet this time I'd spent with Ben had been riddled with trouble. Observing Ben's behavior, my attempt at non-judgment was put to the test. Why did I value his help cleaning up over the making of music? Did I secretly see him as lazy? These were perspectives that I thought required my attention, for the anguish they caused me was based on my own valuation.

Still, the reality remained that I was hard-pressed to complete my basic domestic duties and still have the energy and time left to enjoy all of the people that I loved. I longed to manage our household free from a sense of bitterness and imbalance. The kids swept the floors and folded clothes while Seda pitched in by caring for chickens and rabbits. Ben's contribution of washing dinner plates and silverware and playing music a few times a week still did not seem to be a fair trade for what we offered him.

"Will it ever be enough?" he asked me, repeatedly. The question intimated that my thirst for his participation was insatiable, and yet he hated it when I measured, stating my observations of what we each gave to the partnership. I struggled to maintain a sense of generosity and goodwill while delivering the message that he wasn't carrying his share of the load. I had no desire to be in a management position on this; the household was *our* project, not mine. Every one of us who spent time there had a responsibility to contribute, and we also shared an obligation to notify others if they were remiss.

I thought that Ben's response to my request for domestic help was a stereotypical male response due to our culture's predisposition to heap housework on the women of the family. I did not blame him, per se, for being a domestic minimalist. I just felt irritated with myself that I cooked and cleaned to create a home for him that exceeded his expectations. I did not like to expend effort unnecessarily. Looking more deeply at my discontent, I knew that I also wanted a better role model for my boys. Though I could understand Ben's desire to dodge housework—he'd been raised without having to lift a finger, according to his own account—I did not want to accept it, or rather accept the burden it left me with.

One spring some years before, the boys, Seda, and I completed a ropes challenge course together and the experience left me with a felt sense of what it meant to share the load. Standing squarely on the forest floor, I belayed my sons and several other climbers as they made their way up old growth fir trees to platforms and rope bridges that stretched from trunk to trunk. I grasped the rope that secured one climber at a time with the help of the team beside me—an Asian gentleman and his teenage daughter. As the climbers ascended, I watched carefully and slid the extra rope through my hands, holding my part with just enough tension to feel the climber at the end. I took up the slack steadily as they climbed, prepared to hold if they faltered or dropped.

The man beside me and his daughter were tasked with exactly the same work, but they didn't seem to understand that. They laughed and talked in a language I couldn't comprehend, holding the rope loosely or letting one hand go as they gesticulated and focused on each other or the surrounding trees. I reminded them that they had to hold the rope like I did and pointed at the boy we were responsible for up high. They followed my point and nodded, smiling, taking up the rope with two hands for a few minutes before they again let it go slack, leaving me with the full weight of the climber.

An instructor walked over and stood before me in a hard hat and heavy duck canvas coat. "You have to share the load," he told me, nodding his head to my teammates.

"I'm trying," I said, plaintively.

"You have to do it better," he said and walked away.

I pressed my lips together and turned to them. "Look," I explained, "you have to keep the rope taut. There's supposed to be no loop or relaxation in the line. You have to hold it like this." I lifted my hands for them to see. The man and his daughter nodded and smiled. They raised their hands to me, holding the rope as I did. I sighed with relief then returned my gaze to the climber.

The man and his daughter began to laugh and talk again as the rope slackened between their hands. I held my end of the line while I considered my next move. How could I get these people to understand the importance of our job?

"You have to share the load!" barked the instructor, suddenly beside me again. I jumped.

"I'm really trying!" I said. "They forget! I can't keep them on it."

"Look up there!" he said, pointing to the father that we now belayed. "That guy weighs almost two hundred pounds. Are you going to catch him all by yourself if he falls? You strong enough for that? This is a matter of life or death. *Share the load*," he said.

"Okay! I get it. But how?"

"This is your learning for the day," he said. "You figure it out. Just make it happen!"

Good grief, I thought. But there was no time for thinking. I pointed out the discrepancy to my belay partners again and again to keep them on point. We had a guy up there I couldn't hold alone, and if he fell the onus was on me—not me alone, but still on me, no matter how much I'd tried. Fortunately, the man and his daughter decided that they wanted to do something else. They left my team and were replaced with more attentive help. The lesson did not escape me: don't stop asking for people to take responsibility for themselves. If they refuse to step up to the plate, they will likely choose to leave.

Would that be my path with Ben, too? Would I have to find the courage to ask him time and again to take responsibility for his share of the work and accept that if he chose not to, the fit was just not a good one? I realized that the lifestyles we each preferred required different workloads, and our willingness to take up the slack for exactly as much as we wanted in life might lead us in two very different directions, neither wrong nor shameful. I garnered some acceptance for this inevitability and changed his ring tone to Time Passing, which sounded like a time bomb ticking fast in soprano.

Letting Go

IN THE AUTUMN of 2010, my mom rang me just after I dropped off the boys at school. I parked my bike next to the playground and answered her call.

"Hi, honey," she said.

"Hi, Mom." I could tell from the sound of her voice that something was wrong.

"I have some bad news," she told me.

"Okay," I said, unbuckling my helmet and sliding it off my head while I leaned back against the tetherball pole.

"I had some pain in my abdomen, and it turned out to be a tumor. It's a big one. They did a biopsy, and it was cancerous. I'm not sure exactly how bad this is, but it's not good. I've got ovarian cancer."

I stared at the seagulls that wheeled and landed on the blacktop. I nodded, tears welling in my eyes.

"Wow, Mom. That's big news. I'm so sorry. Does it hurt?"

"It does, Kris. But they're going to start me on chemo soon so they can shrink the tumor before they operate. I just want you to know that I love you so much. No matter what happens."

A light emerged in the darkness when I heard her words. I felt so incredibly grateful to be close to my mother. I felt in awe to witness how secure our attachment had grown over the past several years as Seda had transitioned. NVC had transformed my relationship with her just as it had kept my heart open to my former husband when she became a woman. In that moment, on the side of the playground, I felt wonder, hope, and love for my mother and the world. I felt like my heart had been broken open yet again, and this time there was little or no fear in the cracking.

"Mom, I love you," I said. "I love you so much, and no matter what happens, I will always be with you. Nothing can change that or break it. I'm so sorry for any pain you're in, but the cancer—whatever comes of it—can't threaten my relationship with you. And I'm so grateful for that." I squatted with my back against the tetherball pole, tears streaming down my face as I smiled.

"I feel that way, too," said my mother quietly. "We've been through some tough shit together. But we're in a good place, Kris. I'm so happy to see that you and Seda are raising the boys like you are. And I'm glad you're happy with Ben. I'm so proud of you, honey."

In that moment of crisis, I found myself calm and deeply joyful in a way I had not experienced for some time. Like an eclipse to that brightness, I had concerns for my mother's comfort and physical outcome. This could be another major, life-changing transition, after all. And yet, I felt largely unafraid, even liberated from fear. Perhaps I was finally learning to accept circumstances outside of my control. I rode my bicycle home feeling something like elation in love untethered.

I brought the boys down for a family Christmas with my mom, her husband, and my sister. My mother sat in her chair in the living room, wrapped in a beautiful quilt that her dear friend Trudy had made. My sister crafted her signature smoothies for Mom and roasted a prime rib for our dinner. Mom beamed from ear to ear as her grandchildren unwrapped and played with the Lego sets she'd picked out online. "I wish Seda could have been here," she said.

"I know. Me, too," I told her, but Seda had stretched to take time off so I could be with Mom in October. She had little leeway left to ask for more.

"You guys have something really special, Kris, and I'm glad you appreciate it."

I smiled. "I do," I said. "It hasn't been easy. But I do my best."

"I know you do," she said. "And you're such a good mom. But Kris, you think too much. Do you ever just stop for a while? Just try not to think?" I leaned my head against her knee, and my tears began to fall.

"Give it a try, honey," she said, stroking my hair. "Give it a try, huh?" I could hear her smiling.

I felt strangely uplifted at Mom's passing less than a week later and grateful that she was no longer in pain. We had found peace in our relationship and much healing together. I was surprised to find that I could let go so easily, but I felt Mom to be more present with me after her passing than when she was alive. This was a surprising celebration and significantly shifted my experience of loss.

Seda and Ben brought the boys down for Mom's celebration of life. Ben played piano, but perhaps even more sweet to me in those weeks was the tracks he'd made of her voice with mine only one year before the cancer. We had recorded a song I'd written called "Lullaby for the Mothers." Mom and I had been very nervous about singing and being recorded for the first time ever, and our vocals have a quality of tentative innocence, a joint venture in vulnerability. That recording is a gift that I will always cherish.

Winter passed slowly and tearfully for me. Ben spiraled into depression, ostensibly because he was not able to teach full time, and I had little left in me to offer as support. I felt the weight of my mother's passing daily, sometimes hourly, but it felt more like a train moving through me than it did like genuine sadness. Every morning, I woke with a great heaviness in my body. It took a few seconds to recall in my mind the origin of that sensation. The feeling struck me not so much as grief but rather a sense of inner metamorphosis.

I was transitioning into a new way of being alone, mother-less in the world. The history of my birth, childhood, and young adulthood had been stored in our two bodies, and now half of us had moved on. I felt exhausted adjusting to the physical reality even as a stronger spiritual connection between my mother and I grew in her body's absence. This transformation took a tre-mendous effort to assimilate. I felt weary and tender most of the time.

Michelle had heard from a friend that my mother had passed and called to offer her condolences. We hadn't seen each other in years. "I'm sorry I couldn't be there for you, Kristin," she said. A wave of sadness rushed over me at this admittance to what our current relationship was not. I told her that I needed to get off the phone.

I emailed Michelle later that day and begged to be excused for asking to go so suddenly. I told her that I grieved having lost our friendship over Seda's transition. "I am just having a hard time right now," I wrote. "It's breaking my heart that this beautiful person that I parent with doesn't fit into the world you want your children to see. What a loss. For all of us." I didn't know how to connect with her anymore.

Michelle didn't respond. Had I been hasty and impatient, or had I just come to see things from Seda's perspective? Regard-less of what led me to respond that way, the relationship dis-appeared from my radar, and I suffered no more inner conflict around it. Continued practice in letting go.

Remarkably, Ben and I found our peace together that spring working in his garden. I finally realized that while Ben wanted to plant everything, he was really only willing to do minimal care thereafter, so brassicas and tomatoes were most suitable for his space. I learned by watching his garden go dry over and over that kales and collards are quite tolerant of drought, and I employed this strategy in my own plot to great effect. Then, I willingly prepared garden beds at Ben's place for just the plants that would thrive, and I put these in close to the first rainfall of autumn so that the starts required minimal watering from him. Ben was free to plant whatever else he wanted and to care for it accordingly, but I would not participate in that.

After some time, Ben admitted that brassicas were indeed the best fit. Thereafter, we watered and weeded peacefully together, and one chapter of our conflict finally appeared to be at a close. I had learned a vital lesson: words do not always speak our truths, but listening and responding can extend beyond words, even in adult relationships. Transparency and expression are not always to be trusted at face value because people are not always honest with themselves. You would think I'd have learned that from Seda, but life is full of second chances. I changed Ben's ring tone to Xylophone, a tentative, slightly anxious strain that sounded like falling downhill and hoping for the best.

In July, after I returned from staffing an NVC Family Camp on Vashon Island with the boys, Ben told me that he'd applied for a job in Key West, Florida. They had called him for an interview. What was I to say? "It sounds like you're excited about it," I ventured. "And you don't see any other avenue for employment, right?"

"Yeah! I'll have my own classroom, and I'll be on an island again. I can sail! And if everything works out well, I'll send for you and the boys, just like my grandfather did when he came to America."

"Key West sounds like an adult playground, though," I said.

"Well, that's true, but we don't know yet. I went online, and it's beautiful. It's just a coral bump in the sea."

"Not so great for gardening," I said. "But who knows. I guess we'll find out. I'm glad you're living your dream." I put on my Brave Little Toaster smile.

"Thank you for understanding, honey," said Ben. "I wish I could find the work here, but it's not happening. I've put in over eighteen applications in the past year and haven't gotten a single interview. Now I've finally found a school in a beautiful place with an eco-friendly curriculum, and they're actually excited about what I have to offer!"

"I get it," I said. "We'll figure it out. You do what you have to do."

I went home and cried. Ben found a furnished studio apartment on the island and planned his move within the month. We decided we would leave our relationship's closure inconclusive, attempting kindness to us both.

On the night before we parted, Ben set the table for dinner. Vegetables sizzled in the wok and rice simmered on the stovetop as he placed glasses, forks, and napkins at each person's seat.

Trinidad walked into the kitchen. "That's not my glass," he said. Each of us used our own distinctive glass for water every night.

"Oh. It's not?" asked Ben.

"No," said Trin. "And that's not Sam's either." Ben removed the glass from Sam's place and held it aloft.

"That one's Maddy's," said Trin, pointing. Ben set it at Seda's place.

"And this one's mine," he said, taking the glass from Ben's hand and setting it down while suppressing a giggle.

"What's that about?" asked Ben, gruffly.

"Well, it's just that you've been eating with us for years now, and you still don't know which glasses are whose," Trin said. "I don't really get it."

Ben bristled beside me, and I ran my hand gently over his hair then stroked his back, smiling faintly. I'm sure we were all thinking the same thing: we shouldn't have to suffer this much longer.

No Answer

BEN WAS IN Key West for a month before we realized that we weren't through. I suggested that he fly me out for my birthday in October, and he generously did so using his bonus miles. We spent ten days in a suspended honeymoon playing by the sea, spying on manatees, and eating conch fritters. I opened my eyes to the beauty of the island and discovered that there was much there to feed the soul of a child.

Perhaps the boys and I would join Ben after all! I had always wondered if it would be easier to share the load with Ben if we lived full-time under one roof, sharing primary responsibilities between only two adults. This could be our chance to find out. He and I had agreed that we would not discuss the possibility until after my stay was over. He wanted me to just focus on the present and take in what the island had to offer. Ben had a gentle way of bringing me back when I got a little ahead of myself, and I appreciated his invitation to live in the moment.

Our Key West experience left me open and peaceful despite the many unknown variables in my world. On the plane ride home, I talked with my friend Beth and we agreed that extreme pain is likely only spawned by our resistance to change, confusion, ambivalence, and grief. If we could allow these feelings to simply exist rather than always seeking the answers to where they are or are not leading us, then perhaps our lives would be amazing meditations of love. But such difficult feelings obscure our self-connection and identities; without those in place, we have nothing to set anchor to, and adrift, we are often fearful. I guess that sitting quietly with oneself is considered a practice for a reason.

I continued exploring the dichotomy of resistance and surrender in my journal, seeking to understand how uncertainty, transition, and letting go could possibly happen with grace. I poured out my thoughts, unfiltered, then translated them into feelings and needs, getting to the heart of the matter. Sometimes, unexpected angel messages issued forth on the page:

Let it fall . . .
apart
together
into place

Other times, my explorations were heady and philosophical in bent.

I wrote about the birth of my son, Sam. What was my state of mind like then? I remembered challenging myself to welcome and relax into every contraction. I also managed to keep a portion of my mind and heart open and available to myself and others periodically throughout the labor. The result of mastering the moment in this way, integrating my intense psychological and physiological journey with outside circumstances, was exceptionally powerful. I will never forget it.

But there is a difference, I wrote. One expects that the stretching and opening sensation felt in labor's transition will yield a baby. Such a welcome outcome I could easily celebrate and anticipate with each breath under duress. Death was another thing entirely, or at least it seemed to be. How could I stretch my paradigm to accept, even welcome death in its many forms—the death of a loved one, an era, a relationship, a career?

We try to heal ourselves and our relationships, rather than let them go. So, is it even possible to sit with such pain without trying to fix or change it? Not unless we can embrace the letting go as an accomplishment in itself, and that's hard to do without a deep knowing that it's for the best.

Do the trees hold onto their leaves as long as possible in the autumn? Perhaps. There is a culmination of outside factors that dictate timing, but the leaves will always fall in the end, and the trees know this. It is in their sap, having weathered seasons of releasing, generations of acceptance. The germ of this understanding lies dormant in their seeds, marking the beginnings and endings of trees. It's all a matter of seasons passing with seeming infinitude. So, more than anything, our peace and acceptance in transition—and this includes our attachment and devotion—is determined by a deeper spiritual sense of trust, a sense of rightness in letting go.

If that is so, we can rely on no compass made by human hands in such transitions. No amount of prior knowledge or experience can adequately guide us to a place we've never been. The Ambassador of Death who walked people across such divides in my early-transition dream did not exist. If we can envision only one thing, let it be this: we are limited because we only see from where we are. So much of our perception of transition is seated in our lens and our attachments. Where we most need to spend time in transition is deep in our gut while daily we practice letting go.

The stories we take in empower or betray us on our way. They are the outer experiences that shape our inner experiences. The story of an Amish woman birthing quickly after scrubbing her floor and sanding the rocking chair carried me above discomfort during Sam's labor. Can-do stories support can-do lives, opening us to see more possibilities, fostering curiosity, interest, focus, and an intention of connection and healthy being for all. Humility is not only gratitude and selfless consciousness, but also an utter willingness to accept guidance—even if just from our gut. It's hard to know when to let go by *thinking* in the moment. Relief and relaxation come only when we allow spirit to guide us through the storm. Letting go lies in the seed of us all and will be realized *in its time*. Why did I so often forget?

I would end my journaling session with such a question, then fold the black cover shut to ponder for some minutes, holding the book reverently as if it were a passport to another dimension. Strangely, all of my discoveries seemed to be things I already knew, though I had been unable to integrate and use them to change my behavior before. Most of these discoveries hinged on the interplay of my inner and outer experiences while searching for the key to a portal inward where I could hear the guidance of my own intuition and use it to connect gracefully with those around me. From this place, I could effortlessly see the sacred in myself and others and proceed with some measure of joy no matter the circumstances.

A week after I got home, I tried to connect with Ben and had trouble catching him. I began to worry. My visions of rejoining him in Key West were suddenly shaken before I got a chance to explore them with him. The night before we finally reached one another, I dreamt of Ben, a rare occurrence.

In my dream, I looked out from beneath a small covered area—a square shelter mounted on four sticks, and I saw dark storm clouds gathering. Ben was there beside me. I showed him the clouds and told him we had to stay under cover. He looked right where I was pointing and said, "I don't see them. I don't see the problem."

Then, after the clouds grew even more ominous and pressed inward upon us, he took my hand and turned me around to look in the other direction from beneath our square shelter. "You see?" he asked, pointing up. What appeared to be a storm on one side of our cover looked like patchy clouds on the other. I felt befuddled.

I shared this dream with my friend Beth. When I described the covering, she said, "Oh it's a Chuppah! The Jewish bridal tent. I know it well." I had not seen it in that way, and the image only added to my confusion. Why would Ben reassure me under a bridal tent when the storm suggested that all was about to fall apart? I wondered if the dream was a conversation between his soul and mine across time and space, and I had trouble letting it go.

I received an email from Ben the next day telling me that the housing option that we'd hoped would be available to us if I brought the boys had not panned out, and he didn't think that we could make it work. Out of consideration for us both, he felt it best to end our relationship on a sweet note so no one was left hanging if the school renewed his contract at the end of the year and he decided to stay. We talked on the phone briefly, and it sounded like his mind was made up. No words from me could move him. In fact, he apologetically refrained from listening or speaking from the heart at all.

Over the next two months, I struggled to focus on every bit of work before me. I had taken a part-time job in my former field of teaching children diagnosed with autism, so I now worked in the classroom, too. I managed to juggle family and outside employment well enough, but I still felt sad. To make matters worse, Ben called or emailed me every few weeks. Our new on and off relationship, that he refused to admit to, did not compare with the love we had once shared. After a deeply intimate conversation with him just before Christmas, I received no call on the day itself (the first Christmas after the passing of my mother). I was furious and cut him off completely.

"Don't call or email me unless it's absolutely urgent," I told him. And this time, he got it. I changed Ben's ring tone to Alarm, a loud, monotonous, raspy bark that reminded me of a fire drill or an air raid warning. I wanted to remember the pain and not the kindnesses the next time he called.

I had made myself so miserable being officially out of relationship, that I decided I must be ready for a new one. This was more likely a step toward numbness rather than actual healing or wisdom. Early the following year, I met and quickly fell in love with my new piano tuner. Imagine that. He was much older than me but had a son about Trinidad's age. He understood the life rhythms of parenting and was so reasonable that it brought me to tears, quickly healing the wounds accumulated by Ben's short fuse. I was ecstatic and blissfully engaged with everyone around me. I blogged about the power of falling in love because that was my reality, and I was accustomed to writing about what was true for me in the moment.

Somehow, I did not anticipate what would happen next. Perhaps I was naïve, or maybe my subconscious mind had plotted it all along. The Alarm sounded. I had been napping, and I jumped up in a fog. I stood over my bed trying to place what it was I should be alarmed about. Right! It was Ben calling. I sat down with a thud. "No, Ben," I said aloud. "I am *not* answering."

But I did check the message a minute later. "Kristin," he said. "Kristin. I know you told me not to call unless it was urgent. This is urgent. Marry me. I can't do this without you. I don't want to. You were right! We can work it out. We'll find a way . . . " the call cut off. He phoned again, and I did not answer. In the second message, I heard his name being called over the intercom at school as he muttered and hung up. I shook my head in disbelief.

Housewife, I thought. Through fire and flood, feast and famine, I would never find *boring* in the job description. Or maybe that was just my way of working the job.

Part Six

Moving East to West

THE BOYS AND I descended the steps of the puddle jumper into a wave of humid Key West heat on February 29, 2012. What a leap! The glassy-blue gulf gleamed in the midday sun, and Trinidad stood on his toes to see if he could catch a glimpse of it from the airplane steps as we deplaned. Ben would be teaching today, so we hailed a cab to take us to the tiny apartment that we would now call home.

Ben and I had agreed that continuing his lease was the best option. His apartment, one of three in a divided old Key West residence, was in an excellent neighborhood in Midtown between the convenient shopping options of New Town and the bungalow charm of Old Town. Key West has a land area of about seven square miles, so it would be easy to get around by bicycle, as was our custom. Ben had already procured a bike for each of us according to my specifications, and he told me they stood ready and waiting in the side yard.

It had not been easy to leave Eugene, and the course was far from my intentions when Ben's call sounded the alarm that afternoon in late January. I had declined his on-the-spot proposal and asked him to leave me alone. He accepted my refusal, and then asked if we could just process the end of our relationship together for closure so that both of us could heal and move on.

I agreed to this and found him to be remarkably full of empathy for all of my grief around our parting. He did not resist

in fear but dove in wholeheartedly to listen and better understand my experience and the confusion that had transpired
between us. I was in awe to see him so open and dedicated to
loving unconditionally. In the end, my anger faded completely,
and all I was left with was the sense that I was still quite in love
with Ben and needed to follow that path through to its natural
end before attempting a relationship with anyone else. My new
piano tuner was appalled but understanding. After proposing
that he too would happily marry me (even though I was techni-
cally still married), he kindly agreed to let me go.

Seda was supportive of my move with the children. We had
homeschooled the boys since fall, in part because I wanted to
remain flexible around the possibility of moving to Key West.
We both saw what an adventure and learning experience it could
be for them to live on an island in the southeast corner of the
U.S. Seda had recently enrolled in grad school at the University
of Oregon and spent most of her time studying. She imagined
that a three-month family sabbatical could help her get ahead
academically. She also saw that the opportunity provided a way
for Ben and me to finally determine if our partnership would be
long-term.

Seda had read the lengthy emails flying back and forth
between us for the past few weeks, and her thoughts concurred
with my own. "Well, he's doing everything right," she said. I
gave Ben back his original ring tone, the Blues, and wholeheartedly threw myself into making it work—our first ever shared
home and family experience.

The pink taxi pulled up to the front of our new house, and
we dragged our few pieces of luggage down the wood-chip path
between arching green palms and flowering red hibiscus to a tall
wooden gate. I reached over the top, took a spare key from the
rail, and opened the gate into the side yard that would become
our living room. Tiny lizards scampered in all directions upon
our arrival, and Trinidad was on his knees at once in pursuit. A
brick patio across from our front door held a bench, some potted

ferns, and a round glass table under a cheerful green umbrella. I looked around me and smiled then turned the key that let us into the house through the old, purple front door.

The children burst into our apartment, turning their heads in all directions. The size of the place did not daunt them; we were accustomed to small. Still, at about three hundred square feet, our new apartment would likely hold a record for the most humble dwelling my boys would call home. Two single mattresses wedged together filled the entire floor space of the tiny living room under a wooden ceiling fan. A three-foot wide footpath to the kitchen cut between the ends of the beds and Ben's keyboard set up in an alcove two feet deep across the way. A two-burner stovetop/refrigerator/sink combination stood beside a cutting board set on top of a baker's rack with two shelves. The cutting board's foot and a half square horizontal surface would form my only prized countertop. A narrow, walk-in pantry could be found just behind the kitchen. It was the only room in the house with a door and the perfect place for rainy day phone calls or to catch a few minutes' privacy.

Our bedroom could be entered through a doorway between the kitchen and living room. At my request, Ben had crafted a hinge-less, hatch style, make-shift door out of a rectangular piece of wood panel siding attached to a slightly smaller chunk of Styrofoam. When one slid, or rather wedged, it into the door frame, the door formed an effective barrier for sight and sound. Our bedroom was the most spacious room in the house. We had a closet, wicker loveseat, and bistro table with two tall chairs in addition to our comfortable double bed. The air conditioner had been thoughtfully mounted into the window of this room, and the boys and I would spend most of our indoor time there. After touring our new home, the boys and I stepped back out into the yard.

Our landlady came around from her side of the house to welcome us to Key West. The quintessential Key Wester, Lynn looked to be in her sixties, though her chronological age could have fallen a decade on either side. She wore heavy makeup, fitted jeans, and a pastel T-shirt with fringed edges that she later explained was her own design, for sale in a boutique she worked at downtown. Lynn called a friendly hello to us and reached out to hug me, bangle bracelets clinking.

We stood on the patio with our luggage as she waved her long, tan arms to indicate the shared laundry and which parts of the yard were private to each of the three parties living in her subdivided bungalow. We occupied the downstairs back half. Her long, bleached blonde hair shone flaxen in the sun and she beamed at the boys, clearly delighted to delve into this experiment with us. I hoped her enthusiasm would last. The boys had never lived in an apartment or shared a yard before. I prayed that we could manage the sound restrictions and not break the house too badly.

The gate flew open with a bang as Ben, bright eyes shining, wheeled his bike through with one hand. He did not take off his helmet before he caught me up in one arm. "Excuse me!" he said to our landlady and enfolded me into a long, hard kiss. Then, at arm's length, he looked me over. "My God. You've gotten skinny," he said. "We can fix that." Ben squeezed me again and kissed my forehead.

"Hi, guys!" he cried, turning his attention to the boys. Sam and Trinidad gave Ben a big hug, and he wrapped one arm around them both while holding me with the other.

I had no doubt that I'd chosen correctly. Though I loved the piano tuner, I had missed Ben's way of knowing me deeply, intimately, and with full acceptance for all of my animal ways. His eyes, touch, and gentle words in the dark always knew how to find my softest places.

When I'd realized that I needed to follow through with this relationship, I had told Ben that I could only see one way to do it. If he was proposing marriage, then I thought we should try to make it work together with the resources he had in Key West. A long distance relationship would not be enough to rebuild from the conflict we'd had in the two months prior. There was no knowing what would happen with Ben's work the following year, but a three-month trial period at the end of this school year would tell us all whether we had what it took as a foursome to sign up for any commitment beyond that. He agreed.

I appreciated that Ben wanted me to continue my method of schooling the boys (allowing them to learn by following their interests) on Key West rather than looking for work in the three-month period of our stay. He said it just didn't make sense to do otherwise. If we signed on for another year, that would be different. I felt excited about the opportunity to explore my romantic relationship with Ben while also providing a unique educational opportunity for the boys. Key West had great potential after all! I intended to actively volunteer with the kids as a means of contributing on behalf of our family during our stay.

Frankly, I was dubious about whether we could all manage to live under the same roof; we had never done it full time before. The small footprint of our Key West apartment upped the ante, but Ben and I had always talked about the possibility of living on a sailboat together with the kids. Working around each other in our cracker box apartment on dry land would be a decent test to determine whether such a venture would be wise. Ben too was trepidatious about how it would work, but he was willing to move us here and could support us comfortably on his salary without dipping into savings.

Seda, unfortunately, would not be able to contribute financially because the loss of my income meant that she had to cover the house payment on her wages alone, which would be barely enough. No one we knew was looking for housing at the time, and we wondered whether it would be safe to choose someone unknown to rent my room given that she was preoperative trans, and there was a fair amount of trans-phobia out there. The risk is not always where one expects it to be, and even if she felt safe with the person she invited to live with her, what about their friends and family that could drop by at any time?

The five of us were able to support this endeavor as a family unit in the way Seda and I had always worked together: sharing resources. Each person contributed what they most easily could to receive what they most desired. Ben was thrilled that I had joined him and seemed well aware that I was giving up my job and taking risks by uprooting myself and the boys. I felt seen in doing my part as homemaker, lover, and teacher, and I deeply appreciated his supporting us financially so we could give our relationship the best possible trial run. Seda was glad for time alone to study while the boys were delighted with the adventure of a lifetime. The move felt like a good one for us all.

Work and Play

MY JOB IN domestic management had some unique challenges on Key West. With one tiny refrigerator, later upgraded to two, we went to the grocery store at least every other day. Trinidad, Sam, and I loaded our backpacks and the bike trailer with bags of pasta, beans, and what vegetables and fruits we could get our hands on, and then we pedaled home from the store hoping we wouldn't lose a package of toilet paper or loaf of bread that had been precariously wedged into the stack. Once, we biked home with a load that was genuinely too big, and Trin offered his toy handcuffs to hang a bottle of water from my handlebars. That clever strategy lasted us about four blocks before a metal ring cracked and released, sending the bottle on a long skid to break open across a busy intersection. Everyday, life proved to be an adventure.

Happily, the rides home from the shopping center always included a stop at the saltwater pond behind the Winn Dixie. There, we watched long-nosed fish dart between Cassiopeia jellies, the slow dance of iridescent nudibranchs, and the prehistoric mating rituals of horseshoe crabs. My boys knelt by the waterside to watch the show, red and yellow rock crabs scuttling between them, and then went home to do further research. They drew their specimens in sketchbooks and described the habitats, diets, and behaviors of the animals they saw daily.

We noticed that the pond, connected by waterways to the Gulf of Mexico less than three city blocks away, was in need of help. Beer cans and bottles, pizza boxes, discarded clothing, and candy wrappers piled high at the edge of her waters. The boys and I borrowed shopping carts from the Winn Dixie and heaped close to a dozen of them with refuse we collected and bagged. This took us several trips, one or two mornings a week. The boys loved to snake their bodies through the mangroves and pass trash back by human chain to where I stood at the water's edge. They discovered scorpions, snakes, and land crabs in indigo, burnt orange, and gold while we worked side by side. Trin, Sam, and I were constantly astounded with the amount and variety of wildlife that we shared our island with.

I became the volunteer and social organizer for our family. As our weekly trash cleanup neared an end, I landed us a gig helping out at the Key West Wildlife Center. We were first given the familiar task of cleaning a massive chicken pen and watering trees and bushes as needed. Chickens are protected citizens in Key West, and the Wildlife Center controlled their overpopulation by taking in birds that were live-trapped by neighbors as a nuisance and sending them up to the Florida mainland to be used for pest-management on organic farms and orchards. It's an ironic turnaround when the pests become pest managers! By the end of our stint there, the boys had worked their way up to feeding the big birds—frigates and pelicans. We also got certified with Save-A-Turtle to walk Smather's Beach weekly at sunrise looking for turtle nests to cage and protect. I had always wished for fun and easy community service to engage in with my children, and I found that the community of Key West welcomed us with open arms.

Our family also mingled with a like-minded crowd, One Island Family, at the Unitarian Universalist Church. It was the first church that Ben and I had ever felt drawn to attend in our adult lives. We especially enjoyed their holiday potlucks and after-church playdates with new friends.

All of these activities kept us moving through the day, but I still managed to get supper on the table most of the time by five o'clock. Having only two small burners posed a challenge, and one burner proved to be barely functional. After a week, we bought a toaster oven, and that sped things up a bit. By the end of the first month, I had the dance down and usually only needed help if we were cooking for guests. On weekends, Ben would get us a couple of pizzas and we'd pile up on one of the double beds to watch old movies together or play cards.

Ben arrived home from work by 4:30 most days and played with the boys or chatted with me while I finished cooking. I'd never had a lover and parenting partner I got to see so frequently, and I couldn't get over how much fun that was! For most of our lives together, Seda had spent hours working daily on personal projects—her novel, political commentary, or trans-exploration—so we never had an after-work ritual beyond eating and doing the dishes together. Being new to Key West, I was especially grateful that Ben's only personal project was our family. His arrival home marked an oasis of much needed adult interaction for me, and watching him connect with the kids every afternoon nourished me deeply. Ben was ecstatically happy and generous that first month. We all gave and received with joy and ease, a graceful balance that reflected what we saw in the turquoise waters all around us.

On Wednesday nights, the boys and I packed a picnic dinner and loaded it into my bike basket so we could push off as soon as Ben got home and had changed his clothes. Together, we would bike through Midtown and Old Town to our favorite beach at Fort Zachary Taylor Historic State Park. I suggested that we buy an annual pass immediately, and it paid off within a month as we visited the beach at least twice a week during our stay. On Wednesday evenings, we lit a barbecue in the grove of palms just off the beach, then went to swim while the coals turned red and ashy.

The boys played water monster with Ben, a former lifeguard, who tossed them into the air so that they landed with a fantastic splash four feet away. Over and over they snuck up on him and each time he bobbed them down into the water and then hurled them skyward so they fell crashing into the sea. They shrieked and plotted to catch him by surprise as he floated with eyes closed, apparently relaxed and unaware. Between tosses, I sometimes glided to him through the warm, salty water so he could hold me in his arms and rock me gently while the boys swam impatiently in circles around us.

Later, as we ate veggie burgers with avocado and pickle, brushing the sand off of our salad forks, I wondered how a family structure so fluid and unconventional could work so joyfully. I always felt Seda with us in spirit, and I knew she was home immersed in her work and graduate studies, hopefully cocooned in welcome quiet during this season of separation. We all agreed that if Ben's job worked out in Key West long-term, and we decided to stay, Seda would join us there.

I did miss having her around to talk with at the end of the night. I knew I could email or call Seda anytime I wanted, but she was scheduled tightly between school and work. In addition, Seda had doubled her efforts in advocating for non-discrimination in respect to transpeople who needed health care under the City's insurance policy that currently excluded them. She had been working on the exclusion clause with the City for years and was now to the point of threatening a lawsuit. City management had been courteous but unwilling to acknowledge that their policy translated to active discrimination.

At the time, transgender City employees were not covered by insurance for the treatment of GD even though the treatments themselves were covered if required for different diagnoses. For example, a woman could be authorized for an operation to remove her breast if diagnosed with breast cancer or to receive hormone treatment after ovary removal. A female-to-male transperson would *not* be covered by insurance to receive either of those treatments even though the treatments have been deemed medically necessary for GD by the World Professional Association for Transgender Health (WPATH).[1] Although the medical necessity and cost effectiveness of treatment for GD had been well established, the City's self-insured group health plan retained an exclusion denying coverage for such procedures if they were related to gender dysphoria.

The stress of not being seen or considered in regards to basic human rights had begun to take its toll on Seda. In addition to the stress of attending school part-time while working full-time in parking enforcement, the relationship that Seda had with management at her job was now compromised, and bitterness filled her days. Six weeks before we returned to Oregon, she began suffering from panic attacks that emerged from intense gender dysphoria and an overload of stress. She never wished for us to return before the expected date, though she missed us terribly. She could see how the boys, Ben, and I were benefitting from our life on the island, and that thought gave her joy. She was also aware that she had little time for anything other than what she was already doing.

The anxiety attacks and concern about addiction to the medication she took to keep them at bay moved Seda to make a leap of faith and schedule her gender-confirmation surgery for July of 2013. She made her thousand-dollar deposit and wrote the date in ink on her calendar. We weren't sure how we would pay over $20,000 for the surgery if the City did not come through and remove the exclusion in time. I imagined we could hold fundraisers and sell homemade pies to friends and neighbors. There was no question about whether to do the surgery, only the mystery of how we would manage to afford it. Seda was in trouble, and the needed course of action was clear.

I kept tabs on Seda regularly but had a deep trust in my gut that this challenge was a precious part of her path. Seda and I had never shied from hardship, and I knew that the suffering she now endured would be a gift to many who followed in her footsteps. The discrimination she had run up against plagued transpeople across our nation, and Seda had a tremendous sense of urgency now to address it. Only the municipalities of San Francisco, Multnomah County, and Portland had thus far removed such exclusions, and lawsuits were in the works to address the issue elsewhere.

We were all so proud of Seda for her advocacy over the past years that she'd worked for the City. In 2009, she had received the City's Human Rights Award after serving on the Equity and Human Rights Board. Seda had designed and erected a beautiful display in our downtown atrium that pictured and described the life and work of many transpeople in order to educate and build awareness on the topic. The display is still being used annually during Trans Awareness Week in November. Seda and I both knew that she had huge contributions to make in this field. My work was humble by comparison, but each of us did our part as a family to give and receive in a world abundant with opportunities.

Magic at Sunset

TRINIDAD JUMPED INTO the adventure of Key West with both feet. My eldest son could not get enough of swimming in the sea, always testing himself to go farther and farther out past the reef. He loved the colorful fish, sharks, rays, and hermit crabs that hid deep in their whelk shells. He kicked his fins and snorkeled around rocky outcroppings for hours at a time, super-buoyant in the especially salty waters off Key West.

When we had finished swimming, and the park closed around sundown, we biked through Old Town to catch the Sunset Celebration where a group of artisans, performance artists, and craftspeople vended their products and talents. The boys were captivated by the fire-eating jugglers, silver-painted live statues, beds of nails, internationally acclaimed acrobats, and magicians.

Trinidad immediately spied the opportunity there. He had been cultivating his love of illusion since the age of five and had prior experience performing on the streets of Eugene. Trin returned to the plaza the next evening with his deck of cards and a hat for tips. The first lady who went by dropped him a ten-dollar bill. Trinidad was hooked. The kind administrators of the Sunset Celebration tried to give him a place every evening he came to put his number in the lottery. They liked Trin, and they respected and supported kids growing up in the performing arts. Two professional magicians also took up his cause and, before a week was up, Trin was given a little folding table and a shiny yellow rope that he used to keep crowds four feet from his performance area.

Such crowd control was quickly needed. Trinidad, the golden boy in butternut corduroy shorts and a goldenrod polo shirt, drew crowds of up to sixty people at a time. Children balanced on their parents' shoulders or squeezed their way up to the front to see his show. Trin had mastered the art of disappearing sponge balls and several card tricks that flabbergasted onlookers; they did not expect mastery of illusions from an eleven-year-old. Frat boys and retirees deep in their cups hooted and slapped their thighs, dropping ones and fives into his hat.

Trin made an average of $85 for three hour's work, and he divided this up between savings, charitable donations, reinvestment in the act, and spending money. This was a plan that Ben and I agreed with from the standpoint of business partners since his line of work required adult help in transport, set up, and safeguarding. Trinidad was very generous with his family in return and spent most of his pocket money on ice cream for us all at his favorite ice cream parlor, Matthesson's.

It wasn't long before Sam wanted to get in on the act. He couldn't use a keyboard to show off his new ragtime tune because plug-ins on the plaza were at a premium. He considered doing a comedy spoof on Trinidad's magic act and was quite good at it, but it was hard to make this show stand-alone and he wasn't sure he wanted to be parked next to his brother at all times.

One rainy afternoon, Sam searched YouTube and then, with three oranges, discovered the joys of juggling. We got him some actual balls, and he scored a spot on the plaza to earn spending money of his own. Sam was successful but quickly realized that he didn't enjoy marketing himself or his skills to the public. After two hours work, he retreated to sit among the potted plants with his favorite book.

Finally, boredom resulted in creative endeavors for Ben and me as well. After watching sunset from the plaza for the tenth time waiting for Trinidad's shift to conclude, we hatched a plan that involved a grass skirt, a hot pink bikini, an electric pink wig, ukulele, and flowered lei. I searched YouTube to learn how to hula, and we coordinated a routine of song and dance to Hawaiian, jazz, Bob Dylan, and traditional folk songs. I figured you could tell any story with your hands and hips, and I went to it. The hula was perhaps the only dance I could hope to learn in the seven-by-three foot straight and open stretch we had in our tiny home.

One thing after another got in our way of performing the act, and when we finally got down to the plaza, it was a Monday evening—the quietest night of the week. The crowd there was small and slow moving, but one gentleman loved the act and must have filmed the whole thing three times. Many people wandering past snapped a picture or two of Key West Hula Fusion, but the sweetest surprise came when old friends of mine from Eugene rounded the corner and came upon our act. They were vacationing in Key West en route to an overseas destination. We could hardly believe the coincidence, and it punctuated our performance as one of the highlights of my stay on the island.

I will always be grateful to Ben for his sense of adventure. How many people in the world would help hatch such an act? The kids were our greatest fans, as we were theirs. Trin sat on the sidelines offering tips on how to draw a crowd or close the sale. This irritated Ben no end as he had been performing in public for over forty years and felt he should be respected for that. I deflected the irritation with laughter, and Sam cheered heartily whenever he looked up from his book.

The Coconut Man:
A Postcard from Key West

THE COCONUT MAN is long and brown. His small machete hangs from his belt and his faded green shorts are frayed at the bottom like the bark of a coconut palm. His curly dark hair forms a cloud around his face like a question mark. What is next?

The coconut man is not exactly tall; he is lean and his muscles are defined when he moves. He drives a jeep that has coconut palm fronds lashed to the back and sides, coconuts hanging there in all colors and sizes. This is his vending machine, and you see it parked all over town. He puts his machete in and bam! A stem full of coconuts pops right off into his hand. They can be eaten that quick too—nature's fast food, he says. Thwap! Thwap! Thwap! He has chopped the green husk from the top with his machete in three swings. Chunk! He lops the top off and offers the delicacy with a green piece of husk as a spoon.

"You drink the juice first," he says. "Then you scoop out the jelly with the spoon. It is like beer and ice cream," he says. "Beer and ice cream."

My boys are first in line for more, dripping sweat from beneath their caps. They are silent, waiting, and the sun hangs still in the sky like a postcard; time is frozen as the coconut man reaches out with one long brown arm and takes another coconut. Tourists in polyester white and khaki fidget, but the coconut man is on the postcard, too. He does not really see them.

"May I try it?" I ask. The coconut man knows me and is patient. He hands me the knife, brown blade pointed away. He looks out to the sea as if I don't require watching. I pause with the machete, remembering the quick sweep of the arm, daring myself to be coconut man for three graceful swings. Is it too much to ask?

Coconut man turns to me and he is no longer in the postcard now. He sees that I am still standing there with the machete midair, and he knows I need much more than just a coconut. He takes the knife away from me and swings it hard into the flesh of the coconut with an eye on me to be sure I'm watching. He hands the machete and coconut back. I take a breath, then swing the knife back and down into the coconut, tentative against my best intentions. He shakes his head, narrow muscular chest flexing golden under his tank top in the sun. "You have to do it fast and hard," he says.

"How did you learn to do that?" I ask.

"It's what we did when we were kids," he says. "That was how we played. With knives and coconuts, sticks and stones. I didn't try to learn. It just happened."

"And then you moved to Key West to be the coconut man?" I ask.

He laughs, and I see the postcard has been sent long ago now. "No, I was a teacher first in Venezuela where I grew up. My parents were teachers, too. They yell at me when I go home looking like this," he says, glancing down at his clothes. "They want me to look professional, and I did that for awhile. But I don't want to play the game anymore so I come here, and I send money back to my village where there are many people in need. Here, I am just the coconut man. I wear what I want, and I am free."

His broad smile reveals perfectly straight white teeth. He takes my coconut from me. Coconut man corrects my half-swipe with the knife, and in three swift movements the top of my coconut falls onto the sidewalk below. Coconut man's chocolate brown eyes rise to meet mine, and the shutter behind my lens clicks to freeze us there. I wonder what it's like to be that free.

The Bad Egg

TINY YELLOW BIRDS filled the Royal Poinciana tree on the morning that Ben taught us how to make charoset for Passover Seder. My gentlemen and their cutting boards and bowls filled up every square inch of space on our round patio table. I brought out some green apples and set them in the middle. "Where are the rest of them?" asked Ben.

"Oh, you want them all at once?"

"Yes!" he said. "And the wine and walnuts, too." I brought out several more apples and stacked them precariously on top of one another. There were close to twenty. The boys and Ben began to cut. He showed them how to slice the apple into tiny pieces and then mince it further still. When they had one apple minced, he added another to everyone's cutting board and another. Soon, there were piles of chopped apple before each of them, and he showed the boys how to add the walnuts. The pebbly mixture, traditionally reminiscent of mortar in the Jewish Passover story, now spilled off the sides of the cutting boards and the long chef's knives darted further and further afield to capture the wayward piles.

"Here," I said. "Let's put some of this in a bowl so it's more manageable."

Ben glared at me. "I know how to do this," he said.

"Okay. You want to be sure that everything on the board gets chopped to the same consistency, right?"

"Yes," he said.

"May I suggest that you put some of what's on your cutting boards into a bowl so that you can mince faster and more thoroughly with a smaller batch then switch for the other batch you've set aside?"

"You don't have to tell me how to do this!" he snapped. "I have been making charoset since I was five years old, and my mother would add more to the mix all the time while I would just chop and chop and chop. Only I would chop right in the bowl. This is a little weird with the cutting boards, but I know what I'm doing!"

"All right," I said. "Just trying to help." I kept watching, warily. Chunks of apple fell off the board and table onto the ground. Ben glared at me again. The children dodged under the table trying to catch the bits as their big pieces were mixed with little pieces, the mound nearly covering the entire cutting board before each of them.

"Ben, I'm concerned about safety with those knives waving around trying to keep the apples on the table," I said. "Is there a different way we could do this to make a little more space for the kids?"

"You don't have to teach me how to cook, okay? You're not the only one who knows how. We can do this just fine. You should stay out of it. My family has been making this dish for generations, and I know what I'm doing!" he said, the muscles in his neck bulging in the morning sun.

The boys kept their eyes on their cutting boards. Compromises were made, but the air between us crackled with discontent for the rest of the day.

Fortunately, goodwill was restored at the Unitarian Community Seder that night as our family sampled the traditional foods of Passover in feast and celebration. Ben played the grand piano after, and we all cleared the tables and danced, finishing with a Conga line of women who laughed and cheered after too much wine. It was a joy to be in community with Ben in this way, and the hardships of the day were forgiven.

On Easter morning, two days later, the boys tapped lightly on our door at eight o'clock. I had expected this, but I had not thought to warn Ben who liked to sleep in on the weekend. I tiptoed from our bed to deliver small baskets of goodies to each of our beaming children. The boys picked through wrapped chocolates and jelly beans to eat their favorites before presenting me with a bag of plastic eggs leftover from the library egg hunt the week before. I nudged Ben awake and suggested we get up because the boys wanted us to join their egg hunt.

"It's eight o'clock in the morning," he said.

"Yes," I said. "But it's Easter."

"So?"

"So . . . this is what parents do on Easter!" I said, remembering that this was all new to Ben.

"You don't have to if you don't want to," I quickly added. "I can do it alone. They'll probably be okay with that."

"Look, I thought we'd done the egg hunt at the library! I didn't have any idea this was going to happen. How was I supposed to know? Aren't they a little old for Easter baskets anyway? It's eight o'clock in the morning. I want to sleep!"

"Okay," I said stepping back. "There will probably be more egg hunting later if you want to join then. Go back to sleep. We'll see you when you get up."

I wanted so much to be understanding, but my heart ached that I did not have a willing and happy parent companion for the holiday. The children were bent on magic and fun, and I wanted to help them create it as it had been created for me on so many Easter mornings during my childhood.

I wedged the door hatch into place as well as I could from the outside of our room, and the boys and I took our egg hunt outdoors with the lizards and land crabs. Trin and Sam loaded plastic eggs with licorice bits and chocolates from their baskets, and we counted up our findings each time to see who had gathered the most.

After an hour or so, Ben stomped out of the bedroom into the shower that now sported duct tape and a sheet of plastic across one wall where my foot had gone through the rotten drywall beneath the now dismantled tile.

"Hi, honey! Happy Easter," I said.

"Thanks. I didn't sleep much with everyone running around shouting about eggs."

"Oh. Sorry about that. I tried to keep the noise level down by playing outside with them."

I so wished Seda was there—how many dozens of Easter egg hunts had we organized and played along with? In the back yard, in the house, at the park, and at the beach . . . our boys seemed never to tire of hunting for treasure.

I was exhausted by the constant conflict between Ben and me and asked for help from friends. They suggested ignoring the triggered response and just staying in my joy as much as possible. Too exhausted to do much else, I tried that, quietly keeping my focus on the beauty I knew he possessed. It was easier for Ben to regulate his emotions when I remained calm and trusting, and I expect that holding a strong intention for peace proved more powerful than my former willingness to empathize with his every problem.

After a few bewildered responses, he slowly came round and blew up less often. The downside was that Ben could then rightly accuse me of not processing his pain with him. What kind of NVC person was I that didn't want to work on things? However, if I worked on everything he took issue with, I wouldn't have the energy to partner with him.

The joy in my union with Ben was incomparable when it came. I loved to watch him play with the boys. When I saw them all shrieking and laughing while wrestling around, indoors or out, everything felt good and right. He was up for adventure, anything from Hula Fusion to searching out alligators in the Everglades. He played sea monster with the boys at a hotel pool once for so long that I had to go looking for them. Ben was definitely one of a kind.

I could not help but love the man. He knew me so well, and his attentiveness and acceptance could be magical. Every night we slept together intertwined, with him talking in his sleep all night long, hand on my hip or in my hair.

The next morning, I woke slowly to him pressed against me hard.

"Calm down," I said, voice thick with sleep.

"Oh baby," he said, biting my shoulder gently. "I'm gonna be dead a long time." I pressed my lips together, amused, and rolled over to meet him once more.

Like Cats

Sometimes it is better
we are like cats—
don't
talk
much.

I wrap your
sitting back,
purr,
you eat
then stretch two times,
leave and
don't look back.

I go
my way
tail
twitching.

It is better we
fight like cats,

Housewife

claws out
and scowling,
one bite—
a tangle in
dark night
frenzy.

It is better
we cleave like cats,
tight
and turn away.
Pounce!
And sometimes
play,
as words
get in the way.

Fort Zach at Dawn

ON MOTHER'S DAY, Ben told me that I should do with the day whatever I most wanted to do, and I knew immediately what that would be. Ben agreed to take care of the boys for the morning, and I left them all sleeping as I slipped out of our bungalow before dawn and unlocked my pink cruiser from the back fence. I rolled my bicycle quietly out the back gate and let the latch snap closed with a clink behind me. The sun had not yet risen, but the sky cracked open in anticipation with shades of dark amethyst and salmon.

I rode to the gulf side of our island and down the stretch of road by the water's edge. Sea slugs the size of house cats mated against the concrete wall. How could you keep the sea in with a man-made wall of concrete? I wondered. How could you build a road for human traffic beside sharks and puffer fish, nudibranchs and horseshoe crab? I breathed in the sea air, heavy and soft in the morning silence. There were no cars out yet on this first mile of the eastern interstate highway. No cars at all.

My bicycle glided with a soft whir past tiny houses seated at the feet of banyan trees and small businesses closed and shuttered for night. I greeted the glorious new day alone as pink poured into gold behind the dark silhouette of palm trees as I neared the island's southern edge. I coasted into the park entrance and flashed my pass at the woman inside the kiosk.

"Morning!" she said. "The water's warm."

I smiled and bicycled on, parking in an empty rack at the side of the beach. Two people in park uniforms walked the perimeter of the palms tidying the picnic area in preparation for the day ahead.

I carried no bag with me and felt oddly naked as I stepped out onto the sand. Gazing across the water at the nearest rock formation, I saw snow-white pelicans nodding sleepily to one another and gulls calling to their mates.

The sun broke free of the Atlantic, a searing golden ball that spilled its white light into pastel until pinks and purples retreated into blue. I stood and watched it all, quietly. I wore my pink bikini boy shorts and a black fitted T-shirt that clung to my body like a second skin. The morning breeze lifted the hair on my arms, and it stood on end. The coarse sand at my feet was littered with broken shells, and I shifted my weight from one foot to the other, feeling the rough skeletons of the Gulf and Atlantic beneath me. Here was my mother, the sea, named twice—the Gulf of Mexico and the Atlantic Ocean—at the southernmost tip of the east coast, too wild to be described by names in any tongue. Here was my mother, calling me back.

I walked to the water's edge and stood with the warm surf lapping at my ankles.

"What do you want?" she asked me, light reflecting playfully on water.

"I have it," I answered.

"What do you call that?" she wondered, her voice echoing within me between the cries of the gulls.

"All that is open and expansive," I said. "All that is hope and harmony. I have it, but I have not yet collected it all. I'm scattered, but I can gather myself. It's all there," I said.

"It is?"

"Yes," I said, entering the water up to my waist and pushing off the ocean floor so that my breasts dipped below the surface of the sea. "Yes, all abundance. All you have given me."

"Why be unhappy?" she asked.

"I'm not," I said, slipping beneath the surface entirely, feeling the warm salty water in my hair and against my face as iridescent parrot fish darted below, spitting bits of coral so that they fell with bright clinking sounds when they hit the ocean floor.

"I'm not," I said again. "I can't be. I am only made of joy, and only joy resides in me. I am grateful for all of this abundance, the wealth of the sea and land that I am offered. How could I have missed this?" I asked.

"How indeed," she marveled.

"I got a little lost," I said. "I think I thought too much."

"Really," she said.

"Really," I said, breaking the surface of the water as I rose for a breath. Purple and red rock crabs skittered across the rough, blackened outcropping when I took shape before them.

"It's all harmony," I said. "Big fish, little fish, shark, and crabs."

The ocean was silent.

"I am a woman," I said. "I am also more and less than that. I have taken up and let go so many forms. I do not need to be attached."

"You are a mother," she said.

"As are you, but that, too, does not define us," I said.

"It does not," she agreed.

"We are infinite space and possibility," I said.

"We are."

"And there is no expectation to be had of others, just a trusting of all that is to support all that we are: One."

"That is true," she said.

"I thought I would transform into something better," I said. "I was losing patience."

"I know," she said. "But you didn't have to."

"I see that now. I see that all I ever was did not stop taking shape. There is no transition, really, only this movement of collection and coming forward to meet one another like waves at the water's edge."

"That's right," she said. "I have always been here."

"I have, too. Much greater and smaller than my edges. I have been with you. Giving and receiving, life in death." I watched as a red sea star pried open a mussel that clung to the rock. I would not see the creature digest its meal, but I knew that the process only led to one end.

"I have a story to tell," I said.

"You do," said the sea.

"And it all leads to this."

She laughed a light, tinkling laugh. "Will you know it when you hear it?" she asked.

"In my way," I said. "I must trust that."

"You will," she said.

I swam back and forth between the outcropping and the beach several times slowly as the sun lifted brightly above the ocean. The salty water rolled beneath me, raising me up to the cool morning air. There is no separation between earth and air but me, I thought. And I cannot be separate at all.

Leaving Nests Behind

AT THE END of May, we were excited to share our weekly turtle-nest-hunting beach walk with my dear friend Licia and her long-time partner, Francesco, who were brave enough to live with us for a weekend in Key West. Licia and Francesco had flown to Miami from their home in Modena, Italy, to attend a conference. When they heard we were living just a few islands south, they extended their stay to include a visit. I was delighted with Ben's warm and open response to this idea. Not everyone would be up for sharing their three hundred square foot home with friends, even if they were some of the best. I could hardly contain my excitement at the prospect, and he smiled as he tousled my hair, saying, "Yes, yes, yes!"

We managed to squeeze into our indoor space cozily enough at night with Ben and I sharing the living room bed with the boys, one extra mattress added to the footpath. Licia and Francesco slept in our bedroom with the privacy of the hatch. On the last morning of their visit, Ben opted to stay home and enjoy the quiet while Licia, Francesco, the boys, and I walked the beach in search of turtle nests at dawn. Francesco, a professional photographer, brought his camera with a telephoto lens for our Save-A-Turtle mission.

To date that summer, no nests had been spotted on the entire island of Key West. We parked and locked our bikes before taking up our post at the north corner of the beach and waited for the sun to send a golden sliver above the earth. Then we walked slowly south, combing the sand methodically for some sign of turtles. After pacing only thirty yards or so, we came across a nest. Another hundred yards later, a second nest was found!

The boys and I were elated. Francesco snapped pictures of our find, as a beaming Licia helped us measure and document the tracks on our official forms. Other ambassadors of the Save-A-Turtle program joined us with protective cages for the nests. They also showed us how to dig down deep looking for the eggs that would verify the tracks were not a false crawl. We all poked, dug, and brushed away sea grass and sand in search of proof that a turtle had indeed laid her clutch there. In both cases, it was my boys who found an egg first by digging carefully through layers of wet, packed earth and finally into the soft, fluffy sand where the eggs lay protected. This was an egg hunt we would never forget! We celebrated by going out to breakfast with the whole crew, Ben included. Our family felt whole and keen for adventure! I loved being a part of this group, this lifestyle, this beautiful island and planet that fed us in so many ways.

Ben had been given a voucher for a pelagic snorkeling expedition by one of his student's parents, and we took a boat trip out to the edge of the Florida Keys Reef Tract where the oceanic wildlife was most abundant.

The day before we were scheduled to go, Ben's sister in Vermont suffered a fall that left her in a coma. He did not want to cancel our trip but also did not feel like swimming with us for long. He returned to the boat for solitude as the boys and I ventured out to swim with massive tarpon, nurse sharks, rays, and a giant goliath grouper. Communicating with the boys while we swam in the open sea, staying loosely together while each of us explored for ourselves, was an empowering and trust-building experience that I will never forget. The ocean can be a gentle teacher, all magnificence and splendor. I am grateful for every day that she has gifted herself to me as such.

The wild beauty of Key West was needed to balance the tragedy we held as a family during that time. Ben's sister did not emerge from her coma. He, as her chosen next of kin, had to make the decision to put her on and then eventually take her off of life support. I sat beside him on the bed as he spoke with doctor after doctor about prognoses and options. Together, we fielded texts and calls from concerned family members who wanted their wishes to be included in these decisions. Sleepless nights were followed by long, sad days, as Ben's beloved sister slipped further and further from our grasp. Ben let her go in the end, believing that was what she would have wanted most. We held each other and cried.

That afternoon marked the death of a beloved elder sister, a best friend, and even a mother of sorts for Ben, as many older sisters can be. It also marked the beginning of the end for Ben and me as he turned his attention to packing out of Key West so he could head north to clean out her Vermont apartment. Ben's school contract had not been renewed. We would not be returning to Key West. I couldn't easily go with him to Vermont, so the boys and I gathered our belongings to return to Oregon.

Ben put most of his possessions out onto the sidewalk in a free pile, even his cherished tuxedo that I had brought out by request from Oregon. He was devastated about losing his sister, and he let go in every way he knew how. When I placed my hands on his cheeks, Ben only glared at me with eyes so wide that the entire rounds of his irises could be seen. He needed space, he said, and he was fiercely determined to chart his own course without my help, participation, or distraction. He struggled to let go of his sister, and I surrendered to letting go of Ben.

Snapshots 2013

The boys and I return to a loving Seda, fat cats, and a very happy dog. Seda has readied the garden and, within three days, the boys and I plant tomatoes, brassicas, lettuce, winter and summer squash, garlic, and beans.

I work for a second summer at the NVC Family Camp on Vashon Island. Seda joins us this year and, with Seda actively engaged in looking out for the boys, I feel some of the same joy and ease that I felt in my first month at Key West.

Ben returns to Oregon and buys Trinidad's third of the sky blue sailboat. He generously donates $1,000 to Seda's surgery fund then takes a trip to Peru for three weeks.

Ben wants to teach abroad in January of 2014, and I am unwilling to leave since Seda will have her gender confirmation surgery only five months before. I offer to join him later and continue our relationship long distance, but Ben is not interested. He sees this initially as a choice for Seda over him.

Trinidad and Sam enroll in our neighborhood schools, and I resume assistant teaching at the school for children diagnosed with autism. I am also given a new position as Social Groups Coordinator, where I can utilize my skillset in Compassionate

Communication. I love my work and quickly settle in to this full time job outside the home.

Ben and I part ways claiming divergent paths in terms of where we want to be in 2014, but a month later he writes to tell me that although he loves me dearly, he never really wanted to settle down and have a committed relationship and family. He just needs to chart his own course for a while now as part of his bucket list before dying. I am relieved to see Ben's clarity, and it makes perfect sense as to why I felt confused about his inten-tions for four years. I change his ringtone to the default Strum, but he does not call again.

The City of Eugene removes the exclusion clause and trans-people finally receive insurance for needed treatment. Seda's surgery will be covered at 80 percent. She reads the letter at the picnic table then sets it beside her, staring out into the garden without a smile on her face. "Is it over?" she asks me, and she begins to cry.

Loose Ends

A YEAR LATER, I ran into Michelle at the library. She said that David had lost his job and had been hired, just as his unemployment ran out, by a tobacco company. We were standing in the children's section, and it was a good thing, because I would have been kicked out of any other part of the library. I laughed and laughed with one hand clapped tightly over my mouth.

Michelle's eyes grew wide. "Don't laugh," she said. "Why are you laughing?" But her smile broadened, and her eyes lit up seeing the mischief in me.

"I know!" she said. "God works in mysterious ways. And I had a lot of judgment about it for a long time, but God is providing for us, Kristin, and I have to be grateful. Stop laughing!" she admonished and then laughed herself.

"It's so perfect," I said. It was my guess that God had been trying to break down the walls in Michelle's mind for some time. Her mother, who had moved to Eugene to be in the same town with Michelle and her children, had come out as a lesbian, and Michelle had largely stopped communicating with her. Michelle and her family had been rocked at Seda's coming out and had since maintained their stance, mostly David's as I understand it, that Seda was acting outside of God's orders and therefore was an unacceptable role model and family friend. And now, the family's very livelihood depended on a product with greater addictive qualities than almost any other on the planet. The company, in fact, was treating them very well. God had called in the big guns.

"I know," said Michelle. "You understand. You've had to live with confusion and that kind of judgment from others. You get it. But it's been really hard for me!"

I hugged her. I did not ask if we could finally all be friends. I didn't want to ruin the moment. Michelle told me that their family continued to budget creatively so she could stay home while schooling their children. I shook my head in wonder at her strong character and ingenuity.

When I got home that night, I told Seda the story of David's new job, and she laughed until her sides hurt. "Do you think we could give them that lamb from our freezer?" I asked. We had bought half a grass-fed lamb months before and sadly discovered that we had misjudged our liking for the meat.

"Sure," said Seda. "Why not?"

I brought the lamb to Michelle's door and offered her the packages, cut and wrapped. She received them gratefully and said that David wished to thank our family, too. I told her I would pass his words along. We chatted, and I admired their newly purchased home that had a beautiful garden space of their very own.

"God has been very generous with us," she said.

"Yes. Us, too. It's a good thing."

Michelle nodded, and we left our future together open at that juncture.

The Final Chapter

SEDA AND I are still living under one roof together, and many people are impressed by our courage and love. There are some stories I have in mind about this. None of them are fully true, I think, and none are fully false.

Story #1: We are still together because we believe it's best for the kids. This is a convenient story to embrace because it makes us both look good, even a little heroic. Are we tossing aside potential partners and independent living so that our boys will never know what it means to visit their parents, one at a time? Sure, it's possible that the imagined pain from such a split has driven our subconscious minds to create a solution that would instead keep us all together. Well, we are together. It's also true that neither of us have had serious suitors banging down the door, but then, who would come knocking? If suitors were brave enough to navigate our cultural idiosyncrasies, would they know to come to the back door? And, ultimately, who could say for sure whether stepparents and split time would be a benefit or a detriment?

Story #2: I'm just an amazing person. Seda's mom was of this opinion, and I am touched that she thought so. Other friends and acquaintances have said that they are proud of me for doing something so noble. As if I was cut out for martyrdom. I'm a little embarrassed to be so transparent here, but folks, I am not made to suffer. Not even for a cause as worthy as my children. Not consciously anyway.

Story #3: Seda is just an amazing person. This story is more likely to be true. Seda is such a fine partner that I'd be hard-pressed to find someone who could compete. She knocks down walls for me. She cooks *and* does the dishes. She wanders around all day in the rain giving people parking tickets so that we can have three square meals and a roof over our heads. She listens patiently to my frustrations (usually about a lover) and never complains. We daily work on our relationship together until we're both satisfied. She is an incredible parent and domestic partner in every way. I cannot say enough about Seda's merits as my best friend and co-parent. So, it's possible that we're together because she's just too good to let go.

Story #4: I am not good at letting relationships go. Some people believe the grass is greener on the other side of the fence. I am all about celebrating my grass, every last green or yellow blade of it, because I'm just naturally thankful. I don't want to miss out on one gift that I am given, so I make every effort to fully appreciate and cultivate all of my intimate relationships, because relationships are made for the loving! It is an honor to know someone intimately. And besides, despite all the transition in my world, I am not that fond of change.

Story #5: It's all for the best. This, too, is a reassuring version of our story. It implies that our being together at this and every other juncture was meant to be in order to serve the needs of all involved. Very nice in the retrospective lens, but in terms of intentionally deciding what's next, such a view has no practical merit.

Story #6: We haven't figured out anything better yet. This is certainly a true story, though pared down of all heroic dimensions. No worthy partner has surfaced to challenge our beliefs in keeping the family together. Neither of us has mysteriously stumbled upon the fortune it would take to set up individual houses as single parents. We haven't been irritated with each other frequently enough (in fact, it rarely happens) to justify creative financing or housing arrangements that would exclude one another.

Story #6 is not such a bad story, really. It contains a level of contentment that most people don't manage to achieve in domestic partnerships ever. I've been celebrating that for over twenty years . . . why stop now? On the other hand, I'd hate to rule out my old 4-H motto that it's possible to *make the best better*. I can't imagine what better would look like. It could look like four adults and two or more children in our home. (We've gone unconventional before, you know.) It could be a classic split and re-partnering. It could be that we all join the circus. I'd hate to get too rigid in my expectations.

I can hold all of these truths simultaneously, but if I have to walk one, I'll put my feet on the path of Story #6. And if something better does come my way, I'll count my blessings.

Epilogue

AS I REVIEW the final drafts for this book, Seda and I continue to live together on our urban farm. Two years ago, we drove to the bay area of California, so Seda could complete her medical transition by getting the gender confirmation surgery she had so needed and desired. It was the longest we'd ever left the kids, and we relished our time together, much as we had that long, beautiful night that I'd labored to birth Sam. Like a couple of teenage girls, we cranked the volume on the radio, and I hung my feet out the window to the California sun as we cruised south. Seda and I talked and laughed non-stop for four hundred miles. Our conversations didn't pause at the rest areas, because we could now enter the women's room together. I was single then, and our community gathered around to support our kids as the boys cared for our animals and garden.

Since then, Seda has fully emerged from puberty and taken up the reins as a parent. We both work full time and trade off shuttling kids to soccer games and practices. Seda and I hike together early most Saturday mornings on the Ridgeline trail where we can debrief about our week and discuss the kids' ventures. We fight the temptation to go to coffee somewhere afterward to talk longer. We never seem to run out of things to say.

I have been with a man for two years now who brings further grace to my co-parenting with Seda. Richard, a chef by trade and an artist, cooks for our family at least five nights a week.

Kristin and Fred.

Fred, Kristin and the boys.

Seda and Kristin

Photo: Sherri Phillips

Seda and I typically reheat the leftovers for lunch at work. Richard does not just cook; he creates edible art in the kitchen. We are very blessed to sit down as a family every night to his exquisite alchemy. Without Richard, I cannot see how this book could have been written.

My journey with Richard as a couple has intertwined with our journey as a family. He worried initially that he might be uncomfortable when he met Seda, but it just wasn't an issue. He encountered her for the first time on the soccer field where he'd come to join our family for a pick-up game. Within minutes, we were all hooting, laughing, and slapping each other's backs. The boys liked him immediately and so did Seda. Since then, we've

Seda, Kristin and the boys.

Photo: Sherri Phillips

played many more games together as a family on that turf. We celebrate Richard as our father figure on Father's Day, and he leads the boys in preparing outrageous brunches for Seda and me on Mother's Day. Richard and Seda have even started strategizing with each other about how to work around me when I refuse to come in for meals or go to bed when immersed in gardening, writing, or housekeeping projects.

Every day, we co-create our definition of family. It contains the stories of who Seda and I have been and now who Richard has been as well. It contains Trinidad and Sam, changing and morphing daily into young men. It contains the people we love, and the memory of more people we love, as well as those who are distant but near to heart. Our family is daily defined as the past integrates into the ever-present. I still don't pretend to know what's to come. And I'll tell you what: I'm not holding my breath.

Notes

Prologue

1. Thomas E. Bevan, Ph.D., *The Psychobiology of Transsexuality and Transgenderism: A New View Based on Scientific Evidence* (Santa Barbara: Praeger, 2015), 59, 54.

2. Bevan, *The Psychobiology of Transsexuality and Transgenderism*, 173–4.

3. World Professional Association for Transgender Health (WPATH). Standards of Care. http://www.wpath.org/site_page.cfm?pk_association_webpage_menu=1351, accessed May 30, 2016.

4. Helen Boyd, *My Husband Betty* (New York: Thunder's Mouth Press, 2004). Helen Boyd has continued collecting and sharing a wealth of resources for transfolk and their families at www.myhusbandbetty.com.

5. Jennifer Finney Boylan, *She's Not There* (Crown/Archetype, 2013).

6. Nonviolent Communication, also called Compassionate Communication, is a system of communication based on the principles of nonviolence, developed by Dr. Marshall Rosenberg in the 1960's. For more information, see https://www.cnvc.org.

7. Genderqueer: Of, relating to, or being a person whose gender identity cannot be categorized as solely male or female, Merriam-Webster Dictionary, http://www.merriam-webster.com/dictionary/genderqueer, accessed May 30, 2016.

PART THREE

Brunch with Doug and Janet

1. "Queer" once had negative connotations, and still does for some. Gen X-ers and Millennials (including Seda and myself) were the first generations to reclaim it as a positive label.

Hormones

1. (https://groups.yahoo.com/neo/groups/TransFamilySpouses/info)

Seda

1. This website has a smorgasbord of resources for transfolk: (http://ai.eecs.umich.edu/people/conway/TSsuccesses/TSsuccesses.html).

PART FOUR

Together Apart

1. Judith S. Antonelli, *In the Image of God: A Feminist Commentary on the Torah* (Jason Aronson, Inc., 1997).

2. Stereotypical gender roles dictate what is expected of males and females in terms of dress, behavior, and activity preferences. For example, girls are expected to play with dolls in pink dresses indoors while boys are expected to be found outside in the mud playing with dark-colored toy trucks.

PART SIX

Work and Play

1. World Professional Association for Transgender Health (WPATH). Standards of Care. http://www.wpath.org/site_page.cfm?pk_association_webpage_menu=1351, accessed May 30, 2016.

Definitions

To Help Understand Gender and Sexual Orientation

Ally
Someone who speaks or acts in support of another person or group that they are not a part of.

Androgynous
Presenting and/or identifying as neither specifically masculine or feminine.

Bisexual
Describes a person who is romantically, emotionally, or physically attracted to people of more than one sex or gender, though not necessarily at the same time or having equal experience with each; this orientation is determined by the attraction itself.

Butch
Typically describes masculine presentation in a female, but can also refer to masculine presentation in a male.

Cisgender
Refers to someone whose gender identity aligns with the gender associated with their assigned birth sex.

Coming Out
The process of self-acceptance in which a person acknowledges and embraces their sexual orientation or gender identity then takes steps to share it with the world. Coming out often happens over time and in degrees as a person shares the news with their various circles of friends and community.

Drag Queen/Drag King
A man who dresses as a woman or a woman who dresses as a man, typically for performance and not related to a transgender identity.

FTM
Female-to-male refers to someone who identifies as a male after being assigned the gender of female at birth.

Gay
Describes people who are romantically, physically, or emotionally attracted to people of the same gender.

Gender
A person's inner sense of whether they are male, female, both or neither. This may include social, psychological, and emotional traits, as well as outward behavior (gender expression). Both one's inner and outer experience of gender can be influenced by societal expectations.

Gender Binary
Refers to the belief that there are two distinct and opposite genders—male and female—and that everyone must belong in one or the other. Also implies that these genders are biologically determined.

Gender Dysphoria (GD)
The American Psychiatric Association's Diagnostic and Statistical Manual of Mental Disorders 5 (DSM-V) says: "A marked incongruence between one's experienced/expressed gender and assigned gender, of at least 6 month's duration." This diagnosis is usually coupled with symptoms of distress, depression, and/or impairment of psychosocial development or other important areas of functioning.

Gender Expression
Refers to the way that a person expresses their gender in outward behavior, including (but not limited to) dress, mannerisms, hairstyle, and chosen name. Gender expression can be composed of the masculine and feminine in any number of combinations, even androgyny.

Gender Identity
One's perception of oneself as male, female, both, or neither; this is the deeply held sense of one's gender that may or may not align with the gender/sex assigned at birth.

Gender Role
The behavior deemed appropriate for men and women, boys and girls. These roles can vary amongst cultures with strict roles potentially limiting an individual's development.

Gender Role Stereotyping
These are the stereotypes based on cultural beliefs of male and female gender roles. These stereotypes can limit people's aspirations, achievements, and general wellness.

Gender Spectrum
This describes a broad range of gender experiences including and beyond the male/female binary. People may identify themselves as gendered beings somewhere on this spectrum—more masculine, more feminine, shifting continuously—or not on the spectrum at all.

Genderqueer
These people identify their gender as outside the male/female binary, whether including both or neither, and their experience of gender may be static or fluid.

Gender Transition

The process that people may undergo to align their inner and outer experience of gender. There are multiple levels/facets of transition, and transgender people may go through any number or all of these.

- **Social transition** This might include changes in appearance, mannerisms, pronouns, name and hairstyle. One may transition socially in all or only in certain social circles.

- **Legal transition** This is the process of updating documents to reflect a more authentic name and gender identity. Different states have different rules, and this process can be complicated and challenging.

- **Medical transition** Describes medical interventions used to alter a person's body so it is more in alignment with their inwardly perceived gender. These interventions include but are not limited to hormone therapies, electrolysis and surgeries. A transgender person may use any or none of these.

Heteronormative

This is the assumption that heterosexuality is a default sexuality, and this assumption relies on a belief in the default of male or female binary gender expression rather than gender expression falling on a spectrum.

Heterosexism

This is the belief that heterosexuality is the only "normal" or credible sexual orientation. Heterosexism can manifest in explicitly negative comments towards LGBTQ people or can take a more subtle form, marginalizing them by way of assumptions (often unintentional) and small actions.

Heterosexual
Describes a person who is romantically, emotionally, or physically attracted to people of a different gender. Also known as straight.

Homosexual
Describes a person who is romantically, emotionally, or physically attracted to people of the same gender. This term is commonly used in scientific or medical references.

Intersex
This term describes someone born with any number of conditions wherein the chromosomes, hormones, genitalia and/or other sex characteristics are considered not typical of either male or female.

Lesbian
Describes a woman who is romantically, emotionally, or physically attracted to other women.

LGBTQ
Acronym for lesbian, gay, bisexual, transgender, queer and/or questioning. Additional acronyms could be added for asexual, ally, and/or intersex.

MTF
Refers to a transgender person with an assigned birth gender of male who identifies as female.

Outing
Exposing someone's gender identity or sexual orientation to others without express permission.

Pansexual
Describes a person who is romantically, emotionally, or

physically attracted to people of all gender identities and/or sexes. This sexual orientation is determined by attraction to, not experience with, all sexes/genders.

Queer
Some people use this term to identify themselves as not having a fixed or delineated view of their own gender and/or sexuality. This term may still be offensive to some as it has had derogatory connotations in the past.

Sex
Anatomical, genetic, or physiological attributes that define someone as being male, female or intersex. These attributes include external genitalia, sex chromosomes, secondary sex characteristics (e.g. beard) and reproductive structures.

Sex/Gender Assigned at Birth
One's sex at birth is typically determined by a doctor based on external genitalia. One's gender is assumed to align with one's sex, and pronouns are assumed accordingly at birth.

Sexual Orientation
This refers to a person's physical, emotional, or romantic attraction to other people. Various sexual orientations include (but are not limited to) gay, straight, bisexual, asexual, or pansexual.

Sexuality
Describes the way that people experience themselves as sexual beings (hormones, sensitivity of sex organs, psychosocial experiences) from the time they are very young to when they are very old.

Straight
Slang for heterosexual.

Trans
Shortened term for transgender.

Transgender
Describes people who identify as a gender other than the one assigned to them at birth. This may include male, female, both, or neither. Being transgender has nothing to do with the sexual orientation of that individual. Gender identity and sexual orientation are different.

Transphobia
A term that describes hatred toward, discomfort with, or fear of transgender people.

Acknowledgments

Gratitude to Sat Hari Khalsa for empathy, laughter, and telling me to go for it.

Huge thanks to the following for reading, responding, and helping me to shape this story: Anne Stone Coyote, Nathelle Comeau, Michael Thessen, Elisa Mason, and Tamara Cherry.

Thanks especially to Seda Collier for re-re-reading and to Trinidad for coaching me on what to cut as I read aloud on the couch late at night.

Enormous gratitude to Cat Zavis for reading and shining the light on what was missing in the final hour.

Thanks to so many for their encouragement along the way, among them: Rolla Krebs, Jen Timmons, Andrea Watrud, Rachel Browne, Amanda Jo Broughton, Robyn Miller, Peter Wilde, Jennifer Bucholtz, Maria Ladona Schaad, Rachael Mueller, Gisela Bergman, Reid Vanderburgh, and the Other Colliers: Sam, Pam, Katy, and Jake.

Gratitude out the wazoo to Richard Bartlett for the gift of his beautiful heart and for keeping us fed in all ways.

For their angelic presence that got me through at one point or another, a heartfelt thank you to Ce Rosenow, Angie Thompson, Jima, Sue and Steen, Stephanie Bachman Mattei, Inbal Kashtan, Andhi Reyna, Vanessa Fasone, and Tyson Lancaster.

For their ethereal presence and support, I thank my mothers, Akassia Mann and Gaydell M. Collier.

Enormous thanks to the many people who spend countless hours in support of transfolks and their families online and in community, and most especially to Helen Boyd whose books and website (www.myhusbandbetty.com) have amassed a huge number of resources to help people navigating this path with a loved one.

Finally, countless thanks to my son Sam for his laughter, listening, and indefatigable help and support.

About the Author

Photo: Rachel McLain

Kristin K. Collier is an educator and writer. Her words have appeared in The Sun magazine, and her poetry is a frontispiece for Michael and Kathleen O'Neal Gear's *People of the Sea*. She has been teaching Compassionate Communication since 2004. Kristin and her spouse were featured in NPR's program, Snap Judgment, in their Valentine's edition 2012, http://snapjudgment.org/sugar-spice. She lives in Eugene, Oregon with her family. You can find her at www.kristinkcollier.com.

CPSIA information can be obtained
at www.ICGtesting.com
Printed in the USA
FSOW02n1546271016
26618FS